*The
Western Impact
upon
Tsarist Russia*

The Palace of Peterhof, Leningrad   (*Ewing Galloway*)

The Western Impact upon Tsarist Russia

MELVIN C. WREN
University of Toledo

Holt, Rinehart and Winston, Inc.
Chicago   San Francisco   Atlanta
Dallas   Montreal   Toronto   London   Sydney

Preface

ALMOST from the moment of the Bolshevik triumph in 1917 communist leaders sought to create at home and abroad the impression that the new Russia was a unique social phenomenon emerging for the first time in human history. Stalin created among the Soviet people a narcissistic national mystique that hailed a "Soviet" civilization, novel in its definition, heroic in its daring and defiance, fearless in its pioneering, and glorious in its achievements.

Insistence that Russian social culture was unique, however, began before the November Revolution in 1917. Russophiles and Slavophiles had long persisted in the absurd claim that Russian civilization was unparalleled and without precedent. For centuries they had resisted every effort to promote foreign influence; they believed such influence was a sinister plot to destroy the pristine quality of the old Slavic culture. They applauded the enthusiasm with which the Orthodox clergy in the fifteenth and sixteenth centuries had embraced the preposterous doctrine of the Third Rome—the claim that Moscow had become the leader designate of the true faith after first Rome and then Constantinople had fallen into the respective heresies of papal domination and acceptance of Orthodox-Catholic reunion, which was put forward at the Council of Florence.

My purpose here is twofold: to identify the Western influences that came to bear upon Russia, beginning at the birth of the tsardom of Muscovy and continuing until the end of the monarchy, and to observe the emergence of forces dedicated to resist penetration by the West. It will become apparent in this study that there is much of the West about modern Russian or Soviet civilization but that there is much, too, that is not of the West, that is Byzantine or Oriental or a blend of the two. The social culture of the land today is an amalgam of several elements, as indeed is true of the society of any modern state.

In his preface to Wladimir Weidlé's *Russia: Absent and Present,* Richard Hare applauds Weidlé's analysis of Russian culture as "a branch of the Western tree of civilization," even, implicitly, as British, French, German, and Spanish cultures are other branches of that same tree. He supports "a saner and broader view of modern Russia . . . in her rightful historical place among the European family of nations."

Few students of Russian history will want to quarrel with Hare's position. Toynbee surely goes too far in emphasizing Russia's Byzantine origins and in insisting upon their permanent and indelible imprint. However, Russia did pursue a course—whether by choice is of no consequence—that carried her far adrift from the West in nearly every aspect of her social development. For centuries Russia was not a part of the Christian or European cultural stream. Once she had broken the bonds that held her outside, however, she strove mightily to return to her home "among the European family of nations."

Both the aspirations and the anguish of the peoples of modern Russia stem in considerable measure from the efforts of her leaders—lay and spiritual, political and intellectual—to lure or to drive Russian society back into the cultural fold of the West from which it had strayed during the dark centuries of Mongol-Oriental rule. Professor James H. Billington sees her natural setting, her Christian heritage, and her contacts with the West as the three most decisive forces influencing the cultural history of Russia. The acceptance or rejection of the physical environment was not Russia's to decide. Nor for a variety of reasons was there really much choice, by people or even by prince, in the matter of religious affiliation. And the cleavage between Orthodoxy and Catholicism that carried the East Slavs along a path divergent from the West was not of Russia's doing.

The decision to restore the cultural affiliation with the West, on the other hand, was a deliberate one, however slow and halting the emergence from isolation may have seemed. And the decision was never universally popular. Indeed, it inspired bitter and unflagging opposition from men fully as learned, discerning, and dedicated as were those who stubbornly insisted that Russia's salvation lay in embracing Western civilization.

There was much more, of course, to Russia's interaction with Western Europe than the cultural impact in the narrow sense of the term. But wherever or whenever the choice lay between a Western way of doing things and an Eastern, Orthodox, "Slavic," or Russian way of doing things, there was sure to be harsh and inexorable controversy. This was so in matters having to do with appearance and dress, language and literature, music and the graphic arts, faith and conscience, and economic practices and political institutions.

Those Russians who favored the strengthening of ties with the West equated Westernization with modernization. Frequently they associated the West with emancipation—from bondage or autocracy or obscurantism. Without exception they looked to the West for enlightenment. Those Russians who opposed Westernization, who saw all virtue in their own native Slavic customs and institutions, looked upon the West as evil, sinister, and noxious.

The nineteenth century witnessed a prolonged debate between "Westernizers" and "Slavophiles." The reign of Nicholas

I, which spanned the years of most heated controversy, witnessed only one episode in a struggle that had gone on for over three centuries. Nor did the debate terminate with the demise of Nicholas, or even with the end of the dynasty in 1917. Russia's communist rulers have seemed ever since the Revolution to oscillate between deviousness and candor, between suspicion and cordiality, in their relations with the West. And the land's greatest cities, Leningrad and Moscow, seem still, after a half century of communism, to symbolize the contrast between Westernization and Slavicization.

I have said little about the Western impact upon Russian artistic expression. Perhaps this is excusable by arguing that by the nineteenth century a world community of artists, or at least a Western community, had emerged to the point where Tchaikovsky was no more a Russian musician than Beethoven was a German musician. Music had indeed become an international language. Given variations in local setting, Tolstoy wrote not exclusively for Russians, nor Balzac for Frenchmen, nor Emerson for Americans. The short stories and plays of Chekhov are as sad or as amusing to Italians, Spaniards, and Englishmen as they are to Russians. The paintings of Vereshchagin bespeak the idiocy of war to men everywhere.

Russian artists, whatever their medium of expression, embraced the Western or universal schools or movements with far less reservation than Russian society in general. Dostoevsky implied as much when he proclaimed the deep affection of Russian writers for Western Europe. "We Russians have two motherlands —Russia and Europe," he insisted on one occasion; and on another he wrote, "Europe is our second fatherland. . . . To us all Europe is almost as dear as is Russia."

In the transliteration of Russian names I have not tampered with the Library of Congress system in an attempt to approximate pronunciation. There is no easy way of doing so, and the results are often more bewildering than enlightening. Kiselev is pronounced Kee-sell-yoff with the accent on the last syllable; Muravev is pronounced Moor-ah-vyoff with the accent on the third syllable. Less harm results from mispronunciation, however, than from the chaos that would surely ensue if every writer were to invent his own transliteration system.

The list of those to whom I am indebted is a very long one. I want particularly to express my gratitude to three. My mentor, the late Robert J. Kerner, left his stamp upon all the students who passed under his tutelage. Charles Morley has been a gracious and gentle critic for many years. Keith Eubank was extremely helpful in making suggestions throughout the course of preparing the manuscript.

Toledo, Ohio   M. C. W.
December 1970

Contents

CHAPTER ONE

Early Russian Contacts with the West

THE first enduring Russian state with a European rather than an Asiatic orientation had its capital at Kiev on the Dnieper River. A small group of immigrant Norsemen conquered the quarreling Slavic tribes of western European Russia in the mid-ninth century and put together a commercial empire along the "water road," the river network that connected the Baltic with the Black Sea.

For centuries finished goods and oriental luxuries moved north in the longboats of the Norse rulers and merchants of Russia, from Byzantium over the Black Sea up the Dnieper River to Kiev. There, merchants, Norse and Slav, diverted some share of the imports for distribution among the Slavic tribes of the hinterland. The rest of the flotilla and its cargo continued up the Dnieper to its headwaters and then portaged either into the

Western Dvina River and so into the Baltic Sea, or into the Lovat River and across Lake Ilmen to the ancient tribal capital of Novgorod. Here some of the merchants withdrew their boats from the trading fleet to sell or to trade their goods among the natives of northern Russia. The remaining traders moved their boats down the Volkhov River, across Lake Ladoga, down the Neva River to the Gulf of Finland and so into the Baltic, the highway to England and to the cities of northern Europe that lined the river banks and harbors of Germany and France.

The longboats that moved the wares of Constantinople into Russia and Western Europe did not return empty to the Dnieper. They gathered commodities in the West for sale and trade in Novgorod and Kiev, joined the annual flotilla in the capital, and moved down the water road to Byzantium to ex-change the products of the Russian forest—honey, wax, furs, and slaves—for the merchandise to carry north to begin again the trading cycle that gave life to the Kievan state.

Toward the end of the tenth century Vladimir, grand prince of Kiev, accepted Christianity for himself and his people. Priests from Constantinople conducted mass baptisms, beautiful churches rose quickly in Kiev and other Russian towns, and Byzantine missionaries put together an alphabet that permitted the spoken Russian language to become a written one. The new Russian alphabet was a slight modification of the Greek alpha-bet and tended later to divide Russia from the Latin West. Also, the fact that the conversion was to the Eastern—later the Ortho-dox—Church rather than to the Western—later the Catholic—Church bred suspicion and hostility in later centuries between Orthodox Russia and the Catholic West. For many years after the baptism of Vladimir, however, relations with the West were cordial. One of his nieces and three of his granddaughters mar-ried kings of Poland, Norway, Hungary, and France.

The commercial empire on the Dnieper prospered mightily for three centuries. However, when crusaders from the Catholic West sacked Constantinople beyond recovery in 1204, the traders of Kiev lost their market and their source of oriental goods, and the state quickly declined. Civil war wracked the land for generations as the princes of the royal family fought over the throne. And a succession of nomadic tribes flowed into southern Russia from Central Asia to pillage and burn and carry off thousands into slavery.

Isolation under the Mongols

The last important wave of nomads poured out of Asia in 1237. These were the Mongols, whose scattered tribes Genghis Khan had recently welded into a united people. Now Batu, grandson of Genghis, led a huge army against Russia. Torn by princely feuds, bled by earlier nomadic incursions, and sapped of its commercial vigor by the decline of Constantinople, the Kievan state collapsed. The invading Mongols, whom the Russians call Tatars,* sacked and destroyed the great capital on the Dnieper, perhaps the most populous city in Christendom after Constantinople.

For the next two and a half centuries Russia lay under the Mongol or Tatar yoke. The grand prince of Russia, who served only at the pleasure of the Tatar khan and who gathered for the khan the tribute which the conqueror laid upon the land, moved his capital from Kiev to north central Russia, first to Vladimir and later, in the fourteenth century, to the tiny village of Moscow. The heart of the village was a palisaded fort called the Kremlin.

Russia, a rich and powerful independent state in Kievan times, splintered into a hundred small principalities, each headed by a petty ruler whose subjects regarded him not as a political figure but as a landlord. The grand prince of Russia, viceroy to the khan, exercised only such authority as his sovereign khan chose to grant him—that of taxgatherer and later of judge to settle princely disputes. Russia was only a province in a sprawling Mongol Empire that stretched from the Pacific Ocean to the Carpathian Mountains. The capital of this vast empire was Karakorum in eastern Siberia, to which each suc-

---

*The Tatars, a Turkic people, and the Mongols from Mongolia were ethnically unrelated. The horde that entered Russia in the thirteenth century consisted of both Mongols and Tatars.

ceeding Russian or Muscovite grand prince must journey to seek confirmation of his succession and authority.

Within a century of the conquest of Russia, the Mongol Empire was breaking up into autonomous fiefdoms. One of these was the Golden Horde whose khan, now the ruler over Russia, maintained his capital on the lower Volga at Sarai, the site of the later Stalingrad, recently renamed Volgograd. If Moscow was the provincial capital and the residence of the Russian grand princes, the capital of the state of which Russia was now a province was Sarai. Until the end of Mongol rule in 1480, Russia looked for direction to Sarai, the residence of her oriental ruler.

For generations after the conquest most Russians had no contact with the West. Trade was local; it was no longer inter-regional or international. The grand prince of Russia, to say nothing of the lesser princes over whom he exercised a delegated authority, maintained neither relations nor contact with the independent princes of Western or Central Europe. Foreign affairs did not concern him, for he had not the independence to conduct them.

One consequence of Russia's submergence in the Mongol Empire, and the turning of her attention eastward instead of westward, was to impose upon her people a cultural and socio-economic isolation and backwardness from which she would not soon recover. The first generation of Renaissance poets and painters was at work in Western Europe within a few decades after the Mongol conquest. Russia, now almost completely out of touch with the West, took no part in this intellectual and cultural regeneration. Not until the late fifteenth century did Russia break out of its isolation. By that time Erasmus and Luther, Leonardo and Michelangelo, Copernicus and Columbus, were heralding the high Renaissance.

Novgorod and the West

During the centuries of alien rule only northwest Russia escaped Mongol domination. Novgorod, the northern anchor on the water road of Kievan times, managed to maintain almost complete independence from the khan, although at times admitting the overlordship of the Moscow prince and paying its share of the Mongol tribute. Left in large measure to its own devices, the city built a colonial trade empire reaching north to the Arctic and east to the Ural Mountains and into Siberia. From this tributary land the citizens of Novgorod gathered a rich annual harvest of honey and wax and particularly of fur.

The market for the ermine, sable, and blue fox, which came into the warehouses of Novgorodian merchants, lay not in Russia but in Germany, France, and England. The great traders of the city sometimes traveled into the West to sell their fine furs. Most often, however, they left the marketing to Hanseatic merchants. German traders from the League lived in a quarter of the city where they maintained their own homes, shops, breweries, churches, and warehouses.

So prosperous did the great trading republic* become that its wealth excited the cupidity of its western neighbors. The Swedes in 1240 challenged the city's control of the Gulf of Finland, and Pope Gregory IX preached a Catholic crusade against Orthodox Novgorod. The city's Prince Alexander defeated the Swedes on the banks of the Neva in a brilliant victory that earned him the title Nevsky, or "of the Neva." Two years later Alexander Nevsky beat back an attack against Novgorod by the Teutonic Knights, a German order of crusaders who had settled in East Prussia and who now sought to drive east, again with papal blessing.

Lithuania, Novgorod's immediate neighbor to the west, offered a tempting alliance. By the early fifteenth century the Grand Principality of Lithuania had expanded to the east and south and brought under its control the entire course of the Dnieper water road from Smolensk to Kiev and the Black Sea. Many Lithuanians were Orthodox in religion, and many

---

*While Novgorod had a prince, the city chose the member of the princely family whom it appointed to lead its militia, and strictly limited his power. The great merchant families made up an oligarchy that controlled municipal government in quite the same way the cities of Western Europe governed themselves. While the cities of the West managed their own affairs, they did not regard themselves as republics. Novgorod, in control of one third of European Russia, was in effect a republic.

Russians living on land once part of the Kievan state were still devoutly Orthodox although now Lithuanian subjects.

The temptation for Novgorod to join Lithuania increased as the strength of the Moscow princes grew in the fifteenth century and as the Muscovite rulers steadily expanded their own principality until it threatened to inundate Novgorod. The trading magnates of the city stood to gain most from a merger with Lithuania, for such a union would open the trade route down the Dnieper to Kiev and thence overland into Central Europe, a trade route they could not exploit as long as their ties with Muscovite Russia continued.

The wealthy leaders of Novgorod, at the risk of provoking an uprising of the urban masses, elected a Lithuanian in the fifteenth century to be prince of the city. He stayed only a short time, and another Lithuanian later elected to the post also left soon after his arrival. In choosing a foreigner to be prince of Novgorod, however, the citizens had defied Moscow whose princes long had regarded the throne of Novgorod as disposable only within the Russian princely family. Even the khan of the Golden Horde supported Moscow in its claim to be overlord to the Novgorodians and their prince.

As the power of Moscow waxed and that of Lithuania waned in the latter half of the fifteenth century, the ruling families in Novgorod took the fatal step of recognizing the king of Catholic Poland as sovereign over the great republic. They even promised to pay the Polish king the money they had been forwarding to Moscow as their share of tribute to the Mongol khan.

The grand prince of Moscow could not ignore the challenge. He sent one army against the city of Novgorod and another deep into its fur empire in the north. The urban workers, staunchly Orthodox and resentful of their leaders' desertion to Catholic Poland, rose against the ruling class. The combination of internal and external pressures forced the surrender of Novgorod to Grand Prince Ivan III of Moscow. The prince beheaded a few of the leading citizens "for their conspiracy and crime in seeking to take to Latinism [Catholicism]." Novgorod surrendered its right to name its own officials and to govern itself, and the vast fur empire came under Muscovite rule.

Ivan III and the Renaissance West

The first prince in two and a half centuries to rule over an independent Russia, called Muscovy in his day, was Ivan III (1462-1505). At the time of his accession he was only grand prince, a vassal to the khan of the Golden Horde. In 1480, Ivan refused to pay the Tatar tribute and led an army south to meet the khan's troops who were advancing north to punish the Moscow prince. No battle ensued, and the Tatar hoste turned back to its capital on the lower Volga after a summer of posturing and threatening to force payment of the tribute. So ended the Mongol yoke. The Golden Horde was at the point of collapse from internal dissension in any case. Segments of the Horde—the khanates of the Crimean Tatars on the Black Sea, the Nogai Tatars in the valley of the Ural river, Kazan at the great bend of the Volga, and Kasimov in the lower Oka, tributary to the upper Volga—had fallen away and become practically independent.

Ivan III, now independent and owing no allegiance or tribute to any man, began to refer to himself as "tsar"—short for caesar, the title of Roman emperors—but only in correspondence with foreign monarchs. Crafty and cautious as he was, Ivan did not flaunt his imperious title among his own subjects. His grandson, Ivan the Terrible, assumed the title of tsar at the time of his coronation.

As an independent ruler of a sovereign state, Ivan III had then to concern himself with Russia's relations with other sovereign states. Poland-Lithuania—the two countries had joined loosely together in a dynastic union in which the Polish king was also grand prince of Lithuania—was territorially the largest state in Europe. It was also a threat to the expansion of Muscovy, and indeed its ruler claimed Novgorod and other western Russian towns as his own.

Taking advantage of a moment of weakness when the

Polish king and Lithuanian grand prince died in 1492, Ivan III moved an army into Lithuania, ostensibly to relieve the Orthodox subjects of the king from persecution. Before he opened the attack, however, Ivan sent embassies to and received diplomatic missions from Poland's neighbors who might join him in encircling his enemy. He married his oldest son to the daughter of the prince of Moldavia. He welcomed a delegation of Hungarians and sent his chief diplomat to return the courtesy. He entertained messengers from the German emperor, and the two rulers exchanged mutual assurances of assistance against Poland. Ivan signed a treaty of friendship and support with Denmark. That Catholic rulers of the West should join Orthodox Russia against Catholic Poland was hardly surprising. In this age of the Renaissance religious scruples rarely interfered with power politics. Finally, Ivan opened negotiations with the sultan of Turkey, who had won the allegiance of the Crimean Tatars, who in turn were reliable enemies of Poland. Ivan's wars against Poland-Lithuania were successful, and the border lands that Lithuania had seized now returned to Moscow.

The grand prince of Moscow showed his interest in the West not only in diplomacy and war. When his first wife died five years after his accession, Ivan III began a search for another to take her place. His choice fell upon the orphan Sophia Palaeologus, niece of the last Byzantine emperor, now a ward of the pope who gave her sanctuary when Constantinople fell to the Turks in 1453. With the fall of Constantinople, hope stirred in Rome that the Orthodox Russians might recognize the leadership of the pope since the sultan had seized the Byzantine home of their own patriarch. The pope offered his ward Sophia as bride to Ivan III and suggested that Moscow consider an end to the schism between Orthodoxy and Catholicism that had divided Christendom for four centuries. Ivan accepted the marriage proposal but reserved judgment on the suggestion to recognize papal leadership of a united Christian church.

Sophia left Rome in 1472 with a party of Greeks and Italians, including Roman priests and a cardinal. Upon her arrival in Moscow there was a formal debate between the cardinal and Ivan's Orthodox clergymen over the desirability of a union of the two churches. The Russian priests were uncompromising, and the cardinal returned to Rome with word that Moscow would not accept papal control.

Ivan's new wife continued even after her marriage to sign her correspondence as "Imperial Princess of Byzantium." Her position as Byzantine heiress implied a transfer of imperial dignity and authority to Moscow. Ivan seemed to welcome the newly acquired importance of his court. He began to refer to himself as "Tsar of all Rus," thus heralding his claim to all lands ever ruled by Russian princes or inhabited by Russians—Lithuania, for example. After casting off the Tatar yoke he called himself "Autocrat," a term indicating only that he regarded himself as independent. The double-headed eagle of Byzantium now adorned the crest and seal of Moscow; Ivan thus announced his succession to the political and religious position of the eastern emperor.

Sophia had grown up in a spacious palace surrounded by all the pomp and splendor so typical of Roman and particularly of Byzantine court practice. Some of this pomp and formality now appeared at the Russian court. Ivan's princely abode, however, resembled a drafty wooden barn more than a royal palace. Prodded along, perhaps, by an imperious wife, Ivan employed some of the Italians and Greeks who had come in Sophia's train in work on a new palace and new churches, and imported many artists and artisans from Central and Western Europe.

Ivan's foreigners served him in many capacities. A number of them became his advisers in government. The Italian Marco Ruffo and the Greek Demetrios Ralo went as ambassadors to Western courts. Aristotle Fioraventi served as military engineer and master of artillery. Pietro Antonio designed and constructed a new royal palace and the Uspenskii cathedral, and other Italian architects built smaller churches. Italian painters redecorated old churches in need of renovation. An Italian engineer erected a stone wall around the Kremlin. Italian gunsmiths instructed Russians in improved techniques of arms-making. Foreign die-makers introduced improvements in the minting of coins. German craftsmen joined the Venetians and Romans in many enterprises, and German doctors served the royal court.

Ivan's son, Vasily III, continued his father's interest in the West. Italian artists came to Moscow in increasing numbers, many of them fresh from apprenticeship and study under leading Renaissance artists. Russian diplomatic missions appeared at Western courts in sufficient numbers to excite no curiosity. The tsar corresponded with emperors and popes, sultans and Indian potentates, and dared to call Emperor Charles V his brother.

Ivan the Terrible

Vasily's death in 1533 brought to the Russian throne his three-year-old son, Ivan IV. During Ivan's minority a regency council governed in his stead. At the age of seventeen he swept aside the council and called for his coronation as "Tsar of All the Russias."

The new tsar shared his grandfather's interest in the western frontier. When the hereditary line of Polish kings died out, Ivan offered himself as successor. But the assembly charged to elect a new king preferred the French candidate. When the French king left Poland to return to France, Ivan again nominated himself, and again the Poles chose another candidate.

During his long reign Ivan sought to establish firm contact with Tudor England. He went to war against Lithuania in an effort to anchor his frontier on the Baltic. His goal was to open relations with the West, in part to win British naval support against his enemies Poland and Sweden and in part to obtain easier access to the scholarship, the technical skill, the industry, and the trade that the West could provide.

In the reign of Mary I, two English explorers, Willoughby and Chancellor, sailed round the northern tip of Norway in a search for a northeast passage to the Orient. Willoughby died on the way, but Chancellor landed near Arkhangelsk on the White Sea. He and the Londoners who accompanied him journeyed to Moscow where Ivan warmly greeted them. They returned to England with an offer from Ivan to grant London merchants freedom to trade anywhere in Russia, exempt from the dues that Russian merchants must pay. London investors organized the Muscovy Company to take advantage of the tsar's proposal, and Queen Mary offered Russian merchants reciprocal opportunities to trade in England. The Russian ambassador to the English court hired a number of engineers, craftsmen, and doctors who took up residence and employment in Moscow.

Ivan later proposed to Queen Elizabeth a mutual alliance against their enemies in the Baltic. He even offered her sanctuary in Russia should her domestic enemies win out against her, and asked if he might retire to England should he lose his own throne. He besought Elizabeth not to allow her merchants to trade with Poland, and asked that she send him craftsmen skilled in shipbuilding and arms manufacture. The kings of Poland, Denmark, and Sweden urged the English queen, on the other hand, not to provide Russia with the technical skills of the West that Ivan would turn against them. The tsar was keenly aware that, unless he could bring Western knowledge and techniques to his country, Russia might not survive pressure from Poland, Sweden, or Turkey, or a combination of them; the nation's technological backwardness might bring about her destruction.

The Protestant Revolt was stirring religious and political controversy in the West during Ivan's reign, and the Council of Trent was busy at mid-century bringing reform to the Catholic Church. In 1551 the tsar called a church council of his own in an effort to force reforms in the state church. He considered confiscating church lands, as his contemporary Henry VIII had done in England, for many Russian clergymen agreed with him that the church's vast holdings and enormous income were corrupting influences. He never took the step of seizing church property, however, although he frequently laid the church and individual churchmen under heavy fine and taxation.

Orthodox Church practice was badly in need of reform, as the Council of Trent recognized the Catholic Church to be. Ivan deplored the sinful and slothful living of his clergy and the ignorance of many churchmen. He visited the same cruel punishments upon wrong-doing clerics as upon laymen. He did not hesitate to order sinful or plotting priests dragged from their altars and flogged or put to some fiendish torture. But his efforts to reform the church did not survive him and had to be undertaken all over again in the next century.

Ivan's simple-minded son Fedor succeeded him in 1584 and died without heirs fifteen years later. The dynasty that had ruled Russia since the mid-ninth century died with him. Soon thereafter a violent civil war, which Russians call the Time of Troubles, divided the nation against itself. Poland and Sweden sought to gain some advantage by supplying troops to the rebels and by sending armies to steal some land, an action that Russia was helpless to prevent. The civil war grew in part out of the dynastic crisis that attended Fedor's death, and in part out of a bitter class war brought on by the approach of serfdom to the free peasants of Russia. After a bewildering succession of governments, an army of Poles seized Moscow and placed the son of the Polish king upon the Russian throne. He lasted less than two years, when a popular national uprising drove out the hated foreigners and restored the government to a Russian.

The Early Romanovs

A national "Assembly of the Land" gathered in Moscow in 1613 to elect a new tsar. The choice fell upon Michael Romanov, whose great-aunt was the first wife of Ivan the Terrible. This may have comforted those who sought some continuity with the old dynasty. Michael, uneducated, young, and weak-willed, had languished in prison through much of the Time of Troubles. At least he had made no enemies. His father, who during the civil war had become patriarch of Moscow and thus titular head of the Russian Orthodox Church, shared power with his son and, in fact, directed the government through most of the reign. Whatever of policy appeared during the rule of the first Romanov was the work of his father, the Patriarch Filaret. With the return to peace, the government's first concern became the revival of the exhausted nation.

The poor showing of Russian troops against Poles and Swedes during the Time of Troubles prompted Filaret to seek some improvement in army training and equipment. He hired hundreds of foreigners—Germans, Irish, Scots, Englishmen,

Greeks, and even Swedes and Poles—to serve as officers in the Russian army. These foreigners received far higher pay than did native officers, and many took up land and settled their families in Russia. Equipping Russian troops with Western arms was too costly for the impoverished government to contemplate, and Filaret planned to bring in Western technicians to build weapons factories and to teach Russians to operate them. Andrew Vinnius, the Russian-born son of a Dutch immigrant, built the first Russian weapons factory at Tula in 1632.

Germans, Dutchmen, and Swedes came in from the West to teach Russians such skills as goldsmithery, tanning, clock-making, masonry, glass manufacture, and bell making, in which the Russians soon came to excel. In the days of Ivan IV, the government had set aside a suburb of Moscow as a foreign or "German" quarter, where the foreigners lived in their own neat houses, worshipped in their own Catholic or Lutheran churches, and maintained their own schools and shops. By the time of Michael's death in 1645 over a thousand foreign families dwelt in Moscow's German quarter. There as a child Peter the Great listened to tales of the West and may have resolved one day to visit it.

Michael's successor was his son, the gentle Alexis, who, at Filaret's insistence, had received at least some education. Alexis ordered that his first wife's children should have tutors, although he died before he could provide tutors for Peter, the son of his second wife. Alexis put an end to the oriental custom of isolating women at court—well-born daughters saw only male members of their own family until their marriage. He even saw to the education of his daughter, Sophia, which was an extremely daring defiance of hallowed convention.

Westerners streamed into Russia during the reign of Alexis to settle in the foreign quarter of Moscow. Those who came in greatest numbers were the Dutch. Russian trade with the Netherlands became so important that the tsar employed an English agent to manage Russia's commercial interests in Holland. Dutch sea captains, shipwrights, and carpenters settled with their families in Russia and received high salaries to instruct Russians in Western skills. Many Frenchmen, particularly Huguenots fleeing persecution in their own country, joined the Russian service. By the end of the reign in 1676 there were three thousand Scots living in Moscow—Gordons, Grahams, Patricks, Hamiltons, Dalziels, Crawfords, and Drummonds—many of them Catholics who had managed earlier to escape from Cromwell and his Puritan saints.

The dress and manners of the Westerners who lived in the German quarter contrasted sharply with the appearance and habits of the Muscovites who came into the quarter to be fascinated or shocked at what they saw. Western men were clean-shaven or wore only moustaches. They dressed in knee breeches, silk stockings, and buckled shoes, while the Russians wore long, formless, bulky robes and boots. Houses in the quarter were clean and neat, comfortably furnished, attractively decorated, brightened with flower gardens and window boxes. Inhabitants of the quarter ate not with their hands as Russians did but with knife and fork. Women accompanied their husbands to public social affairs, and the sexes rode together in fine carriages through the streets of the capital.

Alexis led the way in popularizing Western customs among his people. He introduced his daughters and wife to mixed society. He rode in a luxurious carriage to performances by his German orchestra, or to the ballet and theatrical school which a German pastor established in Moscow late in the reign.

Without exception the tsar's advisers were men who admired the West and who sought to bring its learning and its skills into Russia. Perhaps the most outspoken advocate of strengthening ties with the West was Athanasy Ordin-Nashchokin who for some years managed foreign affairs. He arranged peace treaties with Poland and Sweden and promoted a combination of Russian traders to improve commercial relations with Sweden. He established postal communication with Poland and proposed a union of Poland and Russia. His candidate for the Polish throne was the oldest son of Alexis, who of course would also become Russian tsar when his father died. He urged Russia's need for an outlet on the Baltic that would make possible direct contact with the West. To facilitate dealing with foreigners, he learned German, Polish, and Latin. In his fondness for Western customs and in his insistence that Russians should adopt improved Western techniques, he stirred the resentment of old Muscovites who called him "the foreigner."

During the reign of Alexis the Russian Orthodox Church went through a sort of reformation in reverse. There was no separation from the official or mother church comparable to the Lutheran or Calvinist revolt from the Roman Church in the West. Instead there occurred a reformation of the official church, conceived and enforced by the patriarch with governmental sanction and support. However, millions of Russians refused to accept the reforms.

The tsar's favorite cleric was a Moscow prior named Nikon, who became patriarch and thus titular head of the Russian Orthodox Church in 1652. The new patriarch was one of those Westernizers of whom Alexis was fond and to whom he looked for counsel.

Nikon made it his first concern to correct the liturgical books and the church service. For many generations church scholars had been urging such a revision. Faulty translation of the liturgy from the Greek had allowed errors to creep into the service, and they had persisted since Kievan times. In spite of the protest of scholars, the church council called by Ivan the Terrible had sanctified the errors. For example, priests used two fingers instead of three in making the sign of the cross, and argued that this symbolized the divine and the human nature of Christ; erroneous translation from the Greek resulted in a misspelling of the name Jesus. The great majority of the clergy, in the ignorance that had made Ivan IV so impatient with his own church, stubbornly supported the retention of these faulty practices in spite of the fact that they were manifestly without foundation.

Nikon set a team of Greek and Latin scholars, all trained at the theological academy in Kiev, the task of correcting the liturgical books and the service. When they had completed the assignment of removing the old errors, the patriarch ordered the alteration of church service to conform to the new translation. Fierce resistance immediately followed, inspired less perhaps by the policy than by the relentless way in which Nikon enforced it.

He personally conducted the search for priests who clung to the old practices and did not hesitate to drive the defiant ones from the pulpit, to harry them into exile, or even to march them off to the torture. His men had orders to search Muscovite homes and to destroy any heretically painted icons they might find.

When Nikon imperiously dictated to the tsar in religious and even in other matters, Alexis ordered the patriarch to trial by a church council that called for his expulsion from office. Neither the tsar nor the council, however, raised any objection to the reforms that Nikon's scholars had inspired. Their objection was to the patriarch's high-handed methods of enforcement. The state church, consequently, retained the Nikonian reforms.

Many churchmen and laymen refused to accept the alterations in the service and continued to practice their religion in the old, error-ridden way. These were the *Raskolniks*, or Old Believers or Old Ritualists, who were to suffer ridicule and official persecution through the centuries. The numbers of those who defied Nikon's corrections grew in spite of, or perhaps because of, the suffering inflicted upon them; in fact, millions of people in mid-twentieth-century Russia followed the old ritual.

Resistance to the changes in the official church grew in part out of anti-Western sentiment. The scholars who rewrote the sacred books all came from the Kiev Academy, which had been under the rule of Catholic Poland for generations. Indeed, Kiev was still Polish territory for nearly a decade after the promulgation of the reforms. There was much resentment, among laymen and clerics alike, that foreigners, and particularly men tainted with Western contact, should presume to dictate to Orthodox Christians in matters of faith.

While Nikon and Alexis may have felt some real need to modernize or at least to correct church practice, their deeper concern surely was to establish the authority of the state over the church, much as Henry VIII had done in England a century earlier. The move toward strong monarchy, so persistent in Western Europe in the sixteenth and seventeenth centuries, had been clearly in evidence in Russia since the time of Ivan III. Imposing royal power upon matters spiritual as well as secular was simply the extension of a pronounced trend. Indeed, Ivan the Terrible had sought, without much success, to tighten control over church and churchmen.

There are striking similarities between the Old Believers and the Calvinists in the West. Both fought the approaching shadow of royal absolutism. Both rebelled at the rigid formality of the state church. Both were puritanical in the moral code they followed. Both praised the virtue of work and were industrious and thrifty in their daily living. Both became great colonizers—the Calvinists in North America and the Old Believers in South Russia and Siberia.

Late in the reign of Alexis there was a widespread revolt, centering in South Russia but aiming at several trends in Russian society that inspired resentment. Stenka Razin, the leader, was a Don Cossack, and thousands of Cossacks, from the valleys of the Don and the Volga and the Dnieper and the Donets, joined the rising. Old Believers supported the rebellion. So, too, did the peasant masses. Soon the entire steppe frontier north of the Black and Caspian Seas was aflame with the burning of the manor houses of the landowning gentry. The recently adopted law code had legally deprived the Russian peasant of his freedom, and in his defiance he joined the banner of Stenka Razin.

While some small measure of slavery had existed in the land since long before the Russian conversion in 988, most tillers of the soil had been free men until well into the fifteenth century. But the Russian peasant was typically a tenant farmer who rented his few acres from a landowning aristocrat, from the church, or from the state. His rent paid only for the land and buildings. Whatever capital he needed for equipment, seed, or livestock he had to borrow, in the absence of banks, from the landowner at high interest rates.

In the closing years of the fifteenth century Ivan III had imposed a legal limit upon the freedom of peasant tenants to move from the estate of one great landowner—noble or monastery or state—to another. To protect landowners from the flight of tenants who were delinquent in payment of rent or interest, the government forbade such tenants to move at any time other than the two weeks spanning St. George's Day, November 26th, when the harvest season was over. To enforce the regulation—particularly to protect a landlord whose peasants might be enticed away to another estate by promise of lower rent or interest—every landowner-creditor received the right to track down and return runaway peasants. In the seventeenth century the state enforced the law by using the army to curb the flight of peasant debtors.

When the state removed all time limits for the forcible return of peasants to the estate from which they had fled, the peasant lost all freedom. Since he was bound at first to the estate and not to its owner, he was a serf. Later his bondage became personal; he was the chattel of the estate owner who, with impunity, could sell him off the land or move him from the field into the manor house to work as a personal servant. He became in every sense a slave, although the term serf continued in use until the emancipation in 1861.

Aside from the economic factors that contributed to the approach of serfdom, there may have been some political justification for bondage in the sixteenth, seventeenth, and early eighteenth centuries when Poland, Sweden, and Turkey threatened the destruction of an independent Russia. The state would not have been able to survive unless its officials could locate the army recruit and the taxpayer. Since only men and boys were the actual or potential recruits and taxpayers, the census taker counted only the males in the population.

The bondage system, as the law code of Alexis in 1649 confirmed it, affected not only the peasantry but all classes of society. Men born into any class—peasantry, gentry, or townsmen—inherited that class status and could not cast it aside. Sons of the gentry must take up army service and, as Peter the Great later applied the law, even prepare themselves to become officers. Townsmen must live out their lives in the localities of their birth, and each son must succeed to his father's trade.

In some measure the uprising led by Stenka Razin was an expression of opposition to Western influence. The church reform, the new legal code with its enserfment of all classes but especially of the rural workers, the ominous growth of royal power, and the appearance in court circles of Western dress and manners—seemed to many to be the work of the devil. Russia's woes seemed traceable to the growing numbers of Westerners who were entering the country and to the strange foreign ways and ideas to which the nation's leaders were succumbing.

Alexis died in 1676 and Fedor III, his invalid son by his first wife, came to the throne. The new tsar reflected his father's interest in the West, for his tutors had taught him both Polish and Latin. His chief minister, Golitsyn, knew Latin, Greek, and German. Men at court began to appear clean-shaven and dressed in the "German" or Western manner. The feeble Fedor died six years after his accession, leaving a half-witted brother Ivan as one heir and a healthy, vigorous, and intelligent half-brother Peter as another.

By the end of Fedor's reign Western influence had won strong support, particularly in official circles. Whether that influence would continue to grow or subside would depend upon the encouragement it might continue to receive from tsars and their advisers. To the degree that the importation of Western learning and Western habit was producing a cultural and techno-logical revolution in Russia, it was a revolution bursting forth not from the bottom of society but from the top.

The period of Russia's bold advance toward firm contact with Western Europe in the sixteenth and seventeenth centuries coincided with a prolonged time of stress and trouble in the West. Religious unrest was at least brewing in England, France, the Germanies, and Hapsburg lands during the reign of Ivan III, and religious war wracked the continent from Poland to Spain and from Sweden and Denmark to southern Italy at various times from the early sixteenth century to the late seven-teenth. In one instance of religious strife in the seventeenth century, Catholic Poland and Lutheran Sweden jostled each other for territory in Orthodox Russia during and immediately after the Time of Troubles.

Russia's entry into the mainstream of European affairs also came at a time when the new nation-states of the West were engaging in a struggle for power more ruthless and devastating than any the Middle Ages had witnessed. Early in the sixteenth century the battle lines seemed simple to identify: Protestant

Europe was fighting Catholic Europe. Quickly, however, there was a blurring of ideological lines, and Catholic and Protestant powers joined forces to attack or fight off another Catholic and Protestant alliance. Russia became a factor of some significance in the closing stages of the religious wars of the early seventeenth century and a force of some strength to be courted by both sides. Her indifference to the religious issues involved, if indeed the Western contestants had not also completely lost sight of them, made her participation in the conflict a naked power struggle.

CHAPTER TWO

The Petrine Revolution

THE next in line of succession after Fedor III was Ivan, his brother. But Ivan was a sickly idiot, nearly blind and subject to fits. There was also a ten-year-old half-brother, Peter, the son of Alexis's second wife. It was patent that Ivan could not rule alone, and after a threat of revolt by troops faithful to Ivan's sister Sophia, a popular assembly acclaimed the joint succession of Ivan and Peter. Sophia served as regent. Russia thus came under the rule of two tsars. Seven years later, when his half-sister plotted to murder the two tsars and mount the throne herself, Peter seized Sophia and threw her into a convent. He and his simple half-brother continued as co-tsars for another seven years until Ivan's death when Peter became sole tsar.

Peter's Youth

Peter's father died before the child was four years old. Had Alexis lived longer, he surely would have directed his son's education. Fedor had assigned Peter to a tutor of limited intelligence who taught Peter to read and write.

During the regency after Fedor's death Sophia and her lover, Golitsyn, occupied the palace with her brother Ivan and other relatives. However, Peter and his mother, not welcome in the Kremlin, took up residence on a royal estate in the village of Preobrazhenskoe near Moscow. Here the boy roamed at will, his mother apparently unable to control him and the regent Sophia indifferent to his fate.

Peter ran with a gang of boys his own age who came from noble, merchant, and servant families. The young tsar led these "stableboys," as staid elders named them, on mischievous pranks and escapades that terrorized the countryside. Later Peter drilled his friends as two "play regiments," and ordered uniforms and weapons, including artillery, from Moscow. In a barn in a neighboring village the boys discovered an English sailboat in need of repair, and after patching it up they launched it on a nearby river. When he was sixteen years old, Peter transferred his activities to Lake Pereiaslavl, where with the help of some Dutch sailors he built several boats.

Few Russians were as interested in technical matters as the young tsar. This interest led him to the German quarter of Moscow and to associations with Westerners who could nourish that interest. One of his earliest foreign friends was a Dutchman, Franz Timmerman, who taught Peter something of arithmetic and geometry and their application to artillery and fortification. Fascinated particularly with the artillery, the young tsar gave himself the title "Bombardier."

When Peter visited the port of Arkhangelsk on the White Sea in 1693 he met Dutch sailors, and relished the title "Skipper" which they gave him. Thenceforth he smoked the long Dutch pipe so popular with the sea captains from Holland and affected the speech, the rolling gait, the manners, and the dress of a sailor throughout his life. He learned the Dutch language and used it at every opportunity.

Peter acquired intimate friends in the foreign quarter of Moscow, where he spent his time when in the capital. Although he was tsar, he spent little time in the Kremlin. One of the closest of his foreign friends was Patrick Gordon, a Scot nearly forty years Peter's senior, a soldier of fortune who had fought for the rulers of Sweden, Germany, and Poland before signing on with Alexis. Another of Peter's friends was a Swiss, Francis Lefort, twenty years older than Peter, whose ability to consume enormous quantities of liquor rivaled Peter's own. Neither of these companions knew anything of naval matters, but the tsar made them both admirals even before there was a Russian fleet.

The Western Journey

When Peter thwarted Sophia's attempted coup in 1689 and packed her off to a convent, he returned to his playmates, to war games with his play regiments, and to his drinking bouts. His mother managed affairs for him until her death five years later. The young tsar then had no choice but to return to the Kremlin. He took his play regiments with him and turned them into Guards regiments—the Preobrazhensky and Semenovsky regiments were named for the villages where they had fought out their war games. They were the first such distinguished units in the Russian army.

Peter's first important decision was to advance against the Turks who controlled the north shore of the Black Sea. Indeed, that sea was a Turkish lake. The decision indicated no shift in policy from that of his predecessors. War with the sultan or with his vassals had gone on sporadically for two centuries, and Sophia during her regency had twice sent Russian troops into the Crimea. It may be that Peter only wanted warmer water than the White Sea in the Arctic upon which to sail his ships; the Baltic Sea was firmly in Swedish hands, and Sweden, as the tsar later would discover, was a far more formidable foe than Turkey.

In the spring of 1695 the tsar moved his troops south against the Turkish fort at Azov near the mouth of the Don River. Lefort and Gordon commanded the army, while "Bombardier Peter" led the artillery. The attack went on through the summer, but every assault upon the fortress failed and the tsar ordered a withdrawal. He returned to Moscow to plan a campaign the following spring. In preparation for the next year's advance, Peter purchased a galley from Dutch shipyards and ordered the building of others like it on the lower Don River. He would attack Azov by land and by sea. He marched his Guards regiments, together with woodsmen, carpenters, and workers of all kinds, to Voronezh to cut trees and begin the construction of warships. Peter himself lived in a small hut nearby to supervise the work, laboring alongside the men, prodding the laggards, and drinking with Lefort when darkness ended the day's work.

In the spring of 1696, Peter returned to the attack, blocking off the fortress of Azov by sea with his new fleet and besieging it by land. Two months later Azov surrendered. The tsar's new army and navy had performed well. Now Peter began the construction of a naval base—Taganrog, near Azov—and proposed to station a Black Sea fleet at the new base.

Peter anticipated a long war with Turkey in the struggle for control of the Black Sea. He sent young Russians to Venice, England, and the Netherlands to learn more about fortification, gunnery, and shipbuilding. Fifty sons of noble families left immediately on the tsar's orders. Peter also hoped that European allies might join him in a holy crusade against the Moslem Turk. He must visit Western Europe himself to invite other Christian rulers to share with him the glory of driving the infidel off the continent. He thought they surely would welcome his proposal; as recently as 1683 the Turks had advanced to the outskirts of Vienna.

In March, 1697, Peter and a great entourage of two hundred Russian gentlemen with servants, and the clowns and dwarfs whom Russian rulers for generations had gathered about them for their amusement, crossed the frontier and headed toward Riga, a Swedish port on the Baltic. Lefort was in command. The tsar, nearly seven feet tall and rising head and shoulders above all the rest, went along incognito as "Peter Mikhailov" who would study shipbuilding.

At Riga Peter boarded a ship for Königsberg in East Prussia while the rest of the party moved overland. In Königsberg he took lessons in gunnery and received a certificate of proficiency from the post commander. The Russians went on to Berlin where the tsar took a short course in military tactics and received another certificate. From the Prussian capital the party moved on to Hamburg, where Peter took ship for Zaandam near Amsterdam. Here "Master Peter, carpenter of Zaandam," lived in the home of a blacksmith who the previous year had helped build the Russian warships at Voronezh.

After a week of work in Zaandam the tsar went to Amsterdam for a four-month stay. In this Venice of the north that so fascinated him Peter studied mathematics, architecture, navigation, astronomy, and fortification. He wandered through museums and, determined to start one of his own, he bought stuffed swordfish, crocodiles, and embalmed human freaks with which to stock the first Russian museum. He toured hospitals and heard the anatomy lectures of a famous surgeon. He visited a dentist's office and then supplied himself with the instruments with which he would practice dentistry upon his courtiers. He learned something of engraving and printing. He took down copious notes on ship design and construction, sailed small boats on inland waters, and toiled as a ship's carpenter on a galley he contracted to buy.

On invitation from King William III, Peter crossed the Channel in January, 1698, to continue his education in England. Oxford University gave him a Doctor of Laws degree. He observed Parliament from the gallery of the House of Lords and visited the Tower of London, the royal mint, the observatory at Greenwich, the nearby arsenal at Woolwich, and the shipyards at Deptford. He learned a little of clock-making, received a delegation of Anglican bishops, and had his portrait painted by Kneller. And he bought a coffin to serve as a model for Russian coffin-makers.

After four months in England, Peter journeyed to Vienna for a brief visit with Emperor Leopold and planned to go on to Venice to study shipbuilding methods there. In Vienna, however, he learned that the *streltsy*, privileged regiments in the Russian army, were in revolt against his stern rule and were plotting to bring Sophia out of the convent to mount the throne.

He canceled the trip to Venice and hurried home to deal with the uprising.

The rulers to whom he talked in Western Europe encouraged Peter to continue his war against the sultan, but none of them was willing to join him. The immediate threat to tranquillity in the West came from Louis XIV of France, not from the distant Turk. As a diplomatic venture, then, the Western journey was a failure.

The Western journey was a substantial success, however, as an educational experience for Peter. He returned home determined and indeed impatient to force Western learning, skills, customs, and even manners upon his people. Only in this way, he sincerely believed, could Russia emerge from the darkness and ignorance that kept her weak.

A century and more after Peter's death Russian intellectuals quarreled violently over the course the nation should follow in pursuit of her own best interest. The Westernizers insisted that Russia must leave off her backward Slavic ways and become fully a part of Western civilization. The Slavophiles, on the other hand, argued that Russia's salvation—political, spiritual, and philosophical—lay in her clinging to ancient Slavic institutions.

Now Peter may well have been the first of the Westernizers. There was much interest in things Western and much aping of Westerners, of course, long before his time. But there was little of studied policy in Ivan III's employment of Italians to design a cathedral or build a wall around the Kremlin; or in Ivan IV's extension of trade privileges to English merchants; or in Michael's invitation to Swedish and German artisans to settle in the foreign quarter of Moscow; or in Alexis's fondness for riding about Moscow in a Western carriage.

It was quite a different matter with Peter the Great. His employment of Western talents and his appropriation of Western techniques were not done piecemeal or in any random sort of way. They were done deliberately, often defiantly, with determination and with dispatch. They were never done cautiously, hesitatingly, or in any half-hearted spirit of indecision. He embraced Western skills and methods because he regarded them as patently more efficient than the old benighted Byzantine-Oriental ways that had kept Russia backward and sluggish and weak. He equated Westernization with modernization, and modernization with strength. He would make his nation invincible to those enemies who for generations had been threatening Russia along the entire length of her western and southern frontiers. Westernizing and so modernizing Russia would make her strong and invincible and would permit her to win the struggle for her very survival that had gone on ever since the day of independence from the Mongols in the fifteenth century.

Peter, the first Russian ruler to leave his country in six centuries, returned to Moscow in August, 1698, after eighteen months abroad. He left behind many of the young nobles in his party with orders to continue their education in England and Holland. And he brought home with him hundreds of English, Scottish, Dutch, and German sailors, shipwrights, carpenters, teachers, doctors, musicians, and even cooks and gardeners. The population of the foreign quarter of Moscow rose sharply.

Punishment of the Streltsy

Before Peter could apply the lessons he had learned in the West he had to deal with the revolt that had cut short his journey. The plot of *streltsy* leaders to unseat Peter and enthrone his half-sister Sophia had failed even before the tsar left Vienna.

The *streltsy* revolt was to some extent anti-Western. Many were Old Believers. The *streltsy* resented the loss of their privileged position in the army to the new Guards regiments who symbolized Peter's interest in modernization and Westernization. Yet their anti-Westernism was confused, for their idol Sophia was a product of her father's strong interest in the West.

Patrick Gordon, an old Scot who had entered the Russian service in the time of Alexis, had led a loyal army against the rebellious *streltsy* regiments and had forced their surrender. He had tortured scores of the leaders, had hanged many and left their swinging bodies on gibbets along the highways as a warning to others, and had imprisoned hundreds to face Peter's wrath.

Upon his return Peter set up fourteen torture chambers in the village of Preobrazhenskoe to deal out punishment and wring confessions from those charged with complicity in the plot. There was no escape, even for the members of the families of those brought to trial. The hangmen flogged, garroted, beheaded, or buried alive hundreds of men and women. The grim scene went on for days. When the end came to the grisly affair, there was an end as well to the *streltsy* as a political force.

Peter would have had no difficulty justifying his vicious punishment of the *streltsy* had he ever regarded himself as accountable for any act. He would have reasoned that the *streltsy* constituted a threat to strong government, which to him meant good government. He would have reasoned that their sacrifice was necessary to Russia's political, social, and cultural progress. Their attempt to restore Sophia, whom they expected to control, was an attempt to put the administration in weak hands, as the hands of Sophia's grandfather Michael, father Alexis, and brother Fedor had all been weak.

Social Reforms

Even before he had finished settling with the *streltsy*, Peter had begun to make some changes which his Western travels had suggested. He began cutting the beards of the men around him. He did the job himself, as was always his way, and then ordered those whom he had shorn to remain clean-shaven. Those who escaped this first shearing were invited to a huge banquet, and there had their beards cut by a court buffoon. Peter rightly judged the beard to be symbolic of the nation's superstition and backwardness. Church teaching held the beard sacred, the mark of God's creation of man in his own image. To cut it, priests warned, was sacrilegious. The tsar showed his contempt for this nonsense by ordering that any member of the gentry who insisted upon keeping his beard must pay a tax of a hundred rubles—a very large sum for the time—and wear a plainly displayed token indicating that he had paid the tax. He further ordered that any peasant who chose to keep his beard must pay a kopek—one one-hundredth of a ruble—upon entering any town or lose his beard.

Soon the beard disappeared among the gentry, for to wear one was to flaunt one's defiance of the tsar and incite his derision and wrath. But the peasant, who rarely passed through the gates of any town, clung in stubborn superstition to his beard. It became a mark of peasant identification that lasted into the nineteenth century.

Peter was as impatient with the long, bulky robes worn by Russians as he was with beards. Using the long shears with which he had snipped the whiskers of his courtiers, he cut off the long sleeves and shortened the hem lines of the robes worn by men at court. Local police all over Russia received orders to trim the robes of every man who passed through any city's gates. The tsar commanded all officials and members of the gentry to appear in Western or "German" dress. In a matter of months members of the gentry were identifiable in public by their breeches, buckled shoes, and short coat. The peasant—with his long shirt or blouse hanging to his knees and gathered at the waist with a cord, his baggy trousers stuffed into boots or into birch-bark and homespun wrappings around his lower legs, and his shapeless cap—was equally unmistakable.

The *terem*, the exclusion of noble and royal women from contact with men outside the family, had become increasingly unpopular since the time of Alexis, who had abolished it at court. Peter freed the women of all classes in Moscow, and ordered men and women to gather for entertainment at some appointed home at some appointed time. The capital police might order some Moscow citizen to open his home to members of the gentry, to merchants, to officials, to army officers, and even to workers, and each man was to come with his wife. The host received orders to make available space for dancing—Peter had learned dancing in the West—space for card games and chess, and space for smoking and conversation. The host must serve refreshments. Presumably the guests needed no urging to consume the liquor. Russians were notoriously the heaviest drinkers in

Europe. Smoking, which the early Romanovs had forbidden, became popular when Peter set the example and granted to an English merchant a monopoly of the importation of tobacco to Russia.

Until Peter's reign Russia had reckoned time from the date, according to churchmen, of the creation of the world. On January 1, 1700—the year was 7208 according to the Old Russian way of reckoning—the tsar shifted the nation to the Julian calendar and celebrated the occasion with a week of bonfires and parades. While the more accurate Gregorian calendar was in use over most of continental Europe, the English still used the Julian calendar which by 1700 was eleven days behind the Gregorian. January 1, 1700, then, was already January 12, 1700, everywhere west of Russia except in England. The nation clung to the Julian calendar until after the 1917 revolutions, by which time the date had fallen thirteen days behind the Gregorian calendar. Peter must have taken keen pride in addressing his first letter with a recognizable date to a Western sovereign. Appearance was always important to him.

Administrative Reforms

The governmental organization that Peter inherited did not inspire the ruler's confidence nor was it capable of providing honest and efficient administration. Ultimate authority resided solely in the tsar, and so the center of governmental power was wherever the ruler happened at any particular time to be. This caused no problem before Peter's time, for tsars rarely left the Kremlin. Peter, however, spent only a few days each year in the capital, Moscow or later Petersburg. The rest of the time he was leading troops in the field, traveling ceaselessly over Russia, or journeying abroad as he did on more than one occasion.

To provide some stability in meeting his executive responsibilities, Peter appointed a Senate of nine men to head the administration when he was away from the capital. The Senate was answerable solely to the tsar. Its first responsibility was to tighten the collection of taxes and supervise the levy of troops, for the tsar's primary concern was effective prosecution of the wars that went on without interruption except for two years of his long reign. The presiding officer was the director-general of the Senate. He served as a sort of viceroy, signing every decree it issued when the tsar did not attend Senate meetings. The first man to fill the office was Paul Yaguzhinsky, whose authority and power were greater than that of any other man except the tsar himself.

The Senate functioned also as a sort of supreme court of appeals, but this took up little time since the vast majority of Russians were bonded serfs and so not privileged to use the courts of free men. The Senate, which was never a legislative but always an administrative and occasionally a judicial agency, performed in much the same way as did the Privy Council in England and royal councils in other countries. It survived until the Bolsheviks swept it aside in 1917.

From time to time in the sixteenth century there had been an irregular secret police force of sorts. Peter, however, organized a secret political police system and made it a permanent feature of government. The nation would know and fear it from that day forward—through monarchy, republic, and communist regimes—without interruption except for a few years in the early nineteenth century. Its name would change from time to time—Third Section, Okhrana, Cheka, GPU, NKVD, MVD, KGB—but its functions, while later expanding, remained essentially as Peter had defined them. Agents of his secret police force were called "fiscals." Their first assignment was to track down tax evaders, but their broader responsibility was to ferret out discontent and subversion. Paul Yaguzhinsky, the director-general of the Senate, was also the chief fiscal, and as such he had access to information of which even the senators remained ignorant.

During the fifteenth and sixteenth centuries an administrative bureau or *prikaz* had met each responsibility or served each separate function of government. As the principality and tsardom of Muscovy grew, both in territory and in the burdens it shouldered, the number of *prikazes* grew. Before Peter's time, however, there was never any clear demarcation of function from one *prikaz* to another. One sent and received ambassadors as did any foreign office in the West; another handled recruitment and supply of the armed services as did any Western war ministry; still another received and disbursed most government revenue as did any Western treasury. A new *prikaz* to administer Novgorod was added when Ivan III conquered the great republic, and another was formed to handle Siberian affairs when Ivan IV added Sibir to his domain. Each new territorial *prikaz* dealt not only with local administration but handled tax receipts from the district and disbursed from its own funds the monies necessary to the operation of that local administration.

There were some sixty *prikazes* by the time of Peter's accession, many with overlapping functions. The head of each was appointed by the tsar and responsible ultimately to him. The number of such government bureaus and the lack of clear definition of function produced more confusion than efficient administration. And setting a single head over a *prikaz* that received and dispensed income was to invite corruption. Peter fought relentlessly against the dishonesty of his officials and carried constantly with him a cane with which he beat those he caught robbing the treasury. He hanged one governor and broke a chief of the secret police upon the wheel; both had accumulated fortunes by pilfering public funds. But an official told his sovereign that to end corruption was impossible: "In the end you will have no subjects at all, for we all steal."

Peter hoped that reorganizing the administration would put an end to thievery in office. He abolished all *prikazes* and replaced them with Western type administrative departments called "colleges." The executive head of each college was not a single official but a committee or board of several men, usually eleven, most but not all of whom were Russians. There was usually a Russian president and a non-Russian vice-president at the head of each college executive board. The non-Russians might be Swedish prisoners of war or Westerners hired to teach Russians how to operate this collegial type of administration. The practice of assigning government functions to departments headed by a committee rather than by one man was common all over Europe—in Denmark, Sweden, Prussia, and England. Peter adopted the Swedish practice, undeterred by the fact that he was at war with Sweden at the time.

The tsar had first considered adoption of the collegial system of administration when he visited England in 1698. Years later he hired a German civil servant to make recommendations, but first Peter sent him to Sweden for a year to study that nation's reputedly efficient administrative service. However, the first nine colleges did not begin to operate until 1720. In later years the number increased. Each college performed some precise governmental function for the entire nation; none acted for a particular region as some of the old *prikazes* had done. The first nine colleges dealt with state revenue, state expenditure, army, navy, commerce, mining and manufacturing, justice, foreign relations, and "state control" or internal security.

The collegial principle of administrative organization survived for less than a century. Early in the nineteenth century ministries, each headed by a single chief, replaced them. Yet, Peter may have accomplished some things in appropriating a practice proven by the most advanced countries of the West. He supposed, perhaps, that many heads were better than one in directing a government bureau. He may have expected a decline in corruption since every member of each college board worked in full view of his colleagues. One gain he surely realized was the tutelage that the non-Russian vice-president of each college provided for the Russian who sat at his elbow. At the time of his accession there was nothing like a civil service in Muscovy. By the time of his death there was at least a regular way by which officials could receive some training in acceptable procedures.

To provide for the promotion of commoners in the civilian and military services, Peter established a "Table of Ranks," or scale of office, that would admit men of humble origin into the aristocracy as a reward for merit. All offices in civilian and military service were arranged in a hierarchy of fourteen classes. Every civilian and army officer started at the bottom of the ladder and advanced by merit up the scale. A member of the gentry would enter the military as an officer in grade fourteen. But a common soldier who rose to grade fourteen also became a hereditary noble. All civilians who advanced in the civil service from grade fourteen to grade eight became automatically hereditary nobles. The top four civil and military grades constituted the "generality," and those who occupied them held the rank of general.

Peter borrowed the Table of Ranks from Prussia, and he retained the German names for most positions. The Table of Ranks continued in use to the end of the monarchy in 1917 as a sort of organizational chart of government appointments, both civilian and military. The reward of promotion for meritorious service and the custom of beginning at the bottom of the scale and moving up were practices that Peter himself observed. Long before there was a Table of Ranks the tsar began near the bottom as bombardier or captain or naval lieutenant and, tongue in cheek, received promotions from time to time at the hands of the marshals and admirals who commanded his troops and fleets. Not until the victory over the Swedes in 1721 did he accept the rank of admiral of the fleet.

At least while Peter was alive, the Table of Ranks rewarded merit and at the same time held men in rank until they earned promotion. It opened up the ranks of the aristocracy, or gentry or nobility as it is variously called, to deserving commoners. Peter's concern was to create an aristocratic class sufficiently numerous to man the bureaucracy and staff the military with officers. From the moment of his death to the end of the monarchy, Peter's requirement of merit for promotion was ignored. Men won appointment and promotion most quickly by bribery or by having friends or relatives in positions of power or influence.

Peter adopted the Western titles of count and baron. Formerly the only Russian aristocratic title was that of prince. He set the aristocracy apart from the rest of Russian society in dress, in customs and manners, and even in language. German became the preferred language at court, although French replaced it within a generation after Peter's death. The aristocracy had been isolated legally from the rest of society since the time of Alexis. Only the gentry could own land tilled by serf labor.

In an attempt to improve the collection of taxes and the levy of soldiers, always overriding considerations for this ruler of a nation perennially at war, Peter, in 1707, divided his sprawling land into eight huge provinces. A few years later the number rose to fifteen. The tsar appointed a governor to administer each province with the advice of a council appointed by the Senate. The governor must reside in his provincial capital, a departure from earlier practice that allowed area officials to live in Moscow. Officials subordinate to the governor were responsible for tax collection, grain collection, troop levies, and the administration of justice. From this provincial judiciary an appeal lay to the college of justice in the capital, and finally from the judicial college to the Senate.

Peter applied the Swedish model to the organization of local government by dividing each province into counties and each county into districts. The authority of the provincial governor extended only to military and judicial matters. The district became the basic unit of local government. The administrative head of the district was a "land commissar," whose chief responsibility was tax collection. Although Peter accepted the Swedish framework of local government down to the district level, he did not adopt the parish, the essential basic unit in the Swedish system. His justification was that "there are no intelligent men among the peasants" who could assume any official responsibility. Peasants living on state-owned lands, consequently, continued to govern themselves in their own village *mir*, or assembly, under close watch by the police. Peasants, or serfs, living on estates owned by the gentry were in effect the chattels of the landowners who governed them absolutely without let or hindrance.

Swedish and German municipal administrative practices became the model for the government of Russian cities. The first city to which the law applied was the new capital, St. Petersburg. It received a model city council in 1720. A new college of municipal affairs, responsible as were the other colleges to the Senate, called upon other Russian cities to alter their administration to conform to the new model. The college issued a charter setting forth requirements for the organization of municipal government. The charter assigned town dwellers to three categories: the "first guild" consisted of captains of merchant ships, jewelers, doctors, druggists, and wealthy merchants; the "second guild" contained small merchants and artisans; the rest

of the populace—the laborers described as "common people"—
constituted the third group that made up between fifty and
ninety per cent of the urban population at the time. The first
and second guilds voted for city officials who must come only
from the first guild. The members of the city council were
responsible for tax collection, and for the conduct of judicial,
police, and other administrative affairs. These "chiefs of the
city," as the law identified them, must also promote local trade
and industry. Although they won their position on the municipal council by election, they carried out orders of the tsar in-
sofar as such orders affected all citizens, and indeed they acted
with the power and authority of the crown behind them.

In attempting to transplant Swedish practices in central
and local government that had developed and become workable
over many years and many generations, Peter ignored the possibility that they might not work in a new and unprepared environment. He was all too quick to assume that, under the blows
of his cane or the knout of a police official, he could force his
Russians to make imported methods work. Indeed, he never
gave up trying to make them work. His immediate successors,
for the most part, showed no interest in the operation of Peter's
borrowed techniques.

Church Reforms

Even before his journey into the West, high church officials resented Peter's earthy living and his consorting with
foreigners. Joachim, the patriarch who supported Peter's succession at the age of ten as co-tsar, came later to regret his decision.
He hated the foreign quarter of Moscow, which the young ruler
so often visited. His successor, the patriarch Adrian, privately
expressed indignation at the smoking of tobacco and the shaving
of beards. The forced Westernization of the dress and manners
of Russians scandalized churchmen. In his opposition to the
reforms Adrian became a symbol of defiance, and conservatives
looked to the patriarch and other clerics for leadership in pre-
serving the old customs. Peter was not one to permit such defec-
tion to get out of hand.

When Adrian died in 1700, the tsar, whose right it was to appoint a successor, chose not to name a new patriarch. Instead he appointed Stephen Yavorsky to be "keeper and administrator of the patriarchal see." For twenty-one years Yavorsky held the post, trying all the while by flattery and by praising Peter's Westernization to win appointment as patriarch. He did not succeed.

In 1721 the tsar announced a reorganization of the Russian Orthodox Church. A royal order abolished the patriarchate and replaced it with the Holy Synod. The statute explained that ignorant men sometimes regarded the single church head—the patriarch—as equal to, or even superior to, the tsar. If the clergy should defy the tsar, the royal order continued, common people might support the clergy in the belief that surely God must always be on the side of the church. In amazing candor the stat ute declared the authority of the ruler over the church: "When the people learn that church administration is established by decrees of the monarch and decisions of the Senate, they will remain docile and will lose all hope that the clergy will support rebellious movements."

The Holy Synod was a committee, or college, of bishops and monks presided over by a "Director-General of the Holy Synod," a layman appointed by the tsar. This presiding officer, who in Peter's time was an army officer, held the post only at the will of the monarch. Since its governing body came so completely under royal control, the church in Russia from that day forward was simply a branch of the government. Subtler forms of government control of the church existed in England, in some of the German states, in Denmark and Sweden, and even in Catholic countries such as France and Spain.

Peter considered confiscating church lands, as Ivan IV had done before him. Although he did not order secularization, Peter placed episcopal and monastery estates under a "monastery bureau" of the administration. A portion of the income from such estates went toward the maintenance of the church, and the balance went to meet other government expenses, especially those of the military. Surely Peter was not unaware of the confiscation of church lands that Henry VIII had carried through in England, nor was he ignorant of the fact that governments had seized monastic estates wherever Protestantism had triumphed.

In bringing the Russian Orthodox Church to heel, Peter put an end to dual or divided loyalties among his subjects. The state insisted that the allegiance of its citizens be absolute, complete, and undiluted. The tsar said as much in the statute creating the Holy Synod. The Protestant West nearly two centuries earlier had come to the same decision. In Anglican England, in Calvinist Geneva and Scotland and Holland, in Lutheran Scandinavia and Germany, and in Catholic Spain and France— in every state where religion came under explicit or implicit state control—the ruler insisted upon the undivided loyalty of his subjects. The nation-state could not have survived had it allowed its citizens to escape its control by pleading conscience. Peter understood this as well as did Henry of England, Philip of Spain, and John Knox of Scotland.

Military Reforms

In the early sixteenth century the army of the grand princes of Moscow consisted primarily of a gentry militia. By law all able-bodied male landowners and their adult sons were subject to service in time of need. They served until their death or incapacitation and received a money wage and the right to hold land. Indeed, the sovereign granted land to his subjects in military tenure and could recover it in case the tenant proved no longer willing or able to render the military obligation. To augment this irregular and unreliable force, the earliest tsars created a standing army. Regiments of *streltsy* were its chief component.

The *streltsy* originated as a select corps of "shooters"—men armed not with pikes and halberds but with firearms. They dwelt in a special quarter of Moscow, received a good wage and, when not on campaign, enjoyed the privilege of trading at retail without payment of the fees and taxes that ordinary merchants must pay. Ivan IV had enrolled three thousand *streltsy*, but within a century their number had risen to twenty thousand.

Their residence in the capital and their possession of formidable weapons even in peace time made them a political force, a sort of Praetorian Guard. Sophia had won their support when Fedor III died by raising their pay. They had demonstrated riotously on the eve of Peter's departure for Western Europe. Before he returned home they were again in revolt, clamoring for the enthronement of Sophia. Peter dealt savagely with them and destroyed them as a political and even as a military force.

In Peter's first campaign against Turkey in 1695 the *streltsy* performed poorly and the old gentry militia even worse. The Preobrazhensky and Semenovsky Guards—the tsar's former "play regiments"—rendered excellent service, but their strength was well under four thousand men. The Cossacks were another reliable element in the army. These superb cavalry units were drawn from the independent colonies of Russians who in the preceding century had fled to the southern frontier to escape the enserfment that was settling over Muscovite society.

It was the unreliability of most of his army and its sorry showing against the Turks that prompted the tsar to look about for allies. In his travels over Central and Western Europe he was constantly attentive to and inquisitive about other armies and navies and their weapons, equipment, and organization.

When Peter learned on his Western journey that in his quest for allies against the sultan he could rely upon nothing more substantial than sympathy, he shifted his interest to a war against Sweden that might reward him with a strip of the Baltic coast. In this enterprise he was more successful in recruiting allies. Denmark and Poland joined him. Peter quickly concluded a peace with the sultan so that he might concentrate upon this new war that would become his abiding passion.

Peter's interest in a war against Sweden grew out of the fascination of generations of Russians with the Baltic Sea. For centuries after the founding of the first Russian state with its capital at Kiev, the northwestern border had rested upon the Gulf of Finland and the Baltic Sea. Pressure from Poles, Lithuanians, Swedes, and crusading orders of German knights had loosened Russian hold on the sea, and during the centuries of Mongol domination the eastern and southern shores of the

Baltic had come under Lithuanian and Swedish control. Ivan III and Ivan the Terrible had tried to anchor the Russian frontier once again upon the Baltic. So, too, had the early Romanovs.

Once Peter had visited in the West he had only to consult a map to know that the sea offered the easiest access to the lands he had found so appealing. His determination to establish and to maintain contact with the West generated a resolve to break out upon the Baltic. He then would have his "window on Europe." The seacoast so essential to the opening of that window, of course, was Swedish territory. If he could obtain the land only through a war with Sweden, then war there would be.

This "Great Northern War" between Russia and Sweden lasted from 1700 to 1721. It is no exaggeration to insist that Peter's concentration upon the winning of that war lay behind nearly every important decision he made during that twenty-year span. Military reforms obviously contributed to the ultimate victory. But whether the project of the moment were the imposition of some new tax, or the redesigning of the central administration, or the creation of local government, or the inauguration of a school system, or the sending and receiving of embassies, or the creation of a secret police system, or the subjection of the church to royal control, or the ruthless treatment of plotters against his reforms, Peter's first concern was how the project of the moment would affect the course of the war.

The king of Sweden was Charles XII, an eighteen-year-old knight-errant who never outgrew his fondness for war. The young ruler dreamed of emulating his ancestor, the great Gustavus Adolphus, in making Sweden the dominant power in Northern Europe. He succeeded only in arousing the fears of England, Denmark, Prussia, Saxony, Poland, Austria, and Russia. Much to the chagrin of his advisers, he spent his entire reign fighting against Russia, Poland, and Denmark and died in battle against the Danes in 1718. His sister who succeeded him became a constitutional monarch, and the heroic days of Sweden's rulers were over.

When the war opened in 1700, Charles XII quickly disposed of Peter's Danish allies before the Russian army could leave its barracks. But with 40,000 men the tsar besieged the

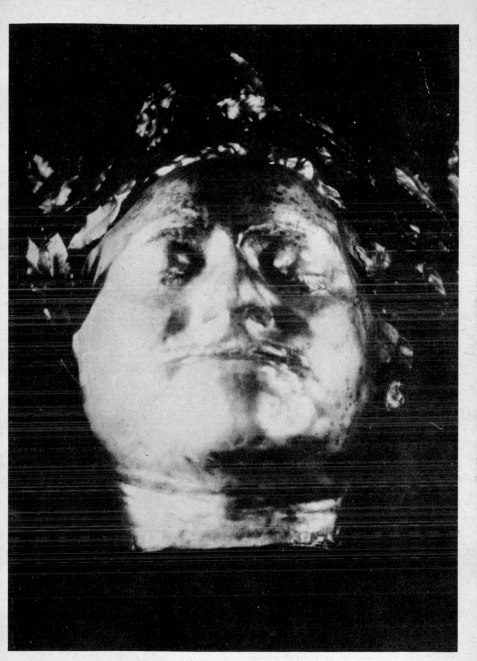

Silver death mask of Peter the Great
(Photo from European)

Swedish fort of Narva on the Gulf of Finland. When Charles advanced with 8,000 troops to relieve Narva, the tsar left the army, turning over the command to a French general who succeeded only in suffering a disaster. The Swedes captured a number of generals, a huge store of supplies, and all the Russian artillery. Europeans laughed in derision at Russia's crushing defeat at the hands of a small force led by a callow youth.

Peter's volunteer and militia army, even with its solid core of Guards, had proved no match for the well-drilled and well-equipped force of Charles XII. After weeping in despair at the news of Narva, the tsar took up the tasks of building a fleet of warships, rebuilding his army, and replacing his artillery. Between the humiliating defeat in 1700 and the proud victory at Poltava in 1709, Peter reorganized the army along Western lines and put recruitment and training on an orderly basis. During those nine years the number of men called to service was not more than 300,000 in a population of perhaps 12,000,000. The total number of men under arms at any moment seldom reached 100,000. When shrinkage occurred through battle casualties, disease, or desertion, each local community was required to replace its fallen or disappearing soldiers with new enlistments.

Army recruits assembled at appointed centers where they received some basic training before joining their units. The artillery imported from the West was the most modern available. English-made flintlocks with bayonets became standard issue to the infantry, and the troops received instruction in using the bayonet as an attack weapon, not simply in defense. The cavalry, perhaps because of the increased strength of the Cossacks, became far more aggressive. Indeed, Peter relied much more heavily upon Cossacks than had any of his predecessors.

It was Peter's new army and his Cossacks who won at Poltava. Once this reliable force had been assembled and molded into an effective army, neither the tsar nor any of his successors ever demobilized it. The men served at frontier posts to meet invasion or at garrisons scattered strategically over the interior to discourage rebellion. The Russian standing army in 1725 was the largest in Europe.

The fascination that the sea had held for Peter in the days of his youth never left him. Its first serious manifestation was the construction at Voronezh of the ships that besieged Azov in the Turkish War of 1696. The building of the naval base at Taganrog proved sterile, and Peter's dream of a fleet on the Black Sea did not materialize because Turkey later recovered the north coast that the tsar had conquered in the 1696 campaign.

The Russian fleet in the Baltic did prove to be permanent. In 1703, only three years after Narva, Peter built a navy yard on the Baltic, and from it warships sailed forth a year later. By the end of his reign the Baltic fleet consisted of over 800 ships manned by nearly 30,000 men and officers. When the new capital, St. Petersburg, rose from the swamps at the head of the Gulf of Finland, the tsar built a strong naval base in the bay and shipyards along the banks of the Neva River that flowed into the Gulf. Very soon after Peter's death, however, the fleet fell into neglect and the ships rotted away. Within ten years only a few were seaworthy, and no officers had been trained to sail them.

Economic Reforms

Peter's interest in stimulating industry and trade grew primarily out of his concern to build and equip a large modern army. His Western visit in 1697 quickened his efforts to build Russian factories to clothe and arm his own troops. Many Western artisans accepted the tsar's offer of high wages to move to Moscow and to set up factories to teach Muscovites their skills. He was not the first ruler, of course, to resent the high cost of importing military supplies and weapons from the West. The first Romanov, Michael, had employed the Dutchman Andrew Vinnius to build the first Russian arms plant in Tula.

Peter was so impatient to expand Russian industry that he applied some of the principles of mercantilism with a vengeance. Mercantilism, the economic doctrine in vogue in Europe at that time, was essentially the vigorous exercise of state control over the economy in order to make the state politically and militarily strong and self-reliant. The tsar protected his infant industries by imposing prohibitively high tariffs on the importation of those commodities he encouraged Russians to produce. In some cases he forbade outright the importation of certain foreign goods.

In the manufacture of some items Peter was the agent less of the founding of an industry than of prodding it into increasing its output. Such was the case in the production of paper, glass, woolens, and some metals.

In many new lines of production, however, the government built plants to turn out uniforms, muskets, gunpowder, canvas, sailcloth, and other items of military and naval equipment. Some of the new factories opened, and occasionally continued for years, under government operation. They were often under the direction of some German, Englishman, or Swede.

Frequently a new government factory, once it had reached the status of a going concern, would become the property of an individual Russian or a private company. Peter often turned over such a plant to private ownership at a fraction of its cost, exempted the firm from taxation for a number of years, guaranteed it purchase orders, and even assigned it a labor force of state-owned peasants.

Some industries prospered and performed respectably in meeting the nation's military needs. By 1701, Russian arms factories were producing 6,000 muskets and bayonets, and within another five years output had risen to 30,000. Peter sent out many exploring expeditions to search for ore deposits, and there were many new finds of industrial minerals. New foundries and armament plants appeared, and ordnance factories produced serviceable field artillery in sufficient quantity to end the dependence upon imports from the West. Early in the war with Sweden, Russian mills were manufacturing all the uniforms needed to clothe the army, although there were frequent complaints about quality.

Peter did not concern himself solely with creating a war industry, however. He encouraged the production of many consumer goods—chinaware, needles, linen goods, leather, brocade, lace, velvet, ribbons, hats, and hosiery. New brickyards and stone quarries were opened to provide fireproof building materials for homes and offices in Petersburg. He urged an increase in the acreage planted to hemp, flax, tobacco, and sugar beets, and supported improvement in sheep breeding and wool growing, so that Russia might produce her own raw materials. He also insisted that the nation have its own silk industry and raise its own silkworms to provide its own supply of raw silk. This venture, however, turned out to be a miserable failure.

Two sources of labor for the new industries were available, whether the plants operated under private ownership or as government enterprises. Most of the workers were state-owned serfs assigned to the factories. Private owners or companies received serfs on permanent loan; they "possessed" but did not own the serfs, whom the census taker identified as "possessional" serfs. No such legal niceties were necessary, of course, when the government used its own serfs in its own plants. Vagabonds, beggars, and prostitutes constituted another source of industrial labor. The police of Moscow received orders to round up "the youths who beg in the streets" and women "to be punished for their faults," and turn such deliquents over to factory owners as conscript labor. Many of Peter's new industrial enterprises were little better than penal institutions. Ten years after the tsar's death, in the reign of the Empress Anne, these conscripted criminals and vagabonds became permanently bonded to the plant owners. The bondage extended to their children, and so there developed a hereditary class of factory slaves.

The industrial surge in the early eighteenth century was not an unqualified success. The armaments industry did so well that Russia no longer depended upon Western artillery pieces or English muskets and bayonets. Paper, glass, and leather industries made good progress, and Peter boasted of the quality of the new textiles. Native merchants insisted, however, that many items of Russian manufacture—needles, hosiery, woolens, silks, brocades, and linen goods—were of extremely poor quality and, even so, cost twice as much as they would have cost if the same goods of better quality were purchased abroad.

Drastic changes in the tax structure came about, without planning, in response to the extreme pressure upon the treasury resulting from Peter's incessant wars. The tsar first resorted to currency debasement. This produced an immediate profit, but it soon disappeared in rising prices. The value of the ruble declined by half during his reign.

Peter next established an administrative office whose assignment it was to propose new taxes. The idea came to Peter from Alexis Kurbatov, a former slave who became one of the tsar's chief advisers and head of the department of tax suggestions. From that moment on there was a continuous rise in the number of items sold and services rendered that became subject to tax. These indirect levies in most cases fell ultimately upon the consumer. There were taxes upon the sale of stamps, hats, harness, boots, hides, leather, watermelons, cucumbers, and nuts. Fisheries and mills paid for a license to operate. Innkeepers surrendered a fourth of their receipts. There was a levy upon private bathhouses graded according to the social status of their owners. The penalty for keeping beards varied from a hundred rubles a year on wealthy merchants and nobles to a kopek on a peasant every time he entered or left a city. Beekeepers paid a fee on each hive.

The government received some income from its monopolies on certain sales or from selling such monopolies to individuals. One public agency bought salt and resold it at twice the cost. Another managed the sale of tobacco after canceling the private monopoly that Peter earlier had sold to an Englishman. Other state monopolies included the sale of chalk, bristles, fats, fish oil, caviar, tar, and potash. The government bought all the coffins in the land and resold them to monasteries at four times the figure it had paid the coffin-makers.

While the ingenuity of Peter's financial advisers was responsible for a heavy burden of indirect taxes upon consumers, the most reliable and predictable revenue came from a direct levy. For years the state had imposed a tax upon each household, and there had been a census of sorts in 1678 to identify the households. The number of dwellings, however, had so increased by 1710 as to make necessary the taking of a new census. However, the census takers discovered a decline of twenty per cent in the number of Russian households, presumably the result of consolidation—the joining of two or more families under a single roof to reduce the tax burden. Another household count in 1716 revealed a further decline, although it was obvious to the officials taking the count that the average dwelling sheltered an increased number of occupants.

The government hit upon a dependable way of reducing the avoidance of the direct tax burden. In 1718 the Senate ordered that every male in the population, "not omitting old men and the latest babies," must pay a poll tax. Russia's first true census—earlier counts had considered only houses—took place in 1719, but as a consequence of widespread evasion and fraud only 3,000,000 males appeared on the rolls. This number did not satisfy the government, and a new census—or what the Russians chose to call a "revision"—was under way by 1721. Local officials first took the count and army officers later verified it. The results were eminently satisfactory. The names of more than 5,500,000 males appeared on the rolls, about 170,000 of whom lived in cities. Since the census bureau took only the names of males, presumably the population, or at least its unfree elements upon whom the census taker focused his attention, approximated twice the census figures.

The Senate pronouncement ordering the new levy called upon every "male soul," or peasant or serf, to pay a specific amount. Revenue from the "soul tax" would go solely toward meeting costs of the military. To arrive at the figure due each year from each serf, the treasury estimated the military budget for the coming year and divided that sum by the number of "souls" on the last census list. Near the end of the eighteenth century it amounted to one ruble per serf. The tax on state-owned serfs was paid into the treasury by the village elders; gentry landowners collected it from the serfs they owned. Each landowner paid for every serf whose name appeared on the preceding census roll, including those who had died and excluding those who had been born since the last "revision."

Before the invention of the soul tax, the unfree rural masses had contained serfs who ostensibly were bound to the estates where they worked, whether state-owned, privately owned, or church-owned. There were also slaves who were the outright chattels of their owners. The imposition of the soul tax obliterated the distinction. From that moment on, since all unfree males or souls were subject to the tax, all became simply serfs in the eyes of the law and the tax collector. Legally slavery disappeared. In fact, since both male and female serfs thus became chattels of the state, of the church, or of some landowner, slavery or "bondage" extended over all rural workers. Serfs were no longer bound to the soil or to the estate. They became the property of their owner, subject to sale individually or by family, but they could be sold only to some other landowner. The state could give its serfs away, as Catherine II gave them away by hundreds of thousands; or it could lend them more or less permanently to some factory operator who could not qualify as an owner of serfs.

The soul tax produced twice as much treasury income as had the taxes in effect at the opening of the war with Sweden. Strangely enough, the soul tax outlived the institution of serfdom by a quarter of a century. A liberal finance minister abolished it in 1886.

Educational Reforms

Russia had no educational system before the beginning of the eighteenth century. The Russian Orthodox Church maintained some scattered schools for the simple training of its own clergy, but there were only a few students in even the largest. Certainly the small number of these rudimentary church schools did not constitute anything like an educational system. There was a theological academy in Moscow and another in Kiev, the ancient capital that had become Russian territory once again in 1667.

Russia's Westernization and modernization—Peter regarded the words as synonymous—could go forward only if there were available for state service and industrial development a great number of men possessing an education and a technical knowledge that Russia in the seventeenth century could not provide. For a century and a half, going back to the time of Ivan III, the emerging nation had employed foreign artists, artisans, and experts of one kind and another. Peter increased the rate at which skilled and educated foreigners entered Russian service. Only recently, however, had Russians gone abroad to study and then to return home with their newly acquired learning. Throughout his reign Peter continued the practice of sending sons of the gentry, and even sons of commoners, to the West for an education.

Soon after returning from his first visit to the West, Peter established in Moscow a "school of mathematical and navigational sciences" to train naval officers. It was the first nonclassical school in Europe, antedating by five years the first German school of the kind. The school's first director was a Scottish professor imported for the position, and foreigners made up the entire staff. Since the school was unique, its graduates were in demand for any official position, and many preferred employment in the capital to service at sea. The tsar later moved the school to St. Petersburg, and it became the Russian Naval Academy. In the last year of his reign nearly four hundred students were attending the school, but twenty years later enrollment had shrunk to a fourth of what it had been in Peter's time.

So promising was the experiment with a school for naval officers that Peter later founded a school to train military engineers and another to produce artillery officers. Both moved to St. Petersburg along with the naval academy. The enrollment in these later academies was modest from the beginning and remained so. The engineering school could only accommodate sixty cadets and the artillery school thirty, and enrollment sometimes fell short of even these modest goals. Russia's first medical school opened in Moscow early in the eighteenth century under the directorship of a Dutch doctor who a few years earlier had founded the first hospital in the capital.

Not all the schools that opened their doors in Peter's time limited their offerings to such practical education as did the service academies. Ernst Glück, a Lutheran pastor from Germany, founded a *gymnasium* or secondary school in Moscow in 1705. The Glück *Gymnasium,* as it was called, offered instruction in modern European, classical, and even oriental languages, in literature, philosophy, ethics, rhetoric, dancing, and horseman-

ship. All the instructors were foreigners. Capacity limited enrollment to a hundred students, although the number in attendance
in 1715 fell to five and the noble experiment came to an end.

The government proposed to establish a system of compulsory elementary education and in 1714 decreed the creation
of two "mathematical" or "cipher" or "navigation" schools in
each province. The teachers were graduates of the naval academy, a fact suggesting that the students would train for the sea.
Boys ten to fifteen years of age were to be chosen by officials from
provincial families of any social class. In an attempt to force completion of the course, a royal decree forbade the marriage of any
student who failed to graduate.

The cipher schools proved to be a disappointment. In the
first year nearly fifty teachers left Moscow to open schools in
the provinces, but over a third of them returned to the capital
because they found no students to teach. And of the 1,400 students enlisted in cipher schools in the first ten years, fewer than
a hundred graduated. Thirty years after the inauguration of this
elementary system, the last eight of the schools became "garri-
son" schools where students trained for a military career under
the instruction of army officers and enlisted men.

The effort to provide the nation with a system of lay education ended in dismal failure. Several factors contributed to that
end. There were no trained Russian teachers, and foreigners
made an unsatisfactory substitute. The curriculum of Glück's
gymnasium was completely unrealistic, and that of the service
academies and the cipher schools dealt almost exclusively with
mathematics. The dragooning of students into classes, and the
stern discipline once they had been forced to enroll, produced
only indifference and hostility. Many more students ran away
from school than stayed on to graduation time.

The new Holy Synod, which succeeded the patriarchate
as the governing agency of the Russian Orthodox Church, established a parochial school system. In contrast to the anemic
lay system, the church schools flourished. By 1725 nearly 3,000
students were enrolled. The great majority of them were sons
of the clergy preparing to follow their fathers' profession. Many

who began their education in church schools later enrolled in the University of Moscow, founded by Peter's daughter Elizabeth.

Peter was in France in 1717 and visited the French Academy in Paris. He returned home to order the founding of the Russian Academy of Sciences. It would encourage scientific research and also promote interest in the humanities by offering courses approximately on a university level. The academy did not open until a few months after Peter's death. The staff consisted of German scholars imported to teach courses in science, philosophy, and literature. Since there were no Russian students qualified to enroll for the program, however, the government also imported a few students from Germany. With only eight students to teach, the seventeen professors often had to attend each other's lectures in order to meet the strict requirements of service that their contracts imposed.

If there was little substantial achievement in the new school system, there was even less in Peter's attempt to raise the cultural level of his people in another respect. There was no public theater in Russia before Peter's time, although his father Alexis had established a school of dramatic arts. While the tsar was in the West in 1697, he attended several stage performances, and in his usual impetuous way he hired a German theatrical troupe to create a Russian theater and to train Russian actors. In Moscow's Red Square, Peter built a theater where dramatic works were performed in both Russian and German. Audiences could not understand German, and the Russian pronunciation of the German actors must have been unintelligible. After only a few performances this first popular theater closed. Private performances continued on occasion, however, at court.

Russia's first newspaper, carrying battle reports, technical information, and accounts of happenings at home and abroad, appeared in 1703. Peter had arranged earlier for an Amsterdam publisher to print books in the Russian language, but the results were not encouraging. So the tsar set up a printing press in Russia and, at the same time, simplified the alphabet. It can hardly be surprising that the first book printed in Russia in the new orthography was an arithmetic text which for the first time used Arabic numerals in place of the old clumsy Slavonic numerals. From that time forward the old orthography fell into disuse except for religious works and came to be called Church Slavonic. Soon after the 1917 Revolution the new government ordered a further simplification of the Russian alphabet.

The New Capital

Peter had hated the old city of Moscow and particularly the Kremlin from the days of his childhood; only in the foreign quarter had he found friends. As he grew from boy to man, he developed a lasting affection for the quarter, not only because of the personal attachments he had formed there, but because of what it stood for—a novel, fascinating, romantic, and progressive way of life, indeed a captivating new civilization. He became enthralled with the tales he heard from the Dutchmen, Germans, Frenchmen, and Scots who lived there, some of whom had dwelt and served in many countries. One imagines the young tsar searching about impatiently for some excuse to visit the West.

His predecessors, with all the interest in Western techniques and amenities that many of them had revealed, never for a moment considered a royal journey abroad. They were content to learn about foreign lands from the visits of ambassadors or from the accounts of Russian travelers. Peter, who seldom trusted the reports about anything that came to him, insisted upon seeing the West for himself.

Moscow represented to Peter all that was backward, archaic, and obscurantist. As the capital of the early princes who had groveled for two and a half centuries before an oriental suzerain, the city retained, from the dress and manners of its inhabitants to the architecture of its buildings, an air half Asiatic and half Byzantine. It was not a modern city to compare with London, Vienna, or Amsterdam. And it housed the patriarch, staunch defender of Orthodoxy and stubborn opponent of innovation.

From the moment of his accession at the age of ten in 1682, Peter spent little time in the Kremlin or anywhere in Moscow except in the German quarter. Soon after his mother's death in 1694, Peter assumed the management of affairs and launched the war against Turkey for control of the north littoral of the Black Sea. One suspects that he left Moscow to serve in the army with some sense of relief. From then on he spent on the average only a few days a year in the old city.

Peter's impetuosity is nowhere more evident than in his decision to build a new capital. He opened the war against Charles XII in 1700 by moving his army into Livonia to the south shore of the Gulf of Finland. The siege of Narva ended in such a rout of Peter's troops that the Swedish king turned his back in contempt upon the Russians. For the next six years Charles fought Russia's ally, Poland, and eventually defeated her.

While the Poles were keeping Charles occupied, Peter gathered a new army and advanced into Ingria. There, where the Neva River flows into the easternmost point of the Gulf of Finland, Peter chose in 1703 to lay out his new capital. This was still Swedish territory. The war had not ended. There had been no peace treaty, nor would there be for another eighteen years. He had no title to this land upon which he proposed, with no more than a squatter's rights, to build.

The site he selected for this new city, St. Petersburg, was a most inhospitable one. The land for miles around was marsh land, and the buildings that went up over the next ten years all rested upon pilings sunk deep into the swampy ground. The tsar put uncounted thousands of his state-owned serfs to work upon the project and drafted many thousands of others belonging to the gentry. Swedish prisoners of war who surrendered after Poltava joined the Russian workers. Contemporaries reported that hundreds of thousands died of exhaustion or disease or cruel treatment. The treasury collected millions of rubles to meet the cost, and it was, in fact, the fantastic burden of paying for the new capital that forced the imposition of the soul tax.

Many have wondered, because of the financial sacrifice and the political risk entailed, at the tsar's choice of a building site. If he wanted a capital where he could be near his beloved fleet, why not simply move the government to Riga, a thriving Baltic port already in existence? Riga belonged to Sweden, but so, too, did the swamp at the mouth of the Neva. He had as much right to the one as to the other.

If Peter ever considered Riga, he must have dismissed it quickly. His new capital must be new in every respect. Riga, although it had a fine harbor, was an old city with narrow winding streets and ancient buildings. Nothing about it, except the Dutch and English ships that called at the port, was Western. Peter, whose supreme confidence in the wonder-working power of Western technology never wavered, wanted a Western capital. Indeed, the Western, non-Russian appearance and character of the city he built have survived revolutions and civil war and communist rule.

While the common unskilled laborers who toiled year after year on the construction of St. Petersburg were natives, the master builders, the engineers, and the architects were usually foreigners. German, Dutch, English, French, and Italian craftsmen and artists earned salaries unheard of among Russians. Their assignment was to design and construct an entire city, not just the buildings to house government bureaus. Every civil servant and military officer was required to move into a new home in the capital. Each must build a house commensurate with his rank or wealth. The site, the size, the design, and the building materials were not matters for the occupant to choose for himself, however; the chief planners and architects made such decisions. To spare his new capital the fires that were the curse of cities of wood houses, Peter ordered all dwellings, as well as public buildings, to be of brick or stone. To assure an adequate supply of materials, he forbade stone construction anywhere else in Russia until St. Petersburg was completed.

The first building to go up at the new site was a small two-storied frame house for occupancy by the tsar when he could spare the time from campaign to watch the slow birth of his capital. It still stands, a haunting monument to the impatience of a restless builder.

This planned city, erected at an enormous sacrifice of money and lives, was ready for occupancy in an incredibly short

Cathedral of St. Isaac, Leningrad   (Photo from European)

time. Nearly 35,000 buildings rose in the decade after the arrival of the first contingent of planners and builders from the West. The Senate moved into its new Petersburg* offices in 1714, and other government agencies and foreign embassies quickly followed. Wealthy merchants and members of the gentry entered the city as soon as their new dwellings were available.

All who moved into St. Petersburg in these early years must have cursed the tsar for his choice of a quagmire upon which to locate the capital. The roads into Peter's "paradise" were almost impossible to negotiate by carriage or wagon even in dry weather, so formidable were the swamps that surrounded the city. But the marshy land made planning easy in one respect. The many canals, which to Peter's delight gave his capital some of the flavor of Amsterdam, were not difficult to cut, and the bridges over them and over the Neva River added to the city's adornment. St. Petersburg quickly earned world recognition as one of the most beautiful of cities.

Western travelers who visited the new capital a generation after its completion expressed amazement and admiration for this "gem of the North." The air of dignity and the magnificence about the city—the Admiralty building, the Hall of the Twelve Colleges, the Fortress of Sts. Peter and Paul, the Winter Palace of the emperors, the churches, the stately town houses of the gentry, the richly stocked shops of the merchants, the broad boulevards or "prospects," the public gardens and fountains and statuary—gave visitors as much to marvel at as they could find in any great city. The bustling docks gave the port an air of prosperity. Peter insisted that imports and exports move through his new capital. By 1800, two thirds of the nation's foreign trade entered and left Russia through the city.

St. Petersburg became a symbol, as the tsar intended it to be, of Peter's determination to make Russia a part of Western civilization. The Empress Catherine II later commissioned the

---

*Officially, the city was Sankt Peterburg—St. Petersburg—but many Russians called it simply Petersburg. In a belated tribute to the first emperor, Petrograd—Russian for "Peter's City"—replaced the German form of the name when, in 1914, Russia and Germany were at war. In 1924, Petrograd became Leningrad or "Lenin's City" after the death of the first ruler of communist Russia.

dedication in Senate Square of a fine equestrian statue of Peter. Later the poet Pushkin immortalized statue and model in his poem "The Bronze Horseman."

Resistance to Westernization

The move toward Westernization had been in preparation for nearly two and a half centuries after the winning of Russian independence from the Mongol yoke. In the thirty years of Peter's personal rule, Russia became so firmly committed to a Western course that later attempts to reverse the trend invariably failed.

To the very end of the monarchy there were individuals and groups in Russian society who fought Western ways and Western thought and influence. In the nineteenth century the quarrel became a philosophical one. The Slavophiles of the 1830s urged Russians to defend their ancient Slavic culture and institutions, and insisted that whatever misfortune or evil befell Russia was the product of pernicious Western influence. The Westernizers argued with as much vigor that Russia's salvation lay in embracing Western culture and technique, and warned that for the nation to hold stubbornly to its outmoded Slavic institutions was to invite cultural and technological stagnation.

Just as Westernization did not originate with Peter the Great, neither did resistance to Westernization begin in his reign. To trace its origin would hardly be profitable; opposition to change in any society seems to be self-generative and indifferent to any call for justification. Orthodox churchmen had stood in the front rank of those who fought innovation. They had done so in the fifteenth century when Sophia Palaeologus had brought Greek and Latin scholars and artists to Moscow. The early Romanovs all had faced resentment at the modest changes they had introduced in their timid ways.

Peter's reforming efforts came upon the Russian people with bewildering speed and this, together with the furious impatience with which he imposed them, provoked open or covert defiance from every segment of society. Churchmen, from parish priests and monks to bishops and archimandrites, spoke out against Western dress and the public appearance of women, just as churchmen had done in the reign of Alexis. They railed against the use of tobacco. They were most bitter over the desecration of the godly image of man when the tsar himself cut off the beards of his courtiers and then in effect forced the upper classes to go clean-shaven. Such sacrilege surely proved Peter to be antichrist, and there was talk that he was not of royal blood but was one of Lefort's bastards. Even Old Believers, who had little cause to agree with clerics of the state church, swore that Peter was the devil incarnate.

Clergymen, however, were not alone in their opposition to the tsar. Young peasants fled into the woods to avoid conscription for labor or for military service. If they did not escape such a draft, they deserted at the first opportunity. Families of serfs and sometimes entire villages disappeared in the night to run away to the frontier beyond the reach of the taxgatherer and the recruiting officer. Many members of the gentry, bitter over the ease with which a commoner could become a noble through the Table of Ranks, gave the tsar only grudging and indifferent service. That some of Peter's most intimate advisers were commoners, or even occasionally former slaves, was hardly palatable to the class that in earlier reigns had monopolized public office. Merchants begrudged the tax exemptions granted so generously to foreigners and to certain nobles. And the tsar honestly believed that even his own son plotted against him.

Alexis was the only child of Peter's first marriage to Eudoxia Lopukhin. The marriage was an unhappy one; the tsar deserted his bride two months after the wedding to rejoin his companions, the riotous "playmates" of his youth. Only rarely did the tsar leave his drinking friends and the dissolute women of Preobrazhenskoe or the German quarter of Moscow to visit his wife and son. The child acquired his mother's resentment at Peter's preference for low-born companions, and his hatred for his father grew even more bitter when Peter drove Eudoxia into a convent. The boy was eight years old at the time. He thenceforth had to live with Peter's sister whom he heartily disliked. He studied German and French with foreign tutors, and his father visited him occasionally to check upon his progress. Peter learned that Alexis had no interest in mathematics, gunnery, military engineering, or navigation. That his son preferred the study of religion only added to Peter's disgust. In one way was the son like the father: Alexis drank heavily, but he did not carry his liquor well; when drunk he would muster the courage to tell others of his hatred for his father.

When Alexis was twenty-five years old, Peter warned his son that he must prepare himself to take over the succession, and threatened to force Alexis into a monastery if he refused to heed the warning. The tsar had in mind that the heir should interest himself in the army and navy, and that he should learn something of administration. For such an assignment the tsarevich* was quite unsuited. In answering his father's request, Alexis confessed his lack of ability to govern Russia. He volunteered to surrender his right to the throne—a possibility that Peter would not yet accept—and asked only for permission to live in retirement on some country estate.

When Peter was in Western Europe in 1717 he wrote to Alexis, sternly demanding that his son begin preparation for his succession. The tsarevich, with his father at a safe distance, fled to Naples, but the tsar's secret police traced him there and dragged him back to St. Petersburg. Alexis quickly signed a renunciation of his inheritance, but this did not satisfy Peter. He demanded to know how his son had managed to escape from the capital, who had helped him get away as far as Naples, and who was privy to the plot—Peter was certain that there was a plot—to wipe out the reforms and restore Russia to her former Asiatic Byzantine darkness.

The tsarevich was put to the torture in an effort to pry from him the names of accomplices. Peter ordered the flogging of nuns who might tell him that his first wife Eudoxia was scheming from her convent cell the undoing of all of Peter's work once Alexis could succeed his father. Men tortured beyond endurance admitted the guilt and associations their tormentors accused them of, and Peter's conviction grew that his son had plotted his overthrow. A court of sorts condemned Alexis to death, but it

*Son of the tsar.

was the continuing torture to wring from him still more confession that killed him.

Whether the tsarevich was, in fact, guilty of involvement in any plan to overthrow his father or to undo his work after his father's death is beyond proof. But proof of his complicity, or even the existence of a plot, was unnecessary. Many knew of the son's distaste for his father's new ways. That Alexis consorted with churchmen was common knowledge, and that many and perhaps most churchmen resented Peter and all he stood for was no secret. The fact, then, was that those who hoped for a restoration of the old way of life must naturally have looked to Alexis, conservative as all knew him to be, as the one to turn the clock back. The tsarevich was potentially a plotter whether or not he chose to be.

Peter did not hesitate to sacrifice his own son to the cause of Russia's Westernization. With Alexis dead, the tsar could rest content that those who would turn the nation back along the old benighted way had lost the symbol around whom they could rally.

Diplomatic Entanglements with the West

Petrine Russia became a diplomatic force of some significance when the tsar visited Western Europe in 1697. His hope for allies against the sultan did not materialize, and he ended the war against Turkey soon after his return to Russia. On his way home, however, it began to appear that he might win support against a different enemy.

When he stopped off in Poland to visit King Augustus II, who was also elector of Saxony, Peter and the Polish king agreed to attack Sweden, whose ruler was a rash youth of seventeen. There was no need to spell out what the spoils would be. Some Swedish territory on the south Baltic coast would go to Poland and some to Russia, which would thus obtain a Baltic foothold. Denmark, who joined the coalition, would receive Schleswig, then ruled by the duke of Holstein who was brother-in-law to Charles XII of Sweden.

Peter's decisive victory over Charles XII at Poltava in

1709 signaled the imminent decline of Sweden as a great power and the rise of Russia to a position of dominance in the Baltic. Poland was in such a state of decline that, on the one hand, Peter could challenge the outcome of elections to the Polish throne and, on the other hand, there were suggestions in Berlin and Vienna that a partition of Poland was in order. The political balance in Eastern Europe which had endured for over a century was threatened if not already undone. Austria, Denmark, the Netherlands, Prussia, and the German states saw an immediate threat from the power shift.

The "Great Northern War" between Charles XII and Peter I carried Russian troops into the heart of Europe—to the Elbe and once even into western Germany. The tsar flexed his power by interfering rudely and unceremoniously in the affairs of Poland and a number of German states. He proposed marriage alliances with Western courts, evidence in itself of Russia's emergence from isolation. With the single exception of Ivan III who married Sophia Palaeologus, no Russian ruler had married a foreigner in seven centuries. Peter's son married a German princess; when she died in childbirth, the tsar proposed his son's marriage into the French royal family, but nothing came of it.

Anne, one of Peter's two nieces, was married to the duke of Courland, a province on the south coast of the Baltic lying between the Western Dvina and Niemen Rivers. The duke died a few months later, but Anne ultimately became empress of Russia. Peter's other niece, Anne's sister Catherine, married Charles Leopold of Mecklenburg, whose duchy lay on the extreme west coast of the Baltic directly south of Copenhagen. Their two-month-old grandson momentarily became emperor of Russia in 1740.

Peter betrothed his daughter Anne to the duke of Holstein, nephew of Charles XII of Sweden, but the wedding took place after Peter's death. The product of that marriage was the half-insane Peter III whose wife became the empress Catherine the Great. The other daughter of Peter the Great was Elizabeth, whose marriage to King Louis XV of France Peter had tried to arrange in 1717 when he was in Paris on one of his many Western trips. Since the king was only seven, the French court could give the proposal leisurely consideration and, by the time Louis XV was old enough to marry, Peter was dead. Perhaps the strangest bit of matchmaking in which the tsar indulged was the discussion over the marriage of his five-year-old daughter Natalia to the son of the king of Spain. The conversations bore no fruit, however, for Natalia died two years later.

The marriages of Peter's relatives into ruling families of petty German courts began a practice followed with monotonous consistency by his successors. The Romanovs were accused, not unjustly, of getting their "brood mares from the stables" of stuffy little princely courts in Central Europe. The result, apparent even in Peter's own time, was that Russia often could not avoid involvement in minor feuds and quarrels that sometimes proved embarrassing and even costly.

It was not only the marriage of his own children and nieces that engaged Peter's fascination with foreign entanglement and downright intrigue. One of the most fantastic proposals that Peter ever considered was the offer by Spain in 1718 of a Russo-Swedish-Spanish alliance to drive the Hanoverian George I off the English throne and restore the Stuarts. Sweden was no longer a serious threat to Russia, and the Swedish king might have obtained more favorable peace terms by becoming Russia's ally. The details of the plan were worked out to the point of providing for an expeditionary force of Swedes and Russians to land in Scotland in support of the Stuart Pretender. The fanciful project fell through when Charles XII died shortly thereafter.

Russia's involvement in the affairs of Europe was not always so chimerical as was the Scottish venture. Peter established embassies in many countries and paid frequent personal visits to the spas and capitals of the West. His ambassadors tried, by gifts of gold, gems, and furs, to bribe the diplomats and statesmen of Europe. If Russian ambassadors were not always impeccable in taste and manners, their gifts were always welcome. St. Petersburg was generous in its grant of titles, decorations, and even estates. The duke of Marlborough, one of the great generals of the age and minister to Queen Anne of England, received one of Russia's highest decorations, a costly ruby, a principality, and a generous income.

When the tsar returned to St. Petersburg from the peace negotiations at Nystadt in 1721, the Senate solemnly proclaimed him Emperor and Peter the Great. His successors, of course, also assumed the imperial title, although several great powers were slow to recognize it—Turkey, Austria, Great Britain, France, and Spain recognized it twenty years or more after Peter's death. However grudging the recognition of the title he labored so hard to earn, there was no denying that Peter had brought his country geographically, politically, and diplomatically into the European state system.

Peter's Contribution

The war with Sweden dragged on for over twenty years, for Charles XII was unwilling to surrender the east and south coasts of the Gulf of Finland, and Peter would settle for nothing less. Meanwhile, Russian forces built up an impressive list of victories. The tsar's armies conquered Finland in 1714, and in the summer of that year his Baltic fleet defeated the Swedes brilliantly in the battle of Hangö. The Aland Islands fell to the Russians, giving them an offshore base fifteen miles from Stockholm, the Swedish capital. In 1716 a great war fleet of Russian and Danish ships, with a few Dutch and English vessels, gathered in Copenhagen for an attack against Sweden and the landing of an expeditionary force on the Swedish coast. Peter, on what must have been a glorious occasion for him, was in command. The fleet did not sail, however, for there was little enthusiasm for the project among Peter's allies. His own armies later ravaged Swedish territory in Germany, and the great north German ports of Hamburg and Lübeck bought off Russian generals with heavy ransom. In the summer of 1719 a large Russian army landed on the south coast of Sweden and plundered at will, while a troop of Cossacks advanced to within two miles of Stockholm.

After Charles XII died in battle in 1718, his enemies one by one came to terms with Sweden. Finally, the Peace of Nystadt brought a settlement satisfactory to Peter. Russia received the east Baltic provinces of Livonia, Estonia, and Ingria, including the fine ports of Riga and Reval; she also obtained Karelia which included the flourishing capital St. Petersburg, the Finnish town of Viborg, and the north shore of Ladoga, thus surrounding that lake with Russian territory. Sweden received back Finland.

Perhaps Peter's most spectacular achievement was the winning of his "window on the Baltic." His determination to have that window became unmistakably clear in 1703 when he knocked down a tiny Finnish fishing village at the mouth of the Neva and began boldly and defiantly to stake out the site of his new capital on land that was still the property of the Swedish king. While the breath-taking beauty of St. Petersburg dramatized the tremendous accomplishment to which the tsar had devoted the better part of his reign, it was the greater prize of the foothold on the Baltic that proved more substantial. Now Russia was a Baltic power, both militarily and commercially. St. Petersburg, of course, did not make her so. But no Baltic power could ignore the fleet of warships based at Kronstadt. And Peter's merchant marine, the very size of which British shipping magnates resented as a threat to their own cargo fleet in these northern waters, made Russia a commercial power in the Baltic. The building of new bottoms in the shipyards of the capital, and the loading and unloading at wharves along the Neva of freighters from many lands—England, France, the Netherlands, Denmark, Sweden, Germany, Spain, and later the young United States—marked Russia as the dominant power in the eastern Baltic.

Peter made Russia not simply a Baltic power, or even the Baltic power. He made her a European power of tremendous force. The influence she wielded was not always wholesome. Her interference in European affairs was not always welcome. Surely the same was true of other powers on the rim of Europe—Great Britain, the Ottoman Empire, and the United States. From Peter's day forward, however, Europe could not go its own divided way, oblivious of Russia's concern for and interest in the nations of the West. Not many of Russia's rulers would be so naive as to turn their backs upon Europe and take up some foggy civilizing mission in Asia, as the last German kaiser urged the last Russian tsar to do.

Russia became Western in many ways, but in ways that were most apparent in government and the governing classes. Before Peter's accession the central administration would have been unrecognizable and even unintelligible to a Westerner. By the time of his death in 1725 any knowledgeable Frenchman, Englishman, Swede, Prussian, Spaniard, or Austrian would have understood the administrative pattern of Russia because it would have seemed so similar to that of his own country. He would have recognized the colleges and the bureaus and might have smiled knowingly at the German or Swedish names Peter gave them. He would have nodded approval at the existence of a carefully regulated state church. The Englishman or the Swede might have felt little sympathy for the total absence of any parliament, but the others would have applauded it. This was the age of absolutism in the West. There was no effective popular check upon royal authority in France, Spain, Portugal, Austria, Prussia, and most of the German and Italian states. Peter did not need to look to Byzantium or Asia for lessons in autocracy. His unbounded faith in royal absolutism may have grown in some measure from admiration for things Western and in his satisfaction that autocracy, too, was a Western practice.

Much of the veneer of Western civilization—the manners, dress, habits, taste, technology, artistic and cultural values, and social attitudes—affected the governing classes profoundly and the urban and rural masses hardly at all. This produced a schism, an alienation of upper and lower classes in Russia that made the two extremes on the social scale seem more like two different nationalities or two races than two classes. It also produced a rigidity of class and an almost total lack of mobility from one class to another. In very fact there had been far more class mobility—the rise of a serf to become a free farmer or a merchant or the fall of a noble into serfdom—before Peter's time than there would be for a century and a half thereafter.

The violence and the rapidity of change which Peter wrought in so many aspects of Russian life, and particularly the ruthlessness with which he forced the change, inspired resentment and opposition both in his lifetime and long after his death. In dragging a reluctant and resisting people toward Western techniques and social customs and values, he provoked the criticism of later Russians less in what he sought to do than in his manner of doing it. No one excused his cruelty. With remarkably few exceptions, however, those who deplored his methods condoned or applauded his goals and his achievements. One of Russia's greatest historians, Vasily Klyuchevsky, noted that Peter's reforms often contradicted each other and called attention to "his errors, his hesitations, his obstinacy, his lack of judgment in civil affairs, his uncontrollable cruelty." Finding more in Peter to praise than to condemn, however, Klyuchevsky admires him for "his wholehearted love of his country, his stubborn devotion to his work, the broad, enlightened outlook he brought to bear on it, his daring plans conceived with creative genius and concluded with incomparable energy, and finally the success he achieved by the incredible sacrifices of his people and himself." One of Russia's greatest literary critics, Vissarion Belinsky, praised Peter the Great as the one who "breathed the breath of life into the body of ancient Russia, colossal but prostrate in deadly slumber."

Belinsky made a poor historian. Much of the Westernization that seemed so dramatically and so suddenly to appear in the early eighteenth century had long been in preparation or in various stages of adoption. Aside from a detail here and there, however, the most significant aspect of the Petrine reforms was that they represented the fruition, if not the culmination, of a process of modernization long at work. What was really new about Peter's achievements was less the reforms themselves than the spirit with which he imposed them. His concern was not simply to import Westerners and to savor their ideas. His determination was that the Westerners and their ideas—their civilization—would refashion Russian society in the Western mode. Unfortunately, perhaps, the remaking of Russia was only a partial success.

It was perhaps Peter's doing that from his day forward Russia remained half Western and half Byzantine-Oriental, half enlightened and half benighted, half modern and half primitive, even half slave and half free. To Westerners, Russia and its people suggested endless contradictions and paradoxes.

CHAPTER THREE

Post-Petrine Westernization: The Eighteenth Century

ONE of the least salutary of the changes that Peter the Great imposed upon his country was his alteration of the law of succession. There was really no approved way in seventeenth-century Russia for a new ruler to follow an old one. The Time of Troubles had witnessed various types of confusion over the succession, but this had come to an end with the Romanovs, more by custom than by law. Michael's son succeeded him; the oldest son of Alexis succeeded his father; then the next oldest son of Alexis, Ivan V, succeeded Fedor III but, because no one expected the simple Ivan to manage affairs, his half-brother Peter shared the succession with him and Sophia served them both as regent.

In 1722 an imperial decree proclaimed the right of the ruler to appoint his successor. The emperor's infant son Peter had died earlier, and of his several children only two daughters would survive him. Peter the Great did not avail himself of his new succession law, however. Perhaps he reasoned that he had already named his successor; less than a year before his death there was a coronation ceremony at which his second wife Catherine became empress of Russia. During the thirty-seven years following Peter's death, there were seven rulers of the unhappy land. They came to the throne by intrigue, by plot, and by *coup d'état*. Some reigns ended in natural death, some in assassination, others in imprisonment, and still others in forcible exile. The shortest reign lasted six months, the longest twenty years. One ruler came to the throne at the age of two months and went to the dungeons a year later. An eleven-year-old child became emperor only to die on the day of his scheduled marriage at the age of fourteen.

The German Period

As Peter the Great lay dying early in 1725, some of his favorites, with the support of officers of the Guards, decided that Peter's wife Catherine should succeed him. This choice of the sovereign by a small group of officials or favorites who could count upon the backing of the Guards set the pattern for the *coups d'état* or palace revolutions that would decide every succession in the eighteenth century. Catherine gathered about her a coterie of Germans from the newly acquired Baltic provinces, some as lovers and some as advisers. One was Baron Andrew Ostermann, whom Peter had used as a diplomatic envoy. The baron so enjoyed his privileges as one of the ruler's chief advisers that he schemed to make his position permanent by arranging the marriage of the two chief candidates for the succession—Peter's daughter Elizabeth to her nephew who was Peter's grandson. Although the incestuous arrangement did not materialize, Ostermann managed to continue in high favor under four sovereigns during the next fifteen years.

Catherine I survived her husband by only two years. When she died in 1727, a gathering of favorites and officials discovered her will, probably a forgery, naming Peter the Great's grandson, the son of Alexis, as emperor. The cheers of the

Guards regiments mustered at the palace gates provided a sufficient air of acceptability, and the eleven-year-old boy became Peter II.

The young Peter came under the influence of a scheming clique led by Prince Ivan Dolgoruky, nineteen-year-old companion of the tsar, and by Baron Ostermann. His advisers persuaded Peter to order the return of the capital to Moscow, and St. Petersburg seemed doomed to political extinction. The young tsar contracted smallpox, however, and died on his wedding day in 1730. The male branch of the Romanov line died with him.

For the third time in five years the favorites, Ostermann, a few other high officials, and some Guards officers, debated the succession. From several candidates of equal legality they agreed upon Peter the Great's younger niece Anne, the widow duchess of Courland. This council, self-appointed to direct the succession, offered the crown to Anne on the condition that she accept certain limitations upon her authority. In effect, she must rule according to the wishes of the "Supreme Privy Council" of eight members who were offering her the throne, and she must neither marry nor name a successor without the council's approval. Baron Ostermann was one of those who drafted the conditions offered to Anne, although he came out against them when he found it profitable to do so. Anne accepted the restrictive document when an official delegation from Moscow laid it before her in her Courland capital of Mitau.

The new empress entered Moscow after declaring herself colonel of the Preobrazhensky Guards, an act explicitly forbidden by the limitation of power she had agreed to. Troops loyal to the crown and suspicious of the intriguing Supreme Privy Council begged Anne to cast aside the conditions to which she had subscribed and to restore the autocratic power. Baron Ostermann convinced Anne, who probably needed little convincing, that she was entitled to the throne in her own right and that her succession required neither election nor confirmation. She obliged her supporters by ostentatiously tearing up the pledge she had given.

The duchess of Courland, married at seventeen and widowed a few weeks later, had lived for nineteen years in Mitau with no income other than the unpredictable subsidies she received from Russia. Her pleading letters to royal relatives and such court favorites as Ostermann brought her enough to maintain a modest establishment. A Russian envoy in Mitau served a dual role as director of governmental affairs in Courland and as Anne's lover. When he returned to Russia, Anne shifted her favors to Ernst Biren, a German who occupied a minor post in Mitau. The Supreme Privy Council, in offering Anne the vacant Russian throne, warned her not to bring her lover to Moscow. She ignored the warning, and Biren became a power of great influence in the new administration. Anne's reign, in fact, went down in the nation's memory as *Birenovshchina*—the rule of Biren.

Anne had endured such penury for seventeen years as duchess of Courland that she devoted the last decade of her life to the gratification of every wish. She lavished enormous sums upon unending court functions and the maintenance of costly households at the various royal palaces. She returned the government to Petersburg, where it would remain without interruption until the Bolsheviks moved it back to Moscow. The direction of affairs became the responsibility of a "cabinet" of three men appointed by the empress. Although he was not a member, Biren controlled it while Ostermann served as its chief "minister."

The sovereign's preference for Germans over Russians became apparent in many ways. Biren had to share his carnal knowledge of the empress with Count Karl Löwenwolde, whose two brothers held highly paid court positions. The commander of the Russian armies was Count Burkhard Münnich who became a field marshal. Anne brought many Baltic Germans to Russia with her and found places for most of them by creating a new regiment, the Izmailovsky Guards, and limiting officer appointments exclusively to Baltic German nobles. Count Karl Löwenwolde became its commanding officer.

The Germans who flocked to court during Anne's reign often quarreled among themselves and jostled each other for preferment. Biren and Ostermann contested for dominance over domestic and foreign affairs, although the two might heal their differences temporarily to meet a challenge from some Russian. Through much of the reign Biren, a late arrival among the Germans at court, had to face the opposition of both Ostermann and Münnich, the army commander. Ostermann managed to thwart Biren's design to marry his son Peter to Anne's niece, the probable successor to the empress.

Anne and her German courtiers and lovers ruled Russia for a decade after 1730. On her deathbed she named as her successor her sister's grandson, a two-month-old infant. Biren would serve as regent until Ivan VI reached maturity. But Ostermann, Münnich, and the child's parents—the prince and princess of Brunswick—drove Biren into Siberian exile, and the infant emperor's mother became regent. Münnich assumed leadership as "first minister," but Ostermann pushed him aside and supported Ivan VI's father, against his mother, in the contest over the regency.

The dreary spectacle of Germans fighting other Germans for power to control the government of the Russian Empire came abruptly to an end with a *coup d'état* by Peter the Great's daughter Elizabeth. While Russians had good reason to resent any further prolongation of the German comedy, the impulse to end it came from abroad. The Swedish government insisted that foreign rule in St. Petersburg must end and sent an army into Russia ostensibly to free the land of its carpetbaggers. The possibility of recovering some of the territory lost to Peter the Great must not have escaped officials in Stockholm. France was hoping for Russian support in the War of the Austrian Succession or at least for Russian neutrality, and the French ambassador encouraged Elizabeth to accept the backing of the Guards. When Guards officers begged Elizabeth to drive out the Germans and claim the throne, she accepted the challenge and rode to the royal palace at the head of the grenadier company of the Preobrazhensky Guards. The child emperor Ivan VI went to live out his life in an unlighted dungeon to be forgotten for twenty years and to grow up a helpless simpleton. His mother and father spent the remainder of their lives moving about from one prison to another. Ostermann, Münnich, and other leaders of the past decade received death sentences. The new empress opposed the death penalty—although the harshest of tortures left her indifferent—and so the fallen favorites escaped with lifelong exile to Siberia.

The Daughter of Peter the Great

Elizabeth, born to Peter and his second wife Catherine some years before their marriage, was strikingly beautiful, charming, dissolute, and common. Her father had pressed her candidacy for marriage to Louis XV, the child king of France, and had even arranged for her to take lessons in dancing and in French to equip her for life at Versailles. When the prospect of a French wedding failed to materialize, she agreed to wed the Lutheran bishop of Lubeck, but he died before the ceremony could take place. Her freedom from any sense of decorum allowed her to find solace from these early disappointments in an unending parade of amorous adventures. She enjoyed the company of common men and women, as had her parents, and she generously bestowed her affections upon illiterate Cossacks and muscular Guardsmen.

During the reigns of Anne and Ivan VI, Elizabeth had lived modestly and quietly away from court, trying to escape notice. After coming out of seclusion, however, she devoted much of her time and far too much of the state's revenue to extravagant entertainment and luxurious living. At the time of her death she left a wardrobe of fifteen thousand gowns. So much did she spend on clothing, court functions, lovers, and wars that she had on more than one occasion to demand of officials and even the church a "voluntary" contribution to meet expenses.

Elizabeth announced at the moment of her accession in 1741 that she would rule in the spirit of Peter the Great. This was an implicit promise that the nation's interests and welfare would receive primary consideration. The empress Anne had made the same commitment back in 1730 and then had promptly forgotten it.

The "cabinet" that Anne had appointed to manage the government disappeared when its members departed for Siberia.

Elizabeth revived the Senate, whose importance had ebbed away since the death of Peter the Great and whose responsibilities each new sovereign had transferred to some new administrative agency. The empress also appointed a director-general of the Senate; there had been none for years. She occasionally attended Senate meetings, at least early in her reign. To supervise the maintenance of royal palaces and to arrange the court entertainments of which she was so fond, Elizabeth set up "Her Majesty's Private Chancery," an agency that would continue for a century to function as it did in her time. For attending day-to-day affairs of state the empress had little patience. Such matters so bored her that she often put off for months the signing of important papers.

While some Russian names had appeared among those close to the throne in earlier reigns, the years from the accession of Catherine I to that of Elizabeth had seen Germans in positions of greatest influence. Now the German names disappeared and those who found preferment were Russians—Trubetskoy, Bestuzhev-Riumen, Ushakov, Cherkasov, Cherkassky, Vorontsov, Shuvalov, Olsufev, Razumovsky. And it is hardly surprising that St. Petersburg began to reflect an interest in French learning and culture that cleared the air of the stuffiness the Germans and Balts had brought with them. Versailles was setting the style for every court in Europe, including those in Germany. French manners, dress, language, and art would continue to be fashionable in Russian royal and noble circles until well into the nineteenth century.

The handsome Ivan Shuvalov, one of Elizabeth's lovers, did much to give the reign an air of cultured progress. He had traveled widely over Europe and was an ardent Francophile. In his concern for science and the arts, of which he was a generous patron, he deplored the modest educational facilities that Russia had to offer. In 1754 he drew up a project to establish a university and two secondary schools in Moscow, one of the latter to be open to sons of the gentry and the other to sons of free commoners. So successful were the secondary schools that two others similar to those in Moscow later opened in Kazan, although Shuvalov's hope proved vain that there would be similar accommodations in every large town. The first Russian institution of higher learning opened in Moscow in 1755. It offered programs in law, philosophy, and medicine, emphasizing the humanities in the first two and science in the third. Ivan Shuvalov, who spurned the rank of count that Elizabeth offered him, became the University of Moscow's first curator.

The reign of Elizabeth witnessed the emergence of a Russian literature that borrowed heavily from the West in orientation and technique. Indeed, Russia was still learning from the West in everything from fashions to science, and in many respects the fascination would never end. The father of Russian drama, Alexander Sumarokov, began in this reign to produce tragedies and comedies in some volume. Not only did he write plays but he staged them, for he became director of the first native Russian theater.

Michael Lomonosov, another of the founders of the University of Moscow, was Russia's first great poet. The son of a state peasant, he studied in Russia and for several years in Germany. His influence upon the Russian language was significant, not only through his poems but through publication of his Russian language grammar, the first of any importance. He was a pioneer in physics and chemistry, and taught the first course anywhere in the world in physical chemistry. He was his country's leading astronomer, geologist, metallurgist, mineralogist, and geographer. His discoveries in electricity, optics, heat theory, and the preservation of matter and energy were lost upon his contemporaries and had to be repeated by later generations.

Western artists continued to visit Russia and even took up work and residence there, as they had in the time of Elizabeth's father. An Italian opera company performed at court during Anne's reign, and there were many operatic and ballet performances before Elizabeth. In 1757, Ivan Shuvalov created the Academy of Arts as an agency independent of the Academy of Sciences, which had harbored an art section theretofore. Portrait painting, owing much to Western teaching, made progress. Construction of the costly and ornate Winter Palace began in St. Petersburg at Elizabeth's order. Its designer was Bartolomeo

Rastrelli, whose father had emigrated from Italy and settled in Russia to sculpt for Peter the Great.

Russia's emergence in the early eighteenth century as a European power had introduced her into a quarrelsome family. No longer were her foreign relations a relatively simple matter of dealing with the Eastern European powers—Poland, Sweden, and Turkey—all of whom were declining in strength and importance years before the death of Peter I. In the future Russia's concerns would lie with the vigorous older powers and the emerging younger powers of Central and Western Europe. The nation's conduct of foreign affairs, however, would suffer in the post-Petrine generation from a variety of circumstances, many of them of Peter's own making. Russia's dynastic ties with petty German courts, the European affiliations and sympathies of various rulers and particularly of their favorites, and the frequent struggles over the succession that often involved outside influences, complicated the nation's foreign relations.

The conduct of foreign affairs between 1725 and 1741 was the responsibility essentially of one man, Baron Andrew Ostermann, a Rhineland German who had joined the Russian service at the age of eighteen and served Peter the Great in an assortment of diplomatic assignments. He stayed on in positions of power until the accession of Elizabeth, who exiled him to Siberia along with the other influential Germans of whom the nation had seen quite enough. The elements of Ostermann's foreign policy were simple: alliance with Austria and resistance to France who opposed Russia's interests in Poland, Sweden, and Turkey.

In 1726, Russia joined Austria and Spain in an alliance that promised mutual defense against the hostile camp of Great Britain, France, Sweden, Denmark, and some of the German states including, momentarily, Prussia. Austria also agreed to aid Russia in any future war with Turkey and to assist the duke of Holstein—son-in-law to Russia's Empress Catherine I—in recovering Schleswig from Denmark. It was Catherine's blind devotion to the Holstein interests of her relatives, with whom Ostermann had little sympathy or patience, that provoked the hostility of Denmark and Denmark's allies, Great Britain and France. The early death of the empress removed Holstein as an irritant to Russo-Danish relations, and the two Baltic powers signed a mutual defense pact, directed obviously against Poland and Sweden. Of even greater significance for Europe, as well as for Russia ultimately, was the realignment of the powers after 1730. Austria and Spain drifted apart and the Franco-British alliance broke up over colonial rivalry. The predictable consequence was that Britain and Austria patched up their differences.

The death of the Polish king in 1733 produced an international crisis because the kingship was elective. The French candidate, the father-in-law of the French king Louis XV, was Stanislas Leszcynski who had won election to the Polish throne back in 1704, had fled from Poland five years later, and had recovered his throne in 1711 only to lose it again. His pro-Swedish leanings made him wholly unacceptable to St. Petersburg. The Russian and Austrian candidate was Augustus, the son of Augustus II, the Strong, who had occupied the throne for so long with Russian backing. The Polish Diet chose the French candidate, but hurriedly reversed itself in favor of Augustus III when Russian troops approached Warsaw. During that War of the Polish Succession a Russian army marched deep into Germany to support an Austrian force near Heidelberg against French troops. The likelihood that the Russians would advance to the Rhine subsided when the war suddenly came to an end. Surely no act could more clearly have demonstrated Russia's involvement in the affairs of Europe than the appearance of Cossacks in the medieval university city of Heidelberg. Russia at the time still had no university.

Meanwhile Turkey had chosen to regard Russian interference in the Polish succession as a threat to Turkish interests, and the French ambassador at Constantinople had passed around generous bribes in an attempt to provoke the sultan into declaring war against Russia. Now that the Polish matter had ended to his liking, Ostermann was not reluctant to shift the pressure to the Ottoman Empire, which he regarded as in a state of decline and in danger of imminent disintegration. He hoped also to put an end to the irritating raids out of the Crimea by the Tatars who recognized the sultan as overlord.

The war with Turkey dragged on for four years, although Ostermann had expected only a summer campaign. One Russian army captured Azov, the scene of Peter's fleeting triumph; another drove into the Crimean peninsula and occupied the Tatar capital. Some time later a Russian force advanced across the Prut River into Moldavia, where a group of leaders came forward to offer the crown of Moldavia to the Russian empress. But the Austrians, who joined the war reluctantly in fulfillment of their treaty commitment, provided little assistance and soon withdrew. Russian interest waned and the war came to an end.

By the terms of the Treaty of Belgrade in 1739, Russia retained Azov and its surrounding territory but agreed not to send a fleet into the Black Sea. The long war had been extremely costly in money and men and had brought little reward.

While that Russo-Turkish war was still in progress, the French ambassador in Stockholm was busy with bribes and rumors inspiring anti-Russian sentiment among the Swedes. In the summer of 1741, long after the end of the Russo-Turkish war that might have given it some advantage, the Swedish government sensed an imminent crisis in St. Petersburg and a possible *coup d'état* against the infant Ivan VI. Swedish officials nobly offered to rid Russia of "foreign rule"—the Germans such as Ostermann who were bitterly anti-Swedish—and marched an army toward the Russian frontier. The Russians advanced into Finland to meet it and routed the Swedes in the war's only battle. Elizabeth's succession brought an end to the mild contest. Her firm refusal to return any of the land conquered by Peter the Great left the Swedish government the choice between accepting Russia's terms or facing a further loss of territory. The Peace of Abo in 1743 made Viborg a Russian city by pushing the Western boundary still farther west along the north coast of the Gulf of Finland.

The War of the Austrian Succession began late in 1740 when King Frederick II of Prussia without a declaration of war invaded Austrian Silesia and claimed it for his own. Whatever the legal technicalities Frederick could conjure by way of excuse for his unscrupulous act, the inspiration for the seizure lay in the accession of Maria Theresa to the thrones of the archduchy of Austria and the kingdoms of Hungary and Bohemia. Her father, Emperor Charles VI, had obtained the signatures of nearly every monarch in Europe for the Pragmatic Sanction that approved the inheritance of the Austrian possessions by a woman in contravention of Austrian law. The fact that Frederick William I, father of Frederick II, had agreed to the succession was no deterrent to the cynical son. Bavaria and France joined the tempting feast, expecting to gain valuable territory with little or no opposition from a helpless and beautiful twenty-three-year-old woman. Only in Russia had women ruled in the eighteenth century, and they had not set an example of strength.

Russia was slow to meet her treaty commitment to assist in the defense of Austria, begging the imminence of war with Sweden. Elizabeth's succession produced a contest at court between a pro-French party—the French ambassador who had helped to finance the empress's *coup d'état* and the duke of Holstein, who was Elizabeth's nephew, and his wife Catherine, both of whom ardently admired Frederick II—and a pro-Austrian party headed by Count Alexis Bestuzhev-Riumen who was primarily responsible for the conduct of foreign affairs. The empress listened sympathetically to the persuasive arguments of the pro-French group, but Bestuzhev finally convinced Elizabeth that the Prussian Frederick with French backing was a far more dangerous enemy than Maria Theresa could be.

The war continued off and on for eight years, and for seven years Russia managed to avoid it. Elizabeth finally agreed to a mutual defense pact with Austria, but it would apply only to any future war. Then, four months before hostilities ended, Russia promised, in return for a generous subsidy from Great Britain, to march an army to the Rhine to attack France. The Russian force moved so slowly, however, that an armistice was agreed upon before it could carry out its mission. Russia did not even earn a seat at the peace table.

Bestuzhev continued his tortuous diplomatic maneuvering in the short interval of peace before the next general European war. His primary concern was to isolate Prussia, whose king had so ruthlessly exploited the Austrian succession question and whom Elizabeth and her foreign minister regarded as thoroughly untrustworthy. The empress recalled her ambassador in Berlin soon after the end of the War of the Austrian Succession, and the Prussian minister to Russia left St. Petersburg.

For several years Bestuzhev sought an alliance with Great Britain. Finally in 1755 the two powers agreed that, in return for an enormous British subsidy, Russian troops would defend the German possessions of the Hanoverian king of England against a Prussian attack. Elizabeth resisted Bestuzhev's persistent request that she accept the British offer for such a long time, however, that London began to lose hope of an agreement and came to terms with Prussia almost at the very moment when Elizabeth finally agreed to a Russo-British convention. The treaty soon proved to be meaningless.

Frederick of Prussia, by his seizure of Silesia at the time of Austria's embarrassment over the succession, managed to touch off a diplomatic revolution. Maria Theresa refused to accept as final the loss of Silesia, and her chancellor Count Wenzel von Kaunitz persuaded the government of Louis XV that Prussia, with her Rhineland provinces, posed a sinister threat to the peace of Europe and to the territorial integrity of France as well as Austria. France's shift of policy in 1755 from one of long hostility to Austria to one of alliance with Austria constituted one part of this most famous "Diplomatic Revolution." Another appeared in Great Britain's shift of support from Austria to Prussia. Both Britain and France felt more at ease in opposition camps in Europe, for they were deadly serious in their bitter dual for empire in Asia and North America.

Russia's alignment in the new diplomatic arrangement on the eve of the Seven Years' War constituted no serious break with her traditional foreign policy. During the war she managed to avoid any conflict with Great Britain, whose interests in Eastern Europe had frequently coincided with her own. The real enemy in Elizabeth's eyes was Prussia. Russia's long friendship with Austria would stand firm. Her cooperation with France, however, was a temporary flirtation that would not long endure.

The generals who led the Russian armies distinguished themselves by their caution and by their slowness to take advantage of their victories. In spite of their leadership, however, Russian soldiers defeated Frederick II on several battlefields. The Prussian king lost the battle of Kunersdorf so disastrously— he managed to save only 3,000 of the 50,000 men with whom he began the engagement—that he expressed grave doubt that his country could survive the blow.

Early in the war the Russians overran East Prussia, and the empress determined to retain it when peace came. In 1760, Russian and Austrian troops occupied Berlin for several days and forced the citizens to pay a heavy indemnity. Frederick II paid the Russian general a generous bribe to leave his capital, but the Prussian king suffered nightmares for years at the memory of Cossacks in Berlin.

Elizabeth, whose health had been failing for years, died early in January 1762, and with her death Russia's participation in the war came to an end. Her stubborn insistence upon destroying Prussian military strength and political influence in the affairs of Europe marked Russia as the most uncompromising of Frederick's foes. France was losing one colonial empire in North America and another in India, and her enthusiasm for the war in Europe was rapidly waning. Even Austria had tired of trying to recover Silesia. Had Elizabeth lived, however, Prussia might well have suffered annihilation. Great Britain, Frederick's sole ally, suddenly lost interest in the European phase of the war when George II, king of England and of Hanover, died in 1760. His grandson, George III, felt no concern for continental politics. William Pitt, the prime minister who had so staunchly supported Frederick, left office. And the huge colonial gains in India and North America were all the compensation Britain really wanted for her contribution to the war.

Elizabeth's death proved providential for Frederick II. Indeed, the Hohenzollern rulers of Prussia ever after expressed gratitude for what they remembered reverently as "the miracle." Russia's new ruler was Elizabeth's nephew, Peter III, who was so sentimentally fond of Frederick the Great that he always carried his portrait with him and often kissed the bust of Frederick that he kept in his chambers. Peter survived his accession just six months, but that was long enough to withdraw from the coalition and turn Russian troops around to fight alongside the Prussians against Elizabeth's former allies. At Peter's invitation Frederick II dictated the peace treaty. Its terms provided that Russia should return to Prussia all the territory occupied during the war.

The Empress Catherine II

Peter III, grandson of Peter the Great and grandnephew of Charles XII of Sweden, had married a princess of the poor German principality of Anhalt-Zerbst. Seventeen years after the wedding and six months after his accession, his wife became the empress of Russia. Her lover Gregory Orlov, with the aid of his brothers, had assassinated Peter III to make way for her.

With Peter III out of the way several claimants to the throne had a better right to it than did Catherine. She, indeed, had none. Her own son Paul, whose father Catherine swore was not her husband but Serge Saltykov, had a strong presumptive claim. Ivan VI, who had ruled for a year before Elizabeth imprisoned him, had even a stronger claim. He was the great-grandson of Peter the Great's half-witted half-brother Ivan V, and of his parentage at least there was no doubt. Catherine even considered marrying him in order to strengthen her position, but a prison interview with the sickly idiot changed her mind. His guards later killed him to foil an attempt to free him and enthrone him.

Catherine had lived in Russia some months before her marriage in 1745 to Peter, duke of Holstein and officially proclaimed heir to Elizabeth. The "young court" of Peter and Catherine was for years a center of intrigue among those who worked against Bestuzhev-Riumen and his insistence upon holding firm to the Austrian alliance. During the War of the Austrian Succession the French ambassador worked tirelessly to line up the heir and his German wife in support of the interests of France and her ally Prussia. Catherine's mother served so cunningly and so unscrupulously as a willing agent of Frederick

Catherine the Great   *(Photoworld)*

II to undermine Bestuzhev's influence that finally she received orders to leave Russia. Peter, so enamored of the Prussian ruler that he referred to him as "the king, my master," suffered the humiliation of being closely and carefully watched by Bestuzhev's agents. Catherine, also an ardent admirer of Frederick II, had at one time to appear before Elizabeth to account for her pro-Prussian exertions. Russia's entanglements in the affairs of Central and Western Europe brought the nation little but intrigue and anguish.

Catherine's education, at least to the age of fifteen when she went to live in Russia, was a modest one. The court at Anhalt-Zerbst sought to imitate life at Versailles, however, as did nearly every great and petty court in Europe. From her Parisian governess Catherine acquired a fluency in French and an affection for French culture. Her education advanced to a more sophisticated level as soon as she left Germany, for she must take her place as the consort of a future emperor.

The first instruction the prospective bride received was in the principles of the Orthodox faith. Catherine shed her Lutheranism as cavalierly as she shed her name—she had been Sophie Auguste Frederika—and embraced the teachings of the Eastern Church with obvious relish. She set about with commendable determination to learn the Russian language but, although she mastered it well enough to serve every need, she always preferred French, as did court society all over the continent.

The works of French men of letters, and particularly those of the *philosophes,* made a great impression upon Catherine. She knew Rabelais, Montaigne, Molière, and Corneille and had read Voltaire before she was sixteen. Montesquieu's *Persian Letters* did not impress her, but she became ecstatic over his *Spirit of the Laws.* She read the first volume of Diderot's *Encyclopédie* as soon as it was available. Then she bought his library, put him on salary as royal librarian *in absentia,* and invited him to take up residence in Russia. He accepted the appointment and the salary, and visited Petersburg but did not long remain there.

Catherine corresponded at length with many of the *philosophes* and with the enlightened despots Frederick II, Gustavus

III of Sweden, and Joseph II of Austria who made a grand visit to the new lands that the empress had wrested from Turkey. She showered gifts upon Voltaire, whose disciple she claimed to be, and invited him to Russia. He accepted the gifts and declined the invitation, although he heaped praise upon her even for her share in the infamous partition of Poland. So enthusiastic was he over her enlightened rule, particularly after he quarreled with Frederick II, that he urged her to seize Constantinople and liberate Greece. Indeed, she christened her third grandson Constantine as if to give him a name appropriate to the assignment she and Voltaire had in mind for him.

To Jean D'Alembert, a leading Encyclopedist, Catherine offered the appointment as tutor to her eight-year-old son Paul. If he accepted the offer he might bring any or all of his friends to Petersburg. D'Alembert did not avail himself of her generosity, although he praised her as a noble and benevolent sovereign. His opinion later changed, and he became a bitter critic.

Catherine interested herself in literary movements outside Russia, corresponding not only with the foremost writers and philosophers of the day but also with the leaders of intellectual circles that were the fashion of the time. She kept in touch, for example, with Madame Marie Geoffrin who maintained a literary salon in Paris and with a Frau Bielke who presided over a similar group in Hamburg. The empress herself was a writer of some achievement. Her collected works published early in the twentieth century run to twelve volumes, although the collection does not contain her correspondence. It does include allegories to aid in the education of her grandson Alexander, memoirs, essays, satires, comedies in French and Russian, a history of Russia before the Mongol conquest, and historical dramas inspired by Shakespeare of whose works she was fond.

The first fruit of Catherine's education in the enlightened thought of the Age of Reason was her *Nakaz,* or *Instruction.* No new legal code had appeared in Russia since 1649, and yet every reign, particularly that of Peter the Great, had produced many new laws. There were ten thousand laws on the books by the eighteenth century, many of them obsolete, contradictory, or otherwise confusing. Peter momentarily had considered the appointment of a commission to bring together all laws, new and old, into some sensible and intelligible order. Anne and Elizabeth had convened commissions to put together a revised code, but they had produced only endless debate.

Soon after her accession Catherine began to reflect upon how best to proceed to the issue of a new code. She reasoned that the nation needed more than a simple arrangement in some manageable order of all the laws then in force. She proposed a much more ambitious and comprehensive undertaking—a detailed enunciation of legal principles based upon natural law and the rule of reason, fetishes of this Age of Enlightenment. Upon this rational foundation would rest the new code, which would include those laws already in force that did not violate the new principles and the expurgation of all others. Full implementation presumably would require new laws, some of them departing radically from time-honored practice.

Catherine knew little of Russian law and less of the principles, if any, upon which it rested. She gave little thought to the difficulty of applying to her own strange land—half Western and half Byzantine, half modern and half primitive—principles derived from Western legal systems worked out laboriously over centuries of testing and application.

In 1767 the empress called for the election of a Legislative Commission to revise and recodify the law. Over five hundred delegates assembled in Moscow: 200 towns each chose a representative; there were twenty-eight high officials; peasants on state lands sent eighty; the Cossacks chose fifty; the gentry sent 160; and thirty-four spoke for the subject nationalities east of the Urals. The government did not ask the privately owned serfs to send delegates; their gentry owners could speak for them.

Before the representatives convened in the Kremlin, they received from the empress the *Nakaz,* or *Instruction.* It was a statement of the rational and enlightened foundations upon which, Catherine suggested, the new law code should rest. She spent over two years putting it together, drawing heavily, as she candidly admitted, upon Montesquieu's *Spirit of the Laws* and Beccaria's essay on *Crimes and Punishments.* In over six hundred items the empress set forth the political, economic, religious, cultural, and sociological principles that should guide the policies of the enlightened state. When she completed her painstaking labor, Catherine asked her advisers for suggestions. At their urging she omitted any criticism of serfdom, the nation's most shameful social ill.

The *Instruction,* which earned Voltaire's praise as the finest monument of the century, expressed Catherine's hope to provide Russia with a legal system in harmony with the dictates of the Enlightenment being expounded, if not being practiced, in Western Europe. She believed that the sovereign must be absolute, not only because despotism no matter how benevolent was the fashion of the age, but because the empire was so vast that any authority less than absolute must fail to provide it with the fair-minded and even-handed justice that was Catherine's professed goal. But absolute monarchy must rest upon strict observance of the law by the sovereign as well as upon strict obedience by the subject, for the aim of good government should be "the glory of the citizen, the state, and the sovereign." All citizens must be equal before the law and subject to the same laws; this, of course, would not include serfs who were mere chattels.

She also believed that government must apply itself to the prevention of crime rather than to punishment for it and that punishment should be appropriate to the crime; for example, it would be unjust for a thief and a murderer to suffer the same treatment. There should be an end to torture to obtain evidence and to maiming as a sentence for crime. Only the "utmost necessity" could justify serfdom or slavery, and then only in the interest of the state; yet to free large numbers of serfs, by legislation at a single stroke, would be dangerous. Landlords had been imposing too great a burden of taxes upon their serf villages. Since the empire harbored peoples of many faiths—Catholicism, Islam, Buddhism, Shamanism, Judaism, Lutheranism, Calvinism, Orthodoxy, and others—Catherine urged "a prudent toleration of other religions not repugnant to our Orthodox religion and polity," whatever that may mean.

The Legislative Commission held 200 sessions over a period of eighteen months. Delegates rose to report the wishes of those who had sent them. Some reported only complaints that were petty, carping, and of no national concern. Many, however, raised issues of widespread interest. There was much discontent over high taxes, and indeed government expenditures had risen many times over in the preceding forty years. Many delegates called for a decentralization of government, and the empress later took steps to meet that request. There was broad support for a clear definition of the rights and obligations of each social class, and again this would be forthcoming at least for gentry and townsmen. Delegates representing state peasants called either for an end to serfdom or for some clarification of the rights of serfs and the obligations of landowners to their serfs. Merchants resented the privilege extended to the gentry to maintain industries on their estates and to engage in trade, both privileges that townsmen had once legally monopolized.

Perhaps the Legislative Commission's greatest achievement was the insight it gave the sovereign into conditions in the land she ruled. The debates gave her some direction for reforms she later undertook. But there was no new code of law. A war with Turkey provided whatever excuse was necessary to send the delegates home. Russia would wait another sixty-five years for the revision she so sorely needed.

Catherine took up the work of Peter the Great and wanted men to regard her as his successor. When she employed the French sculptor Étienne Falconet to produce a magnificent equestrian statue of St. Petersburg's founder, she ordered him to inscribe the work in Latin: to Peter the First from Catherine the Second. The implication was clear that she not only accepted the challenge to continue the course he had indicated but that, in effect, no intervening reigns lay between theirs.

If Catherine emulated Peter in his efforts to strengthen Russia, she did so more in the field of foreign affairs than in any other. She interfered, as Peter had done, in the election of a Polish king when the throne fell vacant in 1763. She sent Cossacks and civilian supervisors into Poland to insure the victory of her candidate, the Polish Count Stanislas Poniatowski, her former lover. Frederick II of Prussia cooperated fully with Catherine. Poniatowski soon showed his ingratitude by seeking to make the elective kingship hereditary in his own family and to restore the royal power that had declined almost to insignificance over the preceding two centuries.

In the "defense" of the Polish constitution, with its *liberum veto* permitting a single adverse vote in the Polish Diet to block passage of any measure—a constitutional provision that made effective government and royal leadership impossible—General Alexander Suvorov led a Russian army against the Polish patriots who supported Poniatowski. When, in 1768, Cossacks pursued the Poles to the Turkish border, the Ottoman Empire, ever watchful to take advantage of Russo-Polish friction, declared war upon Russia.

Nothing should have pleased Catherine more than the sultan's attack upon her. She sent a strong army across the Dniester River into the Balkans. Moldavia and Wallachia, the two provinces that later would join as the state of Romania, fell to the Russians, and Cossacks took the city of Bucharest. The Turks fell back across the Danube. Another Russian army occupied the Turkish lands at the mouth of the Don—the Black Sea was a Turkish lake at the time. The empress sent shipwrights and other workmen to the Sea of Azov to build a fleet with which she would attack Ottoman power all along the Black Sea and also advance toward the sultan's capital.

Meanwhile the Baltic fleet left Petersburg for the eastern Mediterranean, proposing to attack Constantinople from the West. Its commander, Alexis Orlov, landed troops in Greece, but the expected rising of Balkan Christians against their Turkish masters did not follow, and the troops returned to their ships. However, Orlov wiped out the Turkish fleet at Chesme in the Aegean in the greatest victory in Russian naval history. And Russian troops occupied several Aegean islands.

The Russian forces that had driven to the Danube in 1770 had little success the following year. An army under Prince Vasily Dolgoruky, however, occupied the Crimean peninsula, chased away the khan who was the sultan's vassal, and appointed a Tatar khan who would do Russia's bidding.

Western capitals began to show restlessness at the spectacular achievements of Russian fleets and armies. The possibility that Russia might liberate the Balkan Christians, and then create a satellite state that would cover the entire peninsula and perhaps include Constantinople, posed a very real threat immediately to Austria and ultimately to all of Central Europe.

The relaxation of pressure came with a suggestion from the wily Frederick II of Prussia that Catherine should slake her thirst for territory by absorbing eastern Poland. He added that Maria Theresa of Austria should receive a share and that he himself would accept something by way of a fee for proposing this First Partition of Poland. Catherine accepted a diplomatic defeat in agreeing to share Poland with the others, for she was already in effective control of Poland and the hapless nation had been a Russian satellite for generations. But involved in the Turkish war, threatened with a Swedish attack on one side and an Austrian advance on the other, faced with a belated revival of Polish national fervor, and implicitly threatened by Prussia, there was little the empress could do but go along with Frederick's suggestion.

Later, at a moment when Catherine was occupied with her second Turkish war, Prussia backed Poland in proclaiming a new constitution that scrapped the debilitating *liberum veto*, made the kingship hereditary, and restored royal power. But when the empress had finished with the sultan, she ordered a hundred thousand Russian troops into Poland and they swept without opposition from one end of the country to the other. Frederick William II, the new Prussian king, backed away from the Russian challenge, and the Polish Diet revived the old constitution in all its weakness. The Second Partition of Poland followed in 1793. Russia and Prussia divided between them half of what had remained after the First Partition.

A national rising of Poles the following year brought down a Prussian invasion from one side and a Russian invasion from the other. A Third Partition in 1795 erased Poland from the map. Austria won a share, Prussia took the Warsaw region, and Russia absorbed what was left of Lithuania and the western Ukraine. By the First Partition, Catherine had taken lands inhabited for the most part by Russian and Orthodox peoples. By the Second and Third Partitions she took in a population predominantly Lithuanian and Uniat, who practiced the Orthodox ritual but accepted the headship of the pope. Russia also acquired most of the Polish Jews.

After the First Partition of Poland, Catherine pressed her war with Turkey that had lain dormant for a year. Suvorov crossed the Danube and threatened Constantinople, and the sultan called for terms. By the Treaty of Kuchuk-Kainardji in 1774, Russia received an indemnity, the eastern shore of the Sea of Azov, and the left bank of the Bug River all the way to the Black Sea. Crimea became ostensibly independent of the sultan, but its fall to St. Petersburg was only a matter of time. Russia returned to Turkey the Balkan lands she had overrun and the provinces of Moldavia and Wallachia she had occupied. She gave up the Aegean islands that Western Europe surely would not have allowed her to retain. She also received, or thought she did, the right to protect all Christian subjects of the sultan, but the treaty provision was couched in such obscure terms that future diplomats wrangled over its meaning.

For several years Catherine and the Austrian Emperor Joseph II discussed the partition of all Turkish territory on the continent of Europe, but they could not come to terms. The empress also had in mind her "Greek Project," the restoration of the Byzantine Empire with her infant grandson, whom she pointedly named Constantine, as its emperor.

With British, Prussian, and Swedish encouragement, Turkey declared war upon Russia in 1787 when Catherine spurned the sultan's demand that she withdraw from the Crimea whose independent khan had turned the peninsula over to the empress four years earlier. Sweden attacked Russia and posed sufficient threat to St. Petersburg to keep Catherine from sending her Baltic fleet to the Bosporus. Suvorov distinguished himself in the Balkans and was on his way to Constantinople when the sultan accepted the terms of the Treaty of Jassy in 1792. He agreed to Russia's seizure of the Crimea, and surrendered to Russia the land between the Bug and the Dniester Rivers.

Catherine undertook once more, in cooperation with Francis II of Austria, to drive the Turk off the European continent. The old empress died in 1796, however, a year after she and Francis had come to terms. Even had she lived, the mounting concern over the French Revolution probably would have forced a postponement of her ambitious project to rid Europe of the Ottoman presence.

Territorial gains during the reign of Catherine II were impressive and of profound importance. The Russian frontier in the south returned to the Black Sea for the first time since the Grand Principality of Kiev had controlled the north shore. The Ottoman Empire was unmistakably in a state of decline, although the Western powers would shore up its strength in an effort to block further Russian expansion down the Balkan peninsula toward the Straits.

Catherine's absorption of the eastern two thirds of Poland was a mixed blessing. The Poles thenceforth were uncompromising in their hatred of alien rule, but of the three occupying powers they were most bitter against the Russians. Furthermore, the empire now shared common boundaries with Austria and with Prussia, later the eastern segment of the German Empire. Russia no longer had a protective cushion along her western frontier, as she had had during the generations when Poland had remained alive and independent but under Russian domination. Her western borders now lay exposed to her strongest potential enemies.

The domestic reforms of Catherine II were far less impressive than the record of her diplomatic and military triumphs. She closed many monasteries and confirmed the confiscation of church lands that her husband in his brief reign had ordered. Peter the Great and earlier Ivan the Terrible had considered the step, but neither had taken it. The former church estates came under the administration of the Economic College, and the revenues they provided went into the general treasury. Thereafter the state met the operational costs of those monasteries allowed to remain open, and it also paid all clerical salaries.

The beginning of a national system of elementary and secondary education is traceable to Catherine's reign. A royal commission submitted a proposal for a comprehensive system of schools, and the empress confirmed it in 1786. The plan proposed a two-year elementary program to provide instruction in reading, writing, and religion. A system of intermediate schools would add a third year of more advanced work in reading and writing, with the addition of some work in history and geography. A secondary system, parallel to the first two but catering to the privileged classes—officials, gentry, clergy—offered four years of instruction in reading, writing, history, geography, mathematics, physics, and mechanics. Catherine borrowed the three-school-system arrangement from Austria, where Maria Theresa had established it as recently as 1775.

Other demands upon the treasury—for buildings in the capital, for wars, for the prodigality of the court, for the suppression of peasant revolts—were too great to permit Catherine to spend much upon education. The secondary schools opened within a year or two of royal approval of the educational plan, but after a moment of enthusiasm the system languished for want of sufficient funds, satisfactory texts, trained teachers, and even students. Many clerical and most merchant families, for whom the system was created, refused to send their sons to the schools which they regarded as a waste of time. The elementary system, designed to provide a two-year school in the principal town of every district or county, fared even worse. Local authorities were reluctant to spend money on schools; few opened, and several of these closed within a year for want of support. However, there was some progress. In a population of 26,000,000 people there were perhaps 16,000 students attending secular and church schools by 1790. There was never any plan, of course, for schools in the villages of rural Russia, although the Legislative Commission had recommended compulsory education for all males.

Standards at the University of Moscow, and at the college operated in conjunction with the Academy of Sciences in St. Petersburg, were far below those of most Western continental universities. Standards at Oxford and Cambridge, however, were probably little above those of Moscow.

One of Catherine's most spectacular contributions to Russian education was the opening of a school for girls in the former Smolny Monastery in Petersburg. One of the two divisions of the school catered to daughters of the gentry, the other to merchants' daughters. All studied Russian, French, history, geography, and simple arithmetic, but the daughters of nobles also received instruction in "courtly manners" while middle-class girls learned needle work and household management.

Some of the gentry frequently enrolled in a school for officer cadets. Many Russian aristocrats imported foreigners, often distinguished ones, to tutor their children. The Swiss liberal, Frederic La Harpe, settled in St. Petersburg in 1782 as tutor to the son of a Russian nobleman. The Encyclopedist Grimm pointed him out to Catherine, who employed him as tutor to her grandson Alexander. Most tutors in the homes of the gentry were French, and young nobles learned to be so much at home with the French language that many preferred it to Russian. They read the works of the Enlightenment, as Catherine's example encouraged them to do. Some nobles enrolled their sons in Western schools after Peter III and Catherine lifted the ban upon foreign travel. For example, Princess Catherine Dashkov, a close friend of the empress, took her son to London to enter him in the famous Westminster School. Five years later she went with him to Edinburgh to study under the economist Adam Smith and the historian William Robertson. At a time when only two students were attending the university of the Academy of Sciences in St. Petersburg there were Russian students in Leipzig, Göttingen, Strasbourg, Paris, Oxford, Glasgow, and Edinburgh.

Peter the Great had laid the foundation for a system of hospitals, and the Empress Anne had expanded the system. Catherine encouraged the immigration of Western physicians and surgeons, and many accepted the high salaries she offered them. Prominent among them were Germans, Scots, and Englishmen. One doctor, Thomas Dimsdale, introduced inoculation against smallpox and vaccinated Catherine and two of her grandsons.

Catherine left a lasting impression upon the architecture of St. Petersburg. She completed much that Elizabeth had begun, and added other works of her own. Of all the great buildings that amazed visitors from the West, one of the most impressive was the Admiralty, a great stone building housing the college or office of naval affairs, an arsenal and magazine, and a workshop.

Next to the Admiralty was the royal residence, the Winter Palace, with its fifteen hundred rooms and its formal gardens. The Empress Elizabeth had ordered the building, awarding the contract to design it to the Italian architect, Count Bartolomeo Rastrelli, who had entered Russia as a boy when Peter the Great had employed his father. Rastrelli also designed the expansion of the Smolny Institute, the school for girls, and the royal palace at Tsarskoe Selo, now Pushkin.

After Elizabeth died in the unfinished Winter Palace, Catherine commissioned the French architect Jean Vallin de Lamothe to add a private or intimate wing which she called the Hermitage. Here she read and worked and entertained Grimm and Diderot when they visited Russia. Later she extended the Hermitage to house the superb collection of paintings that Peter had started and for which she purchased many costly paintings in Western Europe.

To the Hermitage, Catherine also added a theater, designed by the Italian Giacomo Quarenghi, where the empress and her entourage could enjoy the performance of her own plays or of her own translations of Shakespeare. Two official companies of players, one French and one Russian, acted in the new theater. An official opera company, consisting chiefly of Italians but including several Russians, performed French and German and occasionally Russian works. Ballet, a French import, attracted a number of Russians. Opera and ballet written for and performed by Russians originated in Catherine's reign. The great majority of the musicians who played the Western music to which the Russian court listened were Italians, Frenchmen, or Germans, although one official orchestra consisted entirely of Russians.

Catherine's passion for building was responsible for a number of other palaces, all of them of the neoclassical style so popular in Western Europe in the eighteenth century. The Italian Antonio Rinaldo designed the so-called Marble Palace that Catherine intended for Gregory Orlov. Rinaldo also designed a palace in the village of Gatchina, a few miles from Petersburg, where Catherine's son Paul lived during his mother's reign. Quarenghi designed the Alexander Palace at Tsarskoe Selo for the empress's grandson Alexander I. To lay out and care for the formal parks and gardens that surrounded the royal palaces, Catherine imported a number of English gardeners.

One sixth of St. Petersburg's population of 218,000 in 1790 was foreign—not necessarily foreign born or even first generation, but still identifiable by such names as Tooke, Bush, Cameron, Jackson, Rinaldo, Rastrelli, Falk, Panin, and that of the famous Viennese riding mistress, Nanette Mahueu. Many had Russianized their names, as had Denis Fonvizin whose original German name was von Wiesen. Germans were most numerous among the foreigners in the capital, for Catherine continued the earlier practice of encouraging their immigration not only from the Baltic provinces but from Germany. The second most numerous group of foreigners in Petersburg consisted of Britons —Englishmen and Scots for the most part. They served in all ranks and in many occupations; they were admirals as well as common seamen; many were merchants; one was an engraver, another a tailor; still another made musical instruments. There were many Dutchmen, of course, although their immigration had fallen off since Peter's time.

Foreign merchants and manufacturers received every encouragement to settle in Russia under Catherine the Great. They obtained subsidies and tax exemptions and might even purchase serfs to labor in their factories, a privilege no Russian commoner enjoyed. Russia's urban population numbered something over 300,000 at the end of Peter's reign, but it had increased four times over by the time of Catherine's death. The growth was in large measure a reflection of the immigration of foreigners who built their factories in designated towns whose population swelled with the migration, forced or voluntary, of workers from rural areas.

The government built over 100 towns, many of them in the steppe area north of the Black Sea that came under Russian rule after Catherine's Turkish wars. Westerners filled many of the new towns, for the empress invited foreigners, regardless of race or creed except Jews, to settle in the fertile but sparsely populated lands she had conquered. They received tax exemptions, free land, freedom from military service, and the right to practice their religion and govern themselves. Over 20,000 Germans, the most enthusiastic colonists, accepted the invitation, and clustered in tightly knit communities all over the Ukraine and the lower Volga. They married only among themselves, clung tenaciously to their eighteenth-century German language and customs, and held their Russian neighbors in contempt while setting them an example of industry and good farming practice, as Catherine had hoped they might do. The German colonists remained in South Russia, distinct and culturally isolated, until World War II, by which time they numbered 600,000. During the Nazi invasion in 1941, Stalin moved these Volga Germans into Central Asia.

In 1785, Catherine issued a Charter to the Towns of Russia that laid out a plan of local government. The law divided urban residents into six categories—owners of real estate, resident merchants, foreign and nonresident merchants, craftsmen, unskilled workers, and "distinguished" townsmen, a group that included artists, bankers, officials, and university graduates. Each group chose delegates to a city council that met occasionally to determine broad policy lines and to name an executive board to which it would leave control of day-to-day affairs. The appearance of the elaborate machinery of municipal administration was impressive; its operation was disappointing. Police authority rested with an official appointed by the central administration, and other officials had little power and less influence. So insubstantial were the offices provided for by the Charter to the Towns that frequently no elections took place to fill them. Whatever Petersburg needed in the way of local officials it was willing to appoint, usually from the ranks of the lesser gentry.

The empress made some minor alterations in the central administration. She eliminated several of the colleges and assigned their responsibilities to agencies of local government. The economic college and the colleges of the admiralty, the army, and foreign affairs, however, continued to function. The

Senate, to whom the colleges had been responsible in Peter's time, lost much of its authority and became essentially an honorary body. The office of director-general of the Senate continued, although its occupant no longer had much to do with the Senate. However, he became a still more powerful official to whom all sorts of local agencies must report. Catherine's rearrangement of the formal pattern of administration did little to stabilize governmental operations. Russia continued, indeed to the end of the monarchy, to be ruled not by the orderly processes of her governmental institutions but by the whim and caprice of individual officials.

Peter the Great had undertaken only modest reforms in rural local government, in part because of the lack of personnel to staff administrative positions. His administration appointed and sent out into the provinces all local officials. The first responsibility of the gentry, the only class in society whose members might have served as local officials, was to the armed forces. This left no one in the countryside who might satisfactorily have handled administrative assignments. In forcing the gentry into national service Peter had uprooted the class that, quite naturally by virtue of its position as landowner, had managed local affairs for centuries.

Peter's death removed the only force capable of keeping the nobles in service and away from their estates. Members of the gentry quickly left government service when the succession passed to women and children, and no one had the influence or strength to hold them to their service obligation. Peter III only made the emancipation of the gentry official when he freed all members of the class from Peter the Great's law that they must serve the state, either in the armed forces or in some civil capacity.

In 1775, Catherine took steps to meet the need for governmental machinery in rural Russia. To reduce the unwieldy size of some of the huge provinces into which Peter had divided the land, she increased the number from fifteen to fifty. Each province was to contain some 300,000 or 400,000 inhabitants, and each would be divided into ten districts or counties of 30,000 or 40,000 each. The crown appointed a governor over each province, although in some cases two or more provinces were combined under a governor-general. Minor officials on the district level were to be elected by local gentry, merchants, and the few free peasants who rented state-owned land.

When Catherine granted a Charter to the Towns in 1785, she also granted a Charter to the Nobles which confirmed the earlier emancipation by Peter III and extended their rights and privileges. The gentry received the right to elect delegates to assemblies on the district and provincial levels. The delegates would assemble every three years to choose a "marshal" of the nobility and to levy taxes to meet the cost of whatever local enterprises they should accept. It was the provincial marshal of the nobility who would deal with the governor or lay before the empress some request of the provincial assembly.

The charter exempted all members of the gentry from compulsory service and the payment of direct taxes. Neither the title nor the property of a noble could be taken away "without due process of law," and a nobleman was subject "only to the judgment of his peers." Whatever "due process of law" meant at the time was not clear, particularly in the absence of any recent and usable recodification of the law. It was like Catherine, of course, to appropriate a Western expression that had only limited applicability or meaning in Russia.

Catherine's charter relieved the nobles of subjection to corporal punishment. They were free to travel or live abroad. They might dispose of their lands and their chattels—serfs were chattels, too—as they chose. They could operate industrial enterprises on their estates and sell the product at home or abroad without payment of any license or fee. They and they alone were free to own serf-populated land.

From the moment of its legal emancipation the Russian gentry took on some of the characteristics of Western aristocracies. Many nobles dwelt on their estates and personally supervised the industrial or agricultural work of their serfs. The wealthiest maintained town houses in St. Petersburg and Moscow, frequented the theater, ballet, and opera, and were present at every court function. Such men rarely or never saw their estates, but left them to the management of bailiffs who collected the rents or sold the produce and forwarded the income to the landowner who found many ways to squander it.

It was not only the fine palaces and town houses of the aristocrats and the variety of the entertainments they might enjoy that set them apart from the masses. Their tables were set with the finest china from Dresden or Sèvres and laden with a rich assortment of meats, fruits, vegetables, pastries, and imported wines. Their English gardeners raised pineapples, nectarines, and other rare fruits under glass. Men and women of the gentry dressed in rich brocades, silks, and satins. Some of their clothes were made in Russian factories or shops; some were imported from England, France, or Italy. Russians did not, of course, disdain Russian sable or blue fox, or the rare jewels and perfumes that came from the East; these all had been popular among wealthy Westerners for centuries.

There was nothing exotic or costly about the way of life among the unwashed and uncouth mass of Russians. Their houses were wretched, usually lacking a floor, having one room with perhaps a partial partition, and miserably furnished with a few rough-hewn bits and pieces. Tableware was simply made of wood or crude earthen stuff. There was little variety to the food—poor meats, fish, beans, cucumbers, turnips, cheese, tea, and beer or vodka of poor quality. Clothing was fashioned of leather or coarse homespun linen or wool and nearly formless in cut. Footwear and leggings often were made of birch bark and rags. And a male serf was more distinguishable from his wife by his beard than by the clothing he wore.

By Catherine's time upper and lower classes were identifiable not only in the manner of diet, dress, and dwelling. They spoke different languages—the masses spoke a Russian *patois* as coarse as the clothes they wore; the gentry spoke a polished Russian or more often French. Their very smells set apart the upper and nether strata of society: the gentry imported the costliest perfumes from the Orient or from Paris; the distinguishing odors of the lower classes were those of garlic, tallow, and roughly tanned and seldom cleaned sheepskin. The lower classes used the *banya* or steam bathhouse to cater not so much to cleanliness as to health and sport.

Among the gentry there were wastrels and coxcombs, to be sure, particularly among those who hovered around the flame at court. This was as true of the Winter Palace as it was of Versailles. Catherine deliberately followed the pattern of the French court even while she befriended its critics. Yet not all the wealthy nobles who attended royal functions were frivolous fops. Many were patrons and some were practitioners of the arts. Many had received a brilliant education from Western tutors. Some ranked among the most literate and the most liberal men to be found anywhere. Count Paul Stroganov, for example, was a member of the Jacobin Club and became its librarian when he was in Paris during the French Revolution. And the eighteen-year-old Prince Dmitry Golitsyn joined in the storming of the Bastille. Many of the gentry traveled in the West, and they became a part of the international set that gathered at the spas and the casinos, the theaters and salons of Europe from Naples to London and from Paris to Budapest. They were at ease wherever they went, for in their childhood they had learned English, French, and German from maids, governesses, and tutors imported to teach them the languages and the culture of the West.

Catherine's reign ushered in the golden age of the aristocracy. The class enjoyed the almost exclusive privilege of savoring the luxury and opulence of life at a court whose glitter was as dazzling as that of France. It retained the monopoly of land and serf ownership that gentry status carried with it. Peter the Great had completed the process by which the landowning class became a serving gentry. Catherine reversed the situation, and the gentry became the most privileged class not only in Russia but in all Europe.

During the course of the eighteenth century, Russia, or at least upper-class Russia, became Western in appearance, speech, taste, and culture. If the nation took on a Western veneer in practical interests in Peter's time, it became intellectually and culturally Western in Catherine's time. There was no surer evidence of this shift in emphasis from Western material values to Western moral values, at least in part, than the sense of shame creeping over the nation that it could find no solution to the problem of bondage for its agricultural masses.

Catherine's charter confirming Peter III's emancipation of the nobility, and her Charter to the Towns ending restrictions upon the middle class, immediately raised the question of freeing the serfs. The nation's enemies—Poland, Sweden, and Turkey—had all suffered decisive defeat or obliteration. If bondage for some classes no longer was politically excusable, as the emancipation of gentry and townsmen seemed to affirm, then it was no longer justifiable for any class. Freedom for the serfs should follow.

Emancipation of the serfs did not follow. Catherine's own sense of guilt that bondage would not end for the great mass of Russians is evident in the *Nakaz* she wrote for the delegates to her Legislative Commission. The first draft of these instructions carried a strong indictment of serfdom. But the empress softened its tone at the insistence of her advisers and allowed herself in the final draft no more than an expression of hope that the gentry would not abuse their serfs. Almost at this very moment she organized the Free Economic Society and offered a prize to the writer of the most promising solution to the problem of serfdom. The prize went to a Frenchman, but the landowners who constituted the membership of the society refused to recommend the publication of the essay.

The dealing in human livestock was flaunted in city newspapers for all, including foreign travelers, to see. One advertisement listed "two tailors, a shoemaker, a watchmaker, a cook, a coach maker, a wheeler, an engraver, a night workman, and two coachmen" for sale, and the same notice added the availability of "three young racing horses, one stallion, two geldings, and a pack of hunting dogs." An officer advertised a sixteen-year-old girl who could knit, sew, and iron and who had "a nice figure and pretty face." Catherine, always anxious for Westerners to see the best in Russia, must have winced at seeing such notices. Her son, during whose reign these particular advertisements appeared, obviously did not resent them. Her grandson forbade such notices to appear in the newspapers of St. Petersburg or Moscow. His proscription did not extend to the provinces where Westerners rarely traveled.

The serf had no legal relief from unduly harsh treatment

by his owner. The practice of petitioning the sovereign had occasionally been tolerated, but Catherine put an end to it. She forbade serfs, under threat of flogging and banishment to Siberia for life, to appeal to the throne for redress of grievances against their owners.

The overwhelming majority of serfs belonged to a few great landowners. In the late eighteenth century, as a consequence of the division and subdivision of inheritances that had been going on for generations, some members of the gentry owned no serfs at all and had to till their own fields. A third of the gentry owned fewer than ten serfs, and a half owned fewer than twenty. It was the owners of the great estates and of many villages who made the system seem most callous and brutal. When Catherine's grandson Nicholas I ordered a survey of conditions of serf ownership, officials discovered that only twenty percent of the serfs belonged to the lesser gentry, men who owned fewer than a hundred males. The great magnates counted their "souls," their male serfs upon whom they paid the soul tax, in thousands. The three richest landowners in Russia in the late eighteenth century were Prince P. B. Sheremetiev who owned 60,000 souls, Count K. G. Razumovsky who had 45,000, and Count A. S. Stroganov who owned 23,000. Each owned approximately twice that number of serfs, since a soul legally was a male serf, and only the names of males appeared in the census. By 1796 the privately owned serfs numbered nearly 12,000,000 men and women, almost half the population of the land. The state itself owned 9,000,000 or about forty percent of its own people.

While serfdom did not end completely in France until the dawn of the French Revolution, nor in Austria until the reign of Joseph II, nor in parts of Germany until the early nineteenth century, still there was no traffic in human flesh in any of these lands. The term serfdom was a euphemism in Russia for slavery, and nineteenth-century Russian liberals who corresponded with American abolitionists referred to the serfs as "our white Negroes."

That the Russian masses were impatient to win the emancipation that Peter III had granted to the gentry became unmistakably apparent in the uprising led by Emelian Pugachev. In 1773 this poor but free Cossack, who had deserted from the army and escaped from prison, raised the standard of revolt in southeast Russia. Cossacks from the valleys of the Ural, the Volga, the Don, and the Dnieper gathered round Pugachev. So, too, did runaway serfs, Old Believers who suffered persecution for defying the state church, and Turkic tribesmen whose lands had fallen to Russian rule in recent times. Whatever the incentive may have been for any individual or group, the predominant source of discontent was the reluctance of Catherine's government to emancipate all her people.

The Pugachev revolt swept like a scourge over the valleys of southern Russia. Catherine's first war with Turkey kept the army's attention diverted elsewhere than on the Cossack lands where unrest was endemic, and within months there were 30,000 men in Pugachev's ragtag army, looting and pillaging and raping at will, killing officials, torturing Orthodox clergymen, burning the homes of the gentry, and attacking the symbols of authority and repression wherever they appeared. The rebels stormed Kazan at the big bend of the Volga, and threatened to attack Moscow.

Pugachev claimed to be the murdered Emperor Peter III and maintained an imperial court and government as his headquarters moved to and fro over the land. He announced the end of serfdom, taxation, and conscription, and urged the liquidation of the landlord class. Catherine could no longer keep up the pretense she had maintained in her letters to Voltaire that this was just another ordinary Cossack disturbance. With the end of the Turkish war, which the revolt may have hastened, the empress sent battle-seasoned troops against Pugachev. The army, fresh from impressive victories over the sultan, drove the insurgents back to the lower Volga and worked a stern vengeance upon the countryside. Pugachev's own men betrayed him to the imperial commander, and the rebel leader was taken in a cage to Moscow to be hanged, quartered, and burned.

The word *Pugachevshchina* or Pugachevism entered the language as a synonym for peasant revolt with its savage slaughter of landlords and officials and the smoking ruins of manor houses. One of Catherine's commanders told the empress, "It is not Pugachev that matters, but the general indignation." It was a stern warning that the masses might rise again if bondage did not end. Just how to end serfdom became the most persistent problem facing the government until the emancipation finally came about under Alexander II in 1861.

Although spontaneous, scattered, defiant peasant challenges to authority would continue to the end of the monarchy, Pugachev's revolt was the last organized rural uprising. Thenceforth, the Russian countryside was never free of peasant unrest and smoldering hostility, and *jacqueries* were frequent and widespread. Indeed, officialdom came to expect a certain rhythm of dissatisfaction, a certain acceptable annual number of outbreaks sufficiently severe to require army units to quell them. But it maintained regular garrisons in sensitive areas to move mercilessly to douse any spark of hostility.

The plight of the serfs worsened considerably in this golden age of the aristocrats. Perhaps feeling herself indebted to the gentry for maintaining her on the throne to which she had no legal claim, Catherine abdicated almost every control over the individual noble that the state still exercised. The effect was to leave the serf-owner practically unrestricted in his dealing with his human property. Yet he must not kill a serf, for to do so would cost the state a taxpayer and a soldier. There was no legal limit, however, upon the number of lashes a noble might order. And the landlord alone decided which of his serfs would "go for a soldier" when the call came down to provide a certain number of recruits. It was usual for an estate owner to send his most incorrigible young serfs into the military. Since the enlistment period was twenty-five years, nomination for army duty amounted almost to a prison sentence for life.

Catherine's dedication to the principles of the Enlightenment did not wear well. She condemned serfdom in theory, at least in correspondence and in conversation, but gave to her favorites government-owned estates whose 800,000 peasants in effect governed themselves. Thus the peasants of such estates became serfs, the freely disposable property of the new landlord. She paraded her support for education by adding a school of medicine to the University of Moscow, but only one student had graduated by the end of her long reign. She spoke out in her *Instruction* for religious toleration, but made no effort to curb the persecution of the Polish and Lithuanian Jews who had become her subjects after the partitions of Poland.

Peter III abolished the "Secret Chancery," or security police, which had operated under Anne and Elizabeth, and Catherine confirmed her husband's act. Quietly, however, she later revived the dreaded organization, calling it the "Secret Expedition," or privy or unofficial department. Its chief, S. I. Sheshkovsky, the most feared of all officials, flogged two royal ladies in waiting for some trivial offense that irritated the empress.

Catherine's conservatism did not appear suddenly with the outbreak of the French Revolution. The Pugachev revolt broke out in 1773 and provoked her resentment against the serfs whom the empress had talked warmly of helping. The American declaration of independence three years later disgusted her. The storming of the Bastille threw her into a rage; she became hysterical at the news that Frenchmen had dared to defy the authority of their sovereign. She welcomed French nobles who fled in large numbers to St. Petersburg, and ordered every Russian noble living in France to return home immediately. When the news arrived that Louis XVI had gone to the guillotine, she became ill and took to her bed. Writing to Grimm, she stormed that "everything French and even the very name of France should be exterminated." The republicanism with which she had toyed in her thoughts as a young empress went sour for her. The equality, to which she had paid lip service in her *Nakaz,* became a "monster." She called for vengeance against the mob, and branded as "eastern Jacobins" the Polish liberals who urged emancipation of the serfs.

Catherine had her own Jacobins, or so she regarded them, whom she could call to judgment. One was Alexander Radishchev, son of a wealthy landowner, who in 1790 published *A Journey from St. Petersburg to Moscow.* The work eloquently condemned autocracy, bondage, militarism, privilege, and the class structure of Russian society. It called for a rule of law, for freedom of expression, and for individual human dignity. Its

vignettes depicting the degradation of life among the serfs—
the drudgery, the controlled marriages, the sale of human beings, the breakup of families, and the general brutishness of
existence in the villages—were so tenderly and so sympathetically drawn that they were denied republication in Russia for
over a century. Strangely enough, the official censor approved
the first publication of the *Journey*, but when the empress read
it she flew into a towering rage. The government brought the
author quickly to trial and the court condemned him to death.
Catherine commuted the sentence to Siberian exile, from which
Radishchev returned only in the next reign.

Nicholas Novikov was another upon whom Catherine
visited the wrath of her hatred for those who challenged authority. Novikov, a leader of Freemasonry and one of a handful of
outstanding journalists in all Russian history, began his career
as editor of a periodical that dared to question an official journal
favored by the empress. The Masonic Order, which had entered
Russia from the West during Anne's reign, had perhaps a hundred lodges or chapters and over two thousand members, most
of them nobles, in the capitals and provincial towns in 1775 when
Novikov joined the order. At first he seemed to find less appeal
in the secrets and mysteries of Freemasonry that attracted many
than in the humanitarian and social implications of its teachings.
When the order took on some of the coloration of German pi-
etism through the work of some German Masons who moved to
Russia, Novikov's interest shifted to the great moral issues of
the age. He became particularly concerned over the need of the
individual to seek self-improvement in attacking the social ills
that called for correction.

A few years after joining the Masonic movement, Novikov
left St. Petersburg and became director of the printing press
at the University of Moscow. Under his management the press
published hundreds of works, but he chose not to limit himself
to this single enterprise. He purchased and operated several
private presses and became the editor of a number of journals.
As a significant contributor to the intellectual and literary interests of the reign, and particularly as one who set a moral tone
to his writings that implied criticism of sanctimonious pro-
nouncements, he soon attracted Catherine's suspicion.

Novikov, however, was a man of enormous energy who was not content to limit his enterprises to editing and publishing. With his own resources and subscriptions from friends he opened two schools for children of the poor and even financed foreign travel for worthy students. His printing establishment operated a hospital for its workers and dispensed free medicines to those who could not afford them. He poured sums into famine relief during years of poor harvest. Novikov's selfless dedication to the aid of the needy won him the leadership of a devoted following whose contributions made possible the steady expansion of his work.

Catherine's resentment at Novikov's growing popularity and following was his undoing. The empress was suspicious of Freemasonry, perhaps because of its secrecy and mysticism and perhaps because she imagined its concern for the welfare of the underprivileged as somehow an encroachment upon the benevolent despotism of which she insisted upon being the solitary example. Whatever her reason, she closed down his publishing enterprises in 1791 and ordered an investigation of his activities by Sheshkovsky, the infamous and ruthless head of the secret police. Novikov's widespread popularity, particularly among the intelligentsia, made a public trial seem inadvisable, and the empress by a personal order sentenced him to a prison term of fifteen years. After Catherine's death her son and successor freed the prisoner and apologized for his mother's injustice.

Novikov exerted a far more lasting influence upon his country than did Radishchev whose fame abroad has been perhaps more enduring. He sustained over a period of many years a subtle attack against serfdom, autocracy, and the other institutional blights upon society. His wide influence, particularly among the gentry, had much to do with turning many members of the privileged class into philosophical liberals or even active reformers. Through his writings, his work in Freemasonry, and his philanthropies he undoubtedly made a far greater contribution than did Catherine to the popularization of Western thought and values among literate Russians. To Novikov the principles of the Enlightenment made up a code for the individual to live by and for all of society to benefit from.

Catherine treated the Enlightenment at some times as a philosophic exercise or entertainment in which she and her courtiers might indulge, and at other times as an intellectual garment to make herself and Russia acceptable and respectable to the Westerners with whom she conversed and corresponded.

However suspect Catherine's motives and sincerity may be, the fact remains that during her reign Russia turned intellectually and culturally westward, as it had turned westward in more prosaic ways during the reign of Peter the Great. If Peter had begun the administrative and technological Westernization of Russia, then Catherine had led the massive Westernization of Russian thought, which until the latter half of the nineteenth century meant almost exclusively aristocratic thought. The difference between the two reigns is strikingly apparent from the fact that Peter imported technicians, techniques, and tools from the West, whereas Catherine imported the paintings of the Renaissance masters with which to adorn the Hermitage, the annex to the Winter Palace which a Frenchman designed for her. She could have chosen no surer way to advertise the fact that she regarded the finest creations of the West as primarily exotic decorations of the royal palace. Possibly her affectation of liberal ideas was a similar adornment.

The widespread popularity of the works of the *philosophes* and other enlightened writers of the age, which is traceable to Catherine's reign, laid the foundation for the liberal and radical reform movements of the next century. Catherine's grandson Alexander was a product of this imported enlightenment and did much to encourage its further popularization. During his reign that enlightenment made possible a revolutionary movement, the aim of which was to end those shameful institutions, serfdom and autocracy, that Novikov and Radishchev had challenged.

It was not until much later, however, that the enlightenment or Westernization of Russian thought met with anything but suspicion and hostility from the mass of the people. It was the gentry, or a segment of it, that first embraced Westernization. Later Westernization was accepted by the intelligentsia—the literate or educated elements of whatever class, which in the early nineteenth century consisted almost exclusively of sons of the gentry but which expanded after mid-century to include sons of priests, officials, merchants, and even peasants. All of Russia, however, never became completely or uncritically or enthusiastically Western. To skim off the dross and keep what was best of native culture, and to appropriate and adapt the best of what the West had to offer—this was the golden mean to which the nation's finest minds tried to hold.

CHAPTER FOUR

Western Challenge and Anti-Enlightenment

THE short reign of the Emperor Paul, Catherine's son, did little to alter the trend toward Westernization so clearly in evidence at the time of his accession in 1796. His erratic escapades in foreign affairs only bespoke his instability in other matters. His first solemn pronouncement promised a course of peace and deplored the fact that his mother had kept the nation embroiled in a succession of wars. But with Napoleon's seizure of Malta soon after Paul had become Grand Master of the Knights of Malta, the emperor quickly forgot his promise of peace.

In 1798 the Baltic fleet landed a Russian army in Holland to fight alongside a British contingent. No Russian troops had ever fought so deep into Western Europe. Russia's greatest general, Alexander Suvorov, defeated the French in Italy and Switzerland; indeed, at British and Austrian request he led the allied armies to repeated victories over the troops of the French Republic.

Russian forces in Holland fared badly, however, and suffered a disaster that Paul blamed upon the British. And he became furious when a British fleet captured Malta and refused to turn it over to him. He withdrew from the coalition against France, joined Sweden, Prussia, and Denmark in a League of Armed Neutrality to defy British encroachments upon freedom of the seas, closed his ports to British ships, and sent an army of Cossacks to attack British power in India. His assassination ended that wild venture.

Paul's furious hatred for his mother, who in occupying the throne for thirty-four years had kept him from what he regarded as his rightful inheritance, inspired the most capricious measures. He disinterred the body of Peter III and buried it alongside his mother in the Cathedral of Peter and Paul, the resting place of the Romanovs that Catherine had refused to defile with the body of her insane husband after his assassination. He opened the prisons and recalled from Siberia those whom his mother had arrested or exiled, although he soon filled the jails again with others who in some way displeased him. Among those who won their freedom were Radishchev and the emperor's fellow Freemason, Novikov.

While Paul often spoke of doing something to relieve the plight of the serfs, the steps he took in that direction most often seemed calculated to irritate the gentry, whom he distrusted and disliked in general. He permitted serfs to petition the throne but only as individuals and not in groups. He issued an order that no landowner was to work his serfs more than three days a week, but he provided no machinery to enforce obedience. He ordered free and unfree alike to swear allegiance to the new sovereign, thus implying that the serfs were human beings and not chattels; some supposed that now they were free and refused to return to work until driven back by troops. To his favorites Paul gave away royal estates occupied by a half million state-owned peasants who thereby became privately owned serfs.

The emperor repeatedly and deliberately curbed the privileges of the gentry. He ended the landowner's monopoly of serf ownership by allowing merchants to purchase serfs for use as factory workers. He taxed nobles and forced them back into military service in violation of Catherine's Charter to the Nobility. He ordered floggings for nobles found guilty of crime. He delighted in personally insulting aristocrats and forcing arthritic old generals to spend hours marching and drilling troops. He threatened to move Guards regiments, whose officers were sons of the gentry, away from the capital to some frontier post. He took away the nobles' right to petition the emperor, dissolved the provincial assemblies of nobles, and appointed the marshals whom the nobility by Catherine's Charter had received the right to elect.

A small group of aristocrats plotted for years to remove the emperor, whose sanity many questioned. Paul's son Alexander was privy to the scheme but hoped that his father might quietly step aside. When the plotters broke into Paul's apartment early in 1801, however, the emperor resisted and was strangled. The nightmarish reign was over.

Alexander I: The Liberal Years

The search for identity with the West, or at least for intimate association with or participation in Western civilization, was so firmly under way by the end of the eighteenth century as to be almost irreversible. That search would continue to the end of the monarchy and beyond, always meeting bitter and sometimes violent resistance from forces too powerful and too virulent to ignore.

The accession of Alexander I in March 1801 heralded a return, temporarily at least, to the air of enlightenment that had prevailed in the most roseate of Catherine's years. The new emperor was unlike any other enlightened despot, of which he was perhaps the last, in that his grandmother had raised him and with great care had educated him for the role. During his early childhood she had personally directed his schooling. When he reached the age of seven the empress turned him over to a corps

Alexander I   *(Photoworld)*

of tutors, the chief of whom was Frederic La Harpe, a Swiss of avowed liberal and enlightened views. The future tsar studied the works of Plato, Tacitus, Locke, Montesquieu, and Gibbon. La Harpe, who did not conceal his republican sympathies, contributed his own preachments upon the vices of tyranny, the immorality of serfdom, and the moral virtue of liberty and equality.

One of Alexander's first and most exemplary acts was to convene a committee of four young friends, all aristocrats and all educated as he was in the spirit of eighteenth-century Western liberalism, to consider the nation's reform needs and to prepare a constitution for Russia. Of the four, Count Paul Stroganov had been tutored by the French mathematician and revolutionary Gilbert Romme, and while in Paris he had joined the Jacobin Club before Catherine ordered him home. Count Victor Kochubey had been educated in England, a land he knew better than his own. Nicholas Novosiltsev and Prince Adam Czartorysky had lived in England for some time and both were ardent admirers of the British system of government.

The deliberations of Alexander's so-called Unofficial Committee extended over a wide range of conditions calling for correction. A parade of witnesses offered to advise the committee on how to end serfdom for the masses, surely the most pressing need facing the nation. But no acceptable solution to the problem of bondage appeared, nor was there any constitution. The tsar preferred a Prussian or Austrian type of constitution, somewhat liberalized by guaranteeing certain civil rights to all citizens but which established an orderly and efficient administration based upon a modern and just code of law. The committee members agreed that popular restraint upon the monarchical power would make benevolent despotism impossible. But for an enlightened ruler of Russia to grant a written constitution, a Western concept and a shibboleth of eighteenth-century liberals, would be to insure a government of law and make impossible the sort of capricious tyranny that Paul had imposed upon the land.

Although the tsar corresponded with Thomas Jefferson about the American constitution, and a few years later discussed it with the American ambassador John Quincy Adams, Alexander never really intended the sort of constitution that would dilute the autocracy. His discussions with Americans about their institutions revealed no sentiment for democracy, as liberals then and later mistakenly supposed it to do. Yet the very idea of constitution, whatever its strength or weakness, was a Western idea, alien to Russian experience.

When the emperor, after the distraction of his first war with Napoleon, turned his attention once more to the need for reform, he called for suggestions from a commoner, Michael Speransky, the son of a priest. Speransky submitted a constitutional plan that proposed the erection of a system of local and national representative government, the guarantee of certain civil rights, and a precisely drawn modern code of law that would assure an orderly administration no bureaucrat could defile. Elected local assemblies would deal with local problems, and a representative national Duma, or legislature with limited powers, would advise the tsar on domestic issues of national concern. Speransky favored ultimate emancipation of all serfs but urged in the plan that the end of bondage must come gradually.

The emperor was not ready to adopt Speransky's proposal, perhaps because he suspected that, in the absence of an educated peasantry, the effect would be to increase the influence of the aristocracy with whom he had little patience. The local government provisions of the plan came into operation only in 1864, and the proposed national Duma not until 1905. But the very fact that a tsar should ask for and should consider such a suggestion early in the nineteenth century put Russia at least abreast of the most advanced nations in the West.

Alexander's fascination with constitutions never waned. At the Congress of Vienna he insisted that Louis XVIII grant the French people a constitutional "Charter" when the monarchy was restored in 1814. He also called upon the Bourbon rulers of Spain and Naples to grant their peoples charters when they returned. In 1815, Alexander, now king of Poland, granted his Polish subjects a constitution far more liberal than any such document in existence outside the United States. And, at the tsar's order, Novosiltsev in 1819 drafted a Constitutional Charter of the Russian Empire, providing for a federal division of power between provinces and central administration not unlike the American system, and a local and national hierarchy of representative assemblies similar to those Speransky had proposed. Nothing came of Novosiltsev's labors.

Although Alexander was reluctant to grant his people a constitution, he did carry out certain administrative reforms that brought Russian practice into line with that of most Western governments. He replaced the cumbersome collegial departments founded by Peter the Great with ministries, each headed by a single administrator responsible finally to the tsar. The Council of Ministers served as a body to advise the ruler on policy but not to determine it. Similar bodies in the West served in much the same way except, of course, in the British parliamentary system. The emperor also set Speransky, the best legal mind in the nation, the task of studying other law codes in preparation for the issue of a modern code for Russia; there had been no revision since 1649. The new code did not appear, however, until the next reign.

The emperor did take some halting steps toward a solution to the problem of bondage. A royal order in 1803 permitted a noble landowner to free an entire village of serfs but only if they received land along with the emancipation. The village would pay a price, amortized over a period, that would cover the value of the land and also the market worth of the male serf; females apparently did not enter into the price calculation. Although the announcement excited hope among reformers that a solution to the bondage problem had arrived, the results were disappointing. By the end of the reign in 1825 fewer than 40,000 serfs had won their freedom under the pronouncement of 1803, and another 70,000 came under the act during the thirty-year reign of Alexander's successor. The price of freedom and land per male serf varied from 139 rubles to 5,000. Those who took advantage of the act became "free farmers."

Between 1816 and 1819 the tsar ordered the emancipation without land of all serfs in the Baltic provinces of Estonia, Courland, and Livonia. Most of them became tenant farmers subject to the will of the landowners for rent levels. Some, of course, went into industry. The effect of the move was to free the gentry of all responsibility and obligations to the peasants, whose economic condition as a consequence tended to deteriorate.

The problem of serfdom was far more extensive, of course, than the Baltic provinces which had been part of the Russian empire for less than a century. In 1818, Alexander asked his chief adviser at the time, Count Alexis Arakcheyev, to suggest a solution to the serf problem throughout the empire. The count proposed the appointment of a government-funded commission to purchase freedom for the serfs, and the land they occupied, from the gentry. Nothing came of Arakcheyev's proposal.

The contemporaries of Alexander I regarded him as an actor, or an enigma, or a sphinx, and referred to him in those terms. His nature and conduct are to modern observers no less difficult to fathom and judge. Certainly he persisted both in his quest for a proper instrument of reform—plan, charter, or constitution—and in his search for some way to end bondage. But he always drew back from taking the final step that would commit him to a course of vigorous action. He may have concluded that Russia was not ready either for emancipation or for a broader political base—that is, some popular participation in government. He may have felt that the nation at the moment stood more in need of education than of political reform or universal freedom.

Alexander did far more for education than did any of his predecessors, or even all of them together. The finest minds in the land advised the Ministry of Education, at least during the early years of the reign—Czartorysky, Novosiltsev, Stroganov, and Speransky. The tsar divided the nation into six educational regions, with a curator, or director, over each. He provided each region with a university by founding new institutions in Kazan, Kharkov, St. Petersburg, and Vilna, and by reopening the German university in Dorpat. Together with the old University of Moscow, Russia now had six. The curator was the chief administrative officer of the university and supervisor in his region of all secondary schools, of which each provincial center was to have one. In every district there was to be an improved primary school. By the end of the reign the nation had six universities, forty-eight secondary schools, and 337 primary schools, all newly organized and all in addition to church-sponsored schools.

Alexander increased expenditure on education to more than ten times what it had been in Catherine's time, made possible a significant rise in school population, broadened the curriculum at all levels, extended the number of years of schooling available, and pushed the elementary system down to the local district level. His contribution to the development of public education was so substantial that one admirer credits him with creating the Russian educational system: ". . . there was no such thing as a school system before Alexander I; there were schools but no system."

The spectacular strides in education brought Russia abreast of accomplishments in much of the West, at least quantitatively. Russia had far to go to catch up in teacher preparation, but there, too, there was considerable progress during Alexander's reign. Perhaps the most solid achievement was the relegation of church-controlled education to a somewhat minor role. It was publicly financed secular education that made the phenomenal advance. Even in England at the time education remained firmly under church authority.

Attention to educational progress grew in part out of Russia's interest in the West and her determination, in what might have been Peter's words, to "catch up." The best of the nation's leaders had not forgotten Peter's view that, if Russia were to learn from the West, then she must acquire the tools with which to learn. That meant that she must have a school system, and Peter had taken the first step.

If Alexander had maintained his enthusiasm for reform and his interest in progress, the story of education during his reign might have suffered no blemish. But the Ministry of Education later fell under obscurantist leadership and church influence, and the great promise of Alexander's early years quickly faded. The waning of the tsar's enthusiasm for reform was not limited, however, to the field of education.

About the time of Napoleon's invasion of Russia in 1812 a

noticeable change came over Alexander. The liberalism of his early years seemed to give way to conservatism. An interest in mysticism seemed to replace the agnosticism of his youth. He turned to reading the Bible, discussing Christianity with churchmen, and consorting with Quakers and with pietists of various sorts, the most notorious of whom was Baroness Julie von Krüdener. Whether the change came about over shock at the burning of Moscow, or grief at the death of a natural daughter, or remorse at the suffering his people endured from war, no one can say. It was not simply the flight from one extreme to another that often marked his actions, nor that the tsar was just "a bundle of contradictions," as his grandmother recognized, nor that he was the blend of masculine strength and feminine weakness that Metternich thought he saw, nor even the combination of brilliance and laziness that his tutor detected.

Whatever the explanation for the change in Alexander, the change was so marked as to make clear that the enlightenment that had carried over from Catherine's reign and that had persisted through Alexander's early years on the throne was no longer in evidence after the French invasion. A period of reaction in deed and word and anti-enlightenment in attitude gripped officialdom for the next forty years. It is not unreasonable to see the shift as a reaction to the West, as the manifestation of hostility that followed the invasion of 1812 and the suffering it brought with it.

Alexander I: Foreign Adventure

The accomplishments of Alexander I were much more impressive in the field of foreign affairs than in domestic matters. He assumed immediately that Russia shared with the West a responsibility for international developments. He joined coalitions, led his armies to victory, and conducted negotiations at conferences, acquitting himself well in all such endeavors.

Nicholas Novosiltsev, a member of the Unofficial Committee that met with the tsar soon after his accession, went to London in 1804 to present Alexander's proposal for an Anglo-Russian alliance against Napoleon. The tsar urged a joint public statement that the goal of the coalition was to rid France and all Europe of the tyranny of Napoleon and to make it possible for all peoples to choose their own governments. The remarkable Russian proposal went still further to suggest that the peace treaty, when it came, should proclaim the accepted principles of international law and should provide for mediation of international disputes before resort to war. Each nation should be entitled to its natural boundaries, and in case of conflict arbitration should settle the issue. Once France was rolled back to her natural frontiers, she was to be held there by a sort of *cordon sanitaire* of federations of Italian and German principalities.

Novosiltsev's secret mission wrought no diplomatic miracles. Pitt, the British prime minister, praised the tsar's lofty aims but made no commitment about the peace settlement to come. Great Britain agreed to subsidize a Russian army and the two powers undertook to drive France out of Italy, Switzerland, Holland, and Germany. Sweden and Austria joined the coalition.

Napoleon won a signal victory over Austrian and Russian troops at Austerlitz in December 1805 and Austria withdrew from the war. After a lull in hostilities Russian forces lost again to Napoleon at Friedland in the summer of 1807, and the tsar was ready for peace. His troops were demoralized, the British had been parsimonious, and Austrian support was not forthcoming.

The emperors of France and Russia met for the first time in June 1807 in a striking scene on a raft anchored mid-stream in the Niemen River at Tilsit in East Prussia. The details of the peace agreement were far less important—in any case, the treaty remained in force for less than five years—than was Napoleon's offer to share all Europe with the Russian emperor; the Vistula River was to mark the boundary between the two superstates. There could be no surer recognition of Russia's stature as a Western and European power, the equal of the strongest of them all. Seen in another way, Napoleon's offer was a thinly veiled effort to turn Russia away from Europe and the West by holding her behind the Vistula. Haggling between the two emperors over where the boundary line should fall and what should happen to the bits and pieces around the edges—the Balkans, Constanti-nople, and the islands of the Mediterranean—brought no settle-ment.

St. Petersburg society turned bitter over the loss of the war with France and even more so over the alliance, to which Alexander had subscribed at Tilsit, with the godless Napoleon. The depression that followed the severance of trade with England, to which the tsar had had also to agree, made matters worse. French plays were hissed in the theater, and capital society snubbed the French ambassador.

The uneasy Franco-Russian peace ended in the summer of 1812 when Napoleon invaded Russia with a force of over a half million men. Westerners from many lands marched under the banners of this Grand Army, for fewer than half were Frenchmen. With much smaller forces at his command, Alexander chose to fight only delaying actions, falling back steadily deeper into his own land and stretching ever longer Napoleon's supply and communication lines.

The Russians, troops and civilians alike, scorched the earth, killing or driving off the livestock, burning villages, destroying grain supplies, and poisoning the wells, thus forcing the invader to bring with him everything he used. Partisans picked off stragglers, cut down sentries, and drove back foraging parties. The invaders slaughtered Russians, regardless of age or sex, whenever they could catch them; the partisans, on the other hand, took no prisoners and were savage and ruthless with their axes, scythes, and pitchforks.

The Russian commander, fat old Marshal Michael Kutuzov, fought a fierce battle at Borodino just west of Moscow, and then withdrew in good order through and beyond the old capital. Napoleon occupied the Kremlin for five weeks, waiting for a Russian plea for peace that never came. Soon after his arrival in the city, deserted by its inhabitants, fires broke out and raged unchecked since the mayor had pulled out all fire-fighting equipment. The French soldiers looted and pillaged at will, emptied wine cellars, defiled churches, broke furniture for firewood, and carted off art treasures, jewelry, furs, tapestries, and whatever else the citizens had not taken with them when they evacuated. Destruction was so widespread that the history of Moscow divides into a pre-French and a post-French period. Three fourths of the old city fell sacrifice to the occupation.

The unending battle that raged from the moment Napoleon entered Russia, the exhaustion that came with the summer heat, the dysentery and typhus that killed thousands, the partisan raids that took a frightful toll, the loss of horses from shortage of provender and the physical burdens the men had to assume, the collapse of discipline in Moscow, all so weakened the invading force that Napoleon decided late in October to withdraw from Moscow, blowing up parts of the Kremlin as his troops, laden down with plunder, left the city. The retreat became nightmarish, for clouds of Cossacks and partisans hovered along the route, contested river crossings, and herded the French back over the scorched earth of the invasion path, stripped as it was of all food and forage. In mid-December, 30,000 tattered and desperate men, all that remained of the largest army ever assembled to that time, straggled back across the frontier. The Russians at tremendous cost to themselves had successfully defended their homeland in this memorable "Patriotic War."

Kutuzov, who was content simply to rid the land of the invader and who showed no interest in driving Napoleon back to France, died days after the forlorn survivors of the invasion had left Russian soil. Alexander led his army to the field of Leipzig and then at the head of the allied troops into Paris in 1814. After Napoleon's withdrawal to Elba and the conclusion of peace with France, the tsar visited England as an international hero. No Russian army was at Waterloo to take part in Napoleon's final defeat, but Alexander and his troops returned to Paris soon after the battle to dictate the Second Treaty of Paris. During the long sojourn in the French capital Russian officers, nobles all and most of them educated in the works of the Enlightenment, visited the salons of Paris and charmed French hostesses with their brilliance and their impeccable manners. Paris society made an indelible impression upon them.

The powers gathered at Vienna in the autumn of 1814 to redraw the map of Europe after the turbulence of the Napoleonic wars. The deliberations suffered interruption when Napoleon escaped from Elba and returned briefly for the Waterloo campaign that put an end to his violent career. Alexander led a large delegation to Vienna, the chief members of which were two Germans, a Swiss, a Greek, a Corsican, and a Pole. There was no room to question the fact, Alexander assumed, that Russia had saved Europe from the Napoleonic scourge. Now the Russian emperor met with allied leaders and delegations from defeated enemies to reconstruct Europe, particularly Western Europe, and to create machinery that would make impossible another revolutionary convulsion. This was the first international conference of leaders of many Western states in which Russia was a principal.

The Vienna settlement created a kingdom of Poland with the tsar of Russia as the Polish king; while ostensibly the new state was independent, the consequence of its birth was to carry Russian power, symbolized by the presence of the tsar's brother as viceroy in Warsaw, into Central Europe. Russia also received confirmation of her recent conquests of Finland and Bessarabia.

Something of Alexander's mystical inclinations, and something also of his desperate search for peace, came out at the Congress of Vienna in the tsar's proposal of a Holy Alliance. He drafted the treaty, signed originally by the Austrian and Russian emperors and the Prussian king and ultimately by nearly every crowned head in Europe, by which the signatories agreed as "members of one great Christian nation" to treat each other as Christian brothers and to deal with their subjects as fathers with their children. Alexander reasoned that, if rulers and nations could be persuaded to live by Christian precepts, then there would be no war. It must follow that a sovereign who granted his peoples the reforms and the guarantees of rights they merited would escape rebellion and revolution. The lesson of the age, he seemed to believe, was that revolution to bring about reform only brought greater tyranny and precipitated international chaos and war.

Although every ruler except the sultan, the pope, and the king of England subscribed to the Holy Alliance, there was general scorn and derision at such mystical nonsense. Far more substantial was the Quadruple Alliance, by which Russia, Austria, Prussia, and Great Britain agreed to maintain the peace settlement they had arranged at Vienna. They agreed further to meet from time to time to take stock of the international situation. Implicitly Russia was joining the West in promising to move against any government or any revolutionary movement that threatened to imperil the peace.

The first meeting of the Big Four was at Aix-la-Chapelle in 1818. At the tsar's suggestion France, apparently stable and free of the revolutionary virus that she had once spread over the continent, joined the others to form the Quintuple Alliance. Alexander then urged the creation of a league of European rulers pledged to maintain each other's boundaries and political systems. But no delegation showed any enthusiasm for Russian policing of Western Europe, and nothing came of the proposal.

In 1820 the powers met at Troppau to consider joint action in Spain and Italy, where revolutions were threatening to overturn governments the Congress of Vienna had restored. Neither France nor Great Britain officially attended the meeting, but sent observers. The three Eastern powers agreed to answer the call of any government threatened by revolution, as the tsar had proposed at an earlier conference. Then the Congress adjourned to Laibach to hear evidence of revolutions that had broken out in Piedmont and Naples. Alexander offered to march a Russian army into Italy to put down the uprisings. The others politely declined the offer, and Austrian troops suppressed the Piedmontese and Neapolitan revolutions.

News of a Greek rising against the sultan came to the delegates at Laibach, but there was no action upon which they could agree. When the last of these Congresses met at Verona in 1822, the Greeks seemed to be faltering in their effort to win independence, and the powers decided against taking any action. Aside from the fact that the Greeks were Orthodox, Alexander regarded them as no less barbaric and no more deserving of sympathy than the Turks who ruled them. He was consistent, too, in his opposition to revolution wherever it threatened. His work to keep the peace, to deal with Turkey only in consultation with other powers in the Congress system in spite of the pressure of Graecophile Russians to succor their Orthodox brothers, won him the respect and praise of the British foreign minister.

At Verona news arrived that the Bourbon king of Spain was a prisoner of revolutionaries who had proclaimed a republic. Setting aside his personal distaste for Ferdinand VII, Alexander offered to restore the Spanish king, but the powers agreed that France should undertake the assignment. However, Great Britain, whose trade ties with Latin America were strong and profitable, would not hear of great power intervention in colonial efforts to secede from Spanish rule. And the American President Monroe warned against European interference in Western Hemisphere affairs.

From Alexander's time on Russia was a European power of such magnitude that a settlement of Western affairs without taking her towering strength and her huge manpower reserves into consideration would have been inconceivable and indeed rash. In a sense this had been so ever since Peter the Great, although the West on occasion had not shown Russia the respect Peter knew he had earned for her. But Alexander, whom Russian chauvinists hailed as "the man who defeated Napoleon," made secure the nation's position as one of the world's half dozen great powers. In international politics Russia was as much a Western power after 1815 as was Germany after 1870.

Alexander I: The Anti-Enlightenment

Alexander's hostility to revolution wherever it occurred has been taken generally as incontrovertible evidence of his desertion of the liberalism of his youth and his conversion to a course of reaction. This is perhaps unfair to the tsar, for it seems to judge him by the standards not of his own age anywhere in Europe but by those of a later generation in the West. It misjudges both the assumed liberalism of his youth and the supposed reaction of his later years. If Alexander was liberal at the dawn of his reign, it was in the spirit of eighteenth-century enlightened and benevolent despotism, not in the spirit of nineteenth-century democracy. And his swing to the right after 1815 made him seem reactionary perhaps to revolutionary spirits of the nineteenth century and to those who looked back from the twentieth, but he came to rest somewhere near the middle of the political spectrum of his own time. While Metternich gave his name to the age, reaction was no monopoly of the monarchies of Eastern Europe.

Soon after returning home from the Congress of Vienna in 1815, the emperor turned over, in effect, the direction of all internal affairs to his close friend and confidant of many years, Count Alexis Arakcheyev. The count presided over the Council of Ministers whose recommendations reached the tsar only through him. He suggested the names of those appointed to important posts. Impeccably honest and completely loyal to the emperor as he was, Arakcheyev strove to keep unsettling matters from his sovereign, and Alexander was willing to leave domestic affairs to his faithful servant and concentrate upon the less prosaic subject of foreign relations.

The most infamous invention connected with the name of Arakcheyev was that of the Military Settlements. The tsar faced the likelihood after 1815 that the nation would have to maintain a large standing army to keep the peace in Europe; this would be extremely costly and would place a heavy burden of recruitment upon the Russian people. Since enlistment ran for twenty-five years, and since a normal married life for the soldier in the ranks was impossible, army service, especially in peace time, caused bitter resentment.

Arakcheyev proposed that troops be settled on crown lands and that military drill be combined with farming. The soldiers might marry and live in individual cottages built by the government in a village laid out symmetrically, the houses whitewashed and evenly spaced, each with its vegetable garden in the rear. The men would drill at certain hours and march at others to work in the fields. Children, dressed in uniform, would march to a school built by the government. The villagers would live on a military schedule; they would rise and assemble and work and retire to bugle calls. A certain area would be reserved for an army unit, and landowners were compensated and moved off their estates if they lay in an area to be taken over for a military settlement.

The emperor, who only rarely visited the settlements and then on a flying trip of inspection well prepared for in advance, looked upon the experiment as a sort of social reform. It would make possible an orderly and normal life for an army recruit; it would raise agricultural production by introducing advanced Western methods of farm management and animal husbandry; it would extend education to children of serfs; it would raise the standard of living, since better housing and army rations would be available to the soldier and his family and it would ease the financial burden of maintaining a large army. Since Russia had to bear the primary responsibility of keeping the peace of Europe, her military strength could not flag. By the end of the reign battalions of infantry and squadrons of cavalry constituting one third of the army were living in military settlements.

The military colonies came to be centers of deep resentment by those who occupied them. Tasks were standardized and a regular punishment code was applied impartially—so many lashes with a birch rod for each infraction of the many rules. The regimentation of the entire family created particular hostility. "Better that one son should enlist than the entire family enter the army," the peasants came to feel. Before the reign was out revolts in the settlements were commonplace. Alexander, however, seems to have been unaware of the ill feeling the experiment provoked, and he looked forward to the time when the entire Russian army, nearly a million men by 1825, could be maintained in this way.

Another of the emperor's close friends for many years was Prince Alexander Golitsyn, who became director-general of the Holy Synod in 1802. Later he became head of the Office of Spiritual Affairs of Foreign Confessions whose assignment it was to deal with non-Orthodox faiths in the empire. As an intimate friend of the tsar it was he who suggested that Alexander take up reading the Bible, and the emperor continued the practice all through the long war with France. When the tsar approved the foundation of the Russian Bible Society, modeled after the British Society and dedicated to the translation of the Bible into the several languages of the Russian Empire, Golitsyn became its head. In 1816, Golitsyn became minister of education, but to accommodate the various offices he held, his new title was Minister of Spiritual Affairs and Education.

The Ministry of Education had been a liberal and Westernizing force in the land during the early years of the reign. It became unswervingly antiliberal and anti-Western, however, under Golitsyn's ministry. The office came under the influence of religious fanatics, obscurantists, and reactionaries of various hues. One of the worst was Michael Magnitsky, who was appointed curator of the University of Kazan. He drove out "politically unreliable" staff members, named a director of police and "moral affairs," set spies to observe students and faculty, made attendance at religious services mandatory, stripped from the library the works of the Age of Enlightenment, and made the ridiculous charge to the emperor that his brother, the Grand Duke Nicholas, was a freethinker. One of Nicholas's praiseworthy contributions to Russian education when he came to the throne was to dismiss Magnitsky.

Golitsyn appointed Dmitry Runich curator of the University region of St. Petersburg, and a purge similar to that at Kazan was soon under way. Runich immediately dismissed four professors found guilty of "teaching in a spirit contrary to Christianity and subversive of the social order." Their guilt was apparent from sets of students' lecture notes. Golitsyn stood so firmly behind Runich that he proposed to prosecute the professors criminally, but the case was dropped when the Ministry of Education came under a new head.

Golitsyn's successor was Admiral Alexander Shishkov, who believed that Russian universities had become "schools of vice." He proposed to make them centers of nationalistic fervor, antiforeign, anti-Western in spirit, where youths would not idle away their time in "vaporous dreaming." There was some progress, however; education, the Holy Synod, and the Office of Spiritual Affairs of Foreign Confessions each became once again a distinct branch of government.

Although the drift toward reaction in the last decade of the reign was perhaps more the work of Arakcheyev and Golitsyn than of the tsar personally, still Alexander became far more conservative in his own attitudes than he had once been. He referred to those German universities accused of nurturing radicalism as guilty "of all sorts of irregularities, where young people acquire notions that are most opposed to religion and morality."

The event most often identified as decisive in turning the emperor against the enlightened attitudes he had once embraced and encouraged took place in 1820. In St. Petersburg a battalion of the Semenovsky Guards, of which the tsar was honorary colonel, protested against the harsh discipline of its new commanding officer, Colonel Gregory Schwarz. The colonel chose to regard this as mutiny and imprisoned the entire battalion. The tsar was at Troppau when Metternich gleefully told him the news, hinting perhaps in his manner that the emperor had encouraged rebellion by his own liberal protestations.

Alexander heard the news of the Semenovsky "mutiny" in shock and disbelief. Many of the nobles who held officer rank in the regiment were Freemasons, and several were members of secret societies working for reform. That they had nothing to do with promoting the protest against the rigid discipline of Colonel Schwarz was a fact that Alexander chose to ignore. He made up his mind, while still at Troppau, that the mutiny was part of some international plot. He wrote to Arakcheyev: "There is some foreign, nonmilitary inspiration. I attribute it to secret societies."

The Decembrists

During the years when Russian armies were fighting in Central and Western Europe alongside Western Europeans against Napoleon, and especially during the months of armistice and peace when Russian troops were in bivouac on the outskirts of Paris, the officers came to know Western civilization at first hand. These young aristocrats had many social opportunities to meet Westerners—Frenchmen as well as Britons, Germans, Poles, Italians, Danes, and many others.

The young Russians, tutored in the languages of the West and steeped in the philosophy of the Enlightenment which their own sovereign had urged them to study, discovered a civilization far in advance of their own in many sobering ways. They saw in the homeland of their recent enemy a society of free men where there had been no traffic in human flesh for centuries, a society free of class, and a society where all were equal before the law and where all could own property. They found in France a land where many peasants were more prosperous than were many impoverished Russian nobles. They saw a society where literacy, education, taste, and wealth were not the exclusive right of the wellborn.

The impression left upon these young Russians by their firsthand introduction to the West was an indelible one. It made them envious, for themselves and for all Russians, of the civilized life they found all about them. They contrasted the open society they now visited with the closed society whence they had come and to which they must return. In all their pride of having been victorious over an advanced culture, they wanted to see the best the West could offer transplanted to their own unhappy land.

With the return of the army to Russia, a number of officers stationed in Petersburg met occasionally to recount the experiences they had enjoyed in the West and to reflect upon the sad plight of the nation under the blighting influence of Arakcheyev. Many were members of Masonic lodges—Freemasonry had entered Russia from England early in the eighteenth century—where they had imbibed an interest in philanthropy, a concern for mankind, and a fascination with secret ceremonies. Conspiratorial societies were much in vogue in Central Europe, as the reaction of the restoration years made disappointed liberals restless. When the Russian army was in Germany in 1813, many of the future Decembrists explored the workings of the Prussian *Tugendbund,* or League of Virtue, whose members swore an oath of loyalty to the dynasty but vowed also to work for the reform and improvement of Prussian society.

There was also, among the young reform-minded nobles of Russia, a growing impatience and disappointment with the emperor. Alexander's fascination with external affairs soon became manifest. Those who were winning the tsar's confidence in domestic matters were a dreary lot. Yet everyone knew of his earlier liberalism; it seemed reasonable to suppose that he would encourage continued interest in such projects of his own as emancipation and a constitution. Years later, when well-organized secret societies were scheming the overthrow of the dynasty if necessary to win reform, the emperor admitted his responsibility: "I once encouraged such illusions and errors. It is not for me to get upset about these people."

Early in 1816 a number of young Guards officers stationed in the capital—the youngest was nineteen, the oldest twenty-five, and all were of distinguished aristocratic families—organized a secret society, the Union of Salvation. Its ultimate goals were the end of bondage and a constitutional government; it most resented Arakcheyev, the military settlements, slavery and floggings, police brutality, corruption in officialdom, and the gross mismanagement of the judicial system. The broad aims reflected the impact of Western Europe upon the young idealists and, at the same time, some of the goals that the tsar himself had long considered. Their immediate concern was only to tidy up Russian society, to make it a less shameful thing.

The members later decided to organize branches in other cities and renamed the organization the Union of Welfare. They agreed upon a mild and harmless program of activity: members were to undertake some philanthropic work such as organizing hospitals, urging prison reform, and caring for unfortunates. Then the leaders, meeting in Moscow in 1821, decided to dissolve the organization when they learned that the secret police knew of its activities. And some of the most active had been transferred to frontier posts.

Some who were stationed in Petersburg continued to meet secretly and came to be known as the Northern Society. There were some members and correspondents of the group in Moscow. Other former members of the Union of Welfare, now stationed at Tulchin on the Romanian border, gathered together to form the Southern Society. The two societies distrusted each other, partly because of the strong personalities who headed the separate groups, but more especially because their approaches to Russia's problems radically differed.

At the time of its creation the Northern Society numbered

only thirteen, but they included scions of some of the most respected families of the gentry. There was General Michael Orlov, commander of an army division, who spent most of his own fortune providing educational facilities for his troops; Conrad Ryleyev, one of the nation's most promising young poets; Prince Serge Trubetskoy, later leader of the society, who wanted a constitutional convention to reorganize the government; Nicholas Turgenev, head of a department in the Ministry of Finance; Nikita Muravev, heir to vast estates and many thousands of serfs, who ultimately had six cousins in the movement; and Fedor Glinka, adjutant to the governor-general of Petersburg.

Nikita Muravev, first leader of the Northern Society, drafted its constitution, although he never completed it. It proposed to abolish serfdom and grant to the peasants full ownership of their huts, gardens, tools, and livestock. The gentry would retain their estates, for there would be no involuntary distribution of land. There would be an end to the hated military settlements. All men would enjoy the freedoms of expression, association, and conscience, and there would be an end to class, ranks, and titles.

Muravev's political structure followed closely the model of the United States. There would be thirteen provinces, each with its own bicameral legislature, in a federal system of shared powers. The emperor would be a sort of hereditary president with the same sort of administrative responsibility exercised by the American chief executive. A bicameral legislature, which with a two-thirds majority could override an imperial veto of its enactments, would consist of a House of Representatives and a Supreme Duma, both elected but representing different constituencies. A high property qualification would exclude the freed serfs from the electorate, and a still higher one would limit office holders and legislators to the well-to-do.

If the constitutional blueprint of the Northern Society would base the new government upon the American model, that of the Southern Society derived from the Jacobins of the French Revolution. The dedicated leader of the Southern Society, with its headquarters at Tulchin, was Colonel Paul

Pestel whose father was governor-general of Siberia. He drafted the instrument of government and called it *Russkaia Pravda* — Russian Justice.

Pestel proposed the abolition of serfdom and class privileges — titles, ranks, and immunity to taxation. All land would become the property of the state, which would cultivate part of it to provide revenue and to experiment with improved methods. The remainder would go in parcels to anyone who wanted to farm, each to receive enough to provide for his family. Noble landowners would suffer expropriation, but presumably could ask for the use of a small plot on a basis of equality with all other tillers of the soil. Factory serfs would become free wage-earners and would toil alongside criminals assigned industrial labor to work off their sentences. Any man might engage in trade without restriction; private enterprise would receive every encouragement, except that there would be no protective tariffs. Freedom of assembly and expression would be guaranteed, but secret societies would not be allowed. A secret police, to which Russia had long since become accustomed perhaps, would defend the nation against internal enemies, in quite the same way that the secret police had functioned in revolutionary France.

The author of *Russkaia Pravda* had no patience with federalism. The nation would be strongly centralized. Great Russian would become the official and only language, and Orthodoxy the only religion. Minority peoples would lose their identity, with the single exception of the Poles; this was a bid for the support of Polish nationalists. Pestel would annex border areas necessary to Russian security — the Caucasus, Moldavia, Mongolia, and the Kirghiz steppe. And he would establish an independent Jewish state somewhere in Asia Minor, and assemble all Russian Jews at Kiev and march them away to their new homeland.

The central government would consist of an executive Directory of five men, an obvious imitation of revolutionary French practice. A unicameral legislature, elected for five years on a broad suffrage basis, would enact laws, control the ministry, and appoint all civil and military officers. Russia would become a republic, firmly governed from the capital.

The new society would come into existence by overturning the monarch and assassinating every member of the royal family to eliminate all claimants. Muravev objected to such jesuitism when Pestel visited Petersburg in 1824 to discuss inauguration of the new regime. Later meetings did little to settle the deep differences between the Northern and Southern Societies. Some of the Northern leaders, however, agreed with Colonel Pestel that there should be a revolution in the summer of 1826.

The influences to which Pestel was subject are much clearer than are those that affected Muravev, for notebooks in which Pestel jotted down observations gleaned from his readings still exist. His well-educated parents tutored him until he reached the age of twelve, after which he studied in Germany for five years. He returned home in 1809 to spend two years in the Pages' Corps, the highly exclusive military school for members of the gentry.

Pestel's interests came to focus upon political science and political economy, and he read and took extensive notes on the works of Machiavelli, Voltaire, Diderot, Beccaria, Bentham, and the economists Adam Smith, J. B. Say, and Simonde de Sismondi. Aside from his readings, he found much to admire in the career of Napoleon and sympathized with the benevolent despotism that the emperor gave to France. As a consequence of the confused and contradictory influences to which Pestel was subject, his *Russkaia Pravda* proposed a system that would blend authoritarian with liberal and *laissez-faire* features. His associates in the Decembrist movement—so-called from the attempt of the secret societies to alter the succession in December 1825—frequently expressed uneasiness over his Jacobin-like attitudes, and some even suspected him of wanting to become a Russian Napoleon.

While he was at heart loyal to the Russian state, Pestel's loyalty, unlike that of many Decembrists, did not extend to the dynasty or even to the monarchy. Yet he remained convinced that a strong and centralized authority was essential to the effective government of the nation.

Meanwhile, Alexander gave much thought to abdicating and retiring to some vine-covered cottage on the Rhine or even to some sylvan retreat in America. In anticipation of such a retirement, he drew up a will in 1823 which bypassed his next younger brother Constantine, who refused the succession, and named his third brother, Nicholas, to succeed him. The royal family and a few high officials knew of the arrangement.

In November 1825, Alexander died at Taganrog on the Sea of Azov. Everyone not privy to the terms of his will expected Constantine to succeed. Aware of his unpopularity in the army and of the public knowledge that Constantine was next in line, Nicholas actually took an oath of allegiance to Constantine, who as viceregent of Poland was in Warsaw. He officially proclaimed his older brother tsar, but Constantine refused again and reminded Nicholas that the matter had long since been settled. After a prolonged exchange of requests and refusals between Petersburg and Warsaw, and amid growing restlessness in the capital, Nicholas proclaimed himself emperor.

The delay in the succession provided the secret societies an opportunity they could not ignore. When the troops in the capital were paraded in Senate Square and were ordered to swear allegiance to Nicholas, some of the Guards, incited by officers who were members of the Northern Society, refused to take the oath. Three thousand soldiers and officers defied the royal order as men in the ranks shouted "We don't want Nicholas; we want Constantine!" or "Constantine and a Constitution" in the mistaken belief that Nicholas was a usurper who was preventing the birth of a constitutional regime. But 10,000 stood with the government, firing upon the rebels while artillery raked the square. Sixty or seventy died and scores fell wounded. The date was December 14, 1825. The affair came to be known as the Decembrist revolt and the plotters as Decembrists.

The secret police had a roster of members of the societies. They had infiltrated the organizations, in fact, and had reported every move to Alexander who had refused to arrest the conspirators for harboring liberal views he once had shared. Now the police rounded up every member of the Northern Society in the capital. Prince Trubetskoy, the dictator-designate who was to lead the new regime, was found cowering in the Austrian legation. Colonel Pestel was arrested in Tulchin along with other members of the Southern Society.

In less than a week a court tried nearly 600 accused, acquitted half of them, imposed light sentences on half the rest, and laid long prison terms and Siberian exile upon most of the others. Five were to be quartered and thirty beheaded. But Nicholas generously commuted the sentences; the five were hanged and the rest condemned to Siberia at hard labor. Europe was shocked at the sentence. The Polish poet Adam Mickiewicz expressed the disgust many foreigners felt: "A curse upon a people that murders its own prophets."

Historians still disagree over the significance of the Decembrist rising. Some consider it the first Russian revolution, a sort of prelude to 1917. Others regard it as only another aristocratic *coup d'état*, the last of the many eighteenth-century efforts by nobles to interfere with the succession. Surely the second position is wide of the mark; whether the Decembrists fathered the Bolsheviks may be questionable, but the 1825 affair differed from earlier aristocratic episodes in resting upon a detailed program, indeed two programs, of where the revolution should go.

The Decembrist revolt was not the first time members of the gentry had undertaken violent political action to be sure, nor would it be the last. The affair, however, was the first occasion when army officers revolted, and it was the last. Henceforward, the army would remain loyal to the dynasty. The significance lies not in the fact that the Decembrists were aristocrats nor in the fact that they were army officers; they were intellectuals in revolt, the first of a long line.

Another significant fact about the Decembrists, one rarely noticed, was the Western nature of their education, their experience, their values, and their programs. Along with their Western coloration, however, went a conscience about their native land. They were the first of the "repentant nobles," those nineteenth-century aristocrats who accepted the burden of guilt for, and sought in any way possible to atone for, the cruelty and harshness and evils of Russian society.

Of greatest significance surely is the fact that the grand aim of members of both Northern and Southern Societies was to complete the Westernization of Russia. They would erase the two stains that marked the nation as uncivilized and barbaric. Both Societies would end bondage and grant certain fundamental rights to all Russians. And each in a different way would end the autocracy and move the nation toward representative government. They failed, and the Westernization of Russia remained uncompleted to the end of the monarchy and beyond.

Nicholas I: Conservative Bureaucrat

The anti-Enlightenment, which had emerged as a Russian Francophobia after Tilsit and gathered strength during the last decade of Alexander's reign, continued undiminished under Nicholas I. The strong Western flavor of the Decembrist movement was quite enough, in the absence of any other contributing factors, to give the tsar an anti-Western bias. But the new emperor had had conservative tutors and there had been none of the exposure to liberal writings that had distinguished Alexander's education. Nicholas was with the Russian army in Paris in 1814 but had enjoyed the military parades more than the cultural opportunities the city offered.

After the last of the Decembrists had left in chains for Siberia, the new tsar set about reforming the administration. Fascinated as he was with uniforms and parades, and feeling most at ease in the company of generals, he chose his advisers from the ranks of the military, regarded himself as the nation's commander-in-chief, and referred to a department head as "chief of staff for peasant affairs" or "chief of staff for royal charities." He divided His Majesty's Chancery, which was under his direct control and not some semiautonomous bureau, into several sections or departments to handle specific problems; each department reported directly to the emperor. The Second Section, for example, received the assignment to bring in a new law code, and Speransky became its head. The infamous Third Section was the security or secret police.

Nicholas did not set his mind uncompromisingly against reform, as later liberal detractors accused him of doing. But in considering reform he did not intend to permit progress—he hated the very word—so much as he intended to correct administrative abuses. And any reform that would increase the efficiency of autocratic government would have Nicholas's support. But reform had to come from the sovereign, not from any popular source. "I shall always distinguish," he made clear, "those who desire just reforms and expect them to emanate from the legal authority from those who want to undertake them by themselves, employing God knows what means." He had the Decembrists surely in mind when he swore at the time of his coronation that if government needed any correction it would come from the ruler and "not by impertinent destructive dreams."

The emperor regarded bondage as an evil, or so he said in a meeting of advisers. But he hurried on to say that to sweep it away "now" would do more harm than good. He noted that Alexander, whom he greatly admired, had considered emancipation but had abandoned the project. Nicholas felt that the end of bondage was "very far away," and any reflection about it, let alone any action, would "criminally endanger public security and the welfare of the state." The argument that serfdom stamped Russia as non-Western or non-European would have made no impression upon Nicholas. He would have regarded such reasoning as Decembrist and therefore treasonable. That Russia was the last nation in Europe to harbor serfdom the emperor would not have found either shameful or regrettable.

The tsar also was inclined to move cautiously toward ending serfdom because of his conviction that the precipitate abolition of the last vestiges of serfdom in France in 1789 had not prevented revolution. Indeed, it had helped to provoke the revolution.

Ten separate committees met at various times during the thirty-year reign to consider the need for reform, particularly the need to end bondage. The serfs constantly reminded the tsar of the problem, for Nicholas witnessed over 700 revolts. The administration took some cautious steps to quiet unrest, although they accomplished little. Several landowners who abused their serfs had their estates confiscated. Members of the gentry were forbidden to sell serfs in a public market or to break up families, but both restrictions simply repeated royal orders dating back to the eighteenth century. Nobles were denied the right to sell their estates unless the holdings were large enough to assure eleven acres of tillable soil for each male serf. When the new law code appeared in 1832, however, it did not include this limitation.

The timidity of imperial measures of reform became apparent when Nicholas created a new Ministry of State Lands and named Count Paul Kiselev to head it. Although the count was a man of great good will, he faced constant frustration in his efforts to improve the lot of the state peasants, for the tsar was reluctant to provoke the hostility of conservative advisers. But Kiselev managed to bring about some improvement in the life of state peasants. A royal order declared them to be "free inhabitants dwelling on state land" and so not serfs. This implied that none could be given away into serfdom, as Catherine and Paul had given away over 1,000,000 state peasants. The machinery of self-government was refined to the point where these "residents on crown land" elected their own officials to supervise economic, criminal, and police matters.

Kiselev set up a number of model farms, the purpose of which was to teach state peasants improved agricultural methods. He moved thousands of peasant families out of overly congested areas and resettled them where they might enjoy more generous acreages. He even made state funds available for small improvement loans. A number of hospitals appeared on state lands, and Kiselev's ministry employed its own doctors to care for state peasants.

A royal committee on peasant affairs recommended that privately owned serfs receive their personal freedom and allotments of land in return for a money payment, the amount of which the freed men should work out with their former owners. But there was violent opposition from the gentry, and Nicholas refused to force the issue. When the revolutions of 1848 broke out in the West, Nicholas abruptly dropped any consideration of emancipation. As so frequently happened, domestic policy reacted immediately to changes in foreign affairs. Serfdom ultimately would end in response to Russia's failure in a foreign venture.

The spirit of the anti-Enlightenment became readily apparent in education. The organizational pattern introduced under Alexander I continued and, in fact, there was some increase in the number of schools and students. But the educational edifice, with its four levels of instruction, became avowedly an aid to the perpetuation of the class stratification of society. Schools at the parish level served the "lowest classes," and this of course did not include serfs unless their owners wanted them to attend school. Children of merchants, craftsmen, and "other townsmen" might enroll in district or county schools to receive a type of instruction "most useful for their way of life, needs, and practice," that is to say, appropriate to their social status. The secondary schools, which were preparatory to university matriculation, were for children of gentry and officials.

Admiral Shishkov, the minister of education whom Nicholas inherited from Alexander, supported the class nature of the school system. He recommended that the type of educational exposure a student received should be one that fitted his class and "destiny" in life, and not one that encouraged him to seek immodestly to improve his status. Indeed, most ministers of education in the nineteenth century were content with the class structure of Russian schooling. However, one of them, General Paul Lieven who succeeded Admiral Shishkov, did not believe it possible to imitate the class arrangement of some Western educational systems. He pointed out that Russia had no middle class, that commoners legally might enter the gentry through the civil service, that a peasant might become a merchant, and that the richest of the nobles might "touch the foot of the throne" while the poorest of them were "almost lost in the peasantry." Lieven, whose tenure as minister of education was brief, has been described as "being ill at ease with new ideas and having none of his own."

The minister of education whose philosophy set the tone of the reign of Nicholas was Count Serge Uvarov. His Western contacts were extensive but did not infect him with liberalism. His tutor was a French abbé who escaped from the Revolution and availed himself of the sanctuary the empress Catherine extended to so many Frenchmen. Uvarov entered the diplomatic service and served in Vienna and at the court of Napoleon after Tilsit.

In 1832, Uvarov reported on his inspection of the university and secondary schools of the Moscow region. He warned the emperor that students ran the danger of corruption from exposure to the "misty fields" of politics and philosophy, and that education should provide youth with some insulation against infection by "so-called European ideas." Young men should come under "carefully planned leadership" if they were to become "useful and devoted instruments" of the state. The goal of education should be the production of men "with deep conviction and warm faith in the truly Russian principles of Autocracy, Orthodoxy, and Nationality." This trinity, Uvarov insisted, would assure Russia's salvation and guarantee "the strength and greatness of our country." The emperor was so appreciative of the tenor of the report that he named Uvarov minister of education, and the count continued in the post for fifteen years.

Uvarov's trinity—Orthodoxy, Autocracy, and Nationality—made up the philosophical base, called simply Official Nationality, upon which the regime chose to take its stand. The Russian Orthodox Church, the official and only legal religion, was completely under government control. It would be put to effective use as a monitor of morals and conduct toward officialdom. Orthodoxy would serve the system as a creed which would inspire all subjects with meekness, respect, and obedience to the emperor, the military officer, the bureaucrat, and the landowner-serfowner. To disobey or to show disrespect for these symbols of authority, then, would be sacrilegious. Autocracy, the unlimited authority divinely granted to the tsar, was no more subject to question or challenge than was Holy Writ. Nationality held up to veneration the Russian language, the Russian people, Russian culture, and Russia's past. Non-Russian elements in the population were in no way equal to the Russians. This even applied to the blood brothers, the Poles, whom Nicholas detested. Official contempt for other peoples did not extend to Baltic Germans, whom the emperor favored with so many important civil and military appointments. Indeed, a

Russian who rendered Nicholas a service was asked to name his reward. He answered that he would most appreciate promotion to the "rank of German."

Uvarov shared the suspicion of the West that was a hallmark of the anti-Enlightenment. In proclaiming a new statute bringing universities firmly under government control and curbing the self-government that faculties had enjoyed briefly under Alexander, the education minister explained what the statute would accomplish. Among other things it would attract into the universities the sons of the gentry and "put an end to the harmful practice of educating them at home by foreign teachers," and also "reduce the present passion for foreign education." The West symbolized progress against which Uvarov firmly set himself and the ministry he headed. In his responsibility for the nation's educational system he expressed the hope that he would be able to "retard the development of the country by fifty years."

The Minstry of Education became the agency that doused every spark of enlightenment. The teaching of philosophy was halted at the University of Moscow, an institution that Nicholas despised as "the wolf's den." No university might teach higher mathematics, a subject that might promote speculation in other fields. Physiology teachers were careful not to "offend the instinct of decency." There might be no courses in comparative law, and only churchmen might teach logic. Professors of history were required to glorify the nation's past and were not free to discuss the Reformation, perhaps because its heroes challenged authority.

The blight which Uvarov cast upon the field of education was matched by a censorship designed to prevent the slightest breath of criticism against the regime. There was a general law of censorship that charged officials to prevent the publication of "harmful" material. But the general law grew bits at a time, and many bureaucratic offices had or assumed responsibility for censorship. Even the Department of Horse Breeding exercised censorship over the materials it sent to the press. The situation became so hopelessly confused and mired in bureaucratic nonsense that one censor charged that there were many more censors than books published. This battery of "cannon aimed at a flea," as one observer described the censorship, included even the emperor himself. Nicholas presumed to pass upon every literary creation, and urged Pushkin to write "more like Sir Walter Scott."

Strict censorship imposed at the frontier kept foreign publications from entering Russia. Nicholas was particularly suspicious of France, the home of revolution, but Italian, English, and even German publications came under the official ban. The emperor at one time even forbade the admission of foreign sheet music, lest the innocent-appearing notes might constitute some subversive message in code. That Nicholas was keenly aware of the disturbing and liberating consequences of Western contacts was apparent from his stubborn efforts to seal off the nation by heavy-handed censorship, by stifling education, by exclusion of foreign publications, and by sternly limiting Russian travel abroad.

The Third Section, the infamous secret or political police, laid down restrictions upon how Russian authors and editors must treat certain topics. No mention of any secret society might appear in print, for Nicholas never forgave the Decembrists. No writer whose works had been censored could be mentioned in any publication. To publish any journal required official approval. Yet once approved, any publication could be suspended and its editor imprisoned or deported simply for displeasing the censor. Uvarov, the minister of education, expressed the hope that Russian literature might cease to exist.

Birth of the Intelligentsia

One of the most celebrated cases of censorship in this age of darkness involved Peter Chaadayev. A favorite of Moscow society, his home was a gathering place for men and women, nobles and commoners, who shared their host's concern over Russia's cultural and social stagnation. After resigning his commission as an officer in the Semenovsky Guards in 1821, Chaadayev spent several years traveling in the West. Only his absence prevented his involvement with other officers of his regiment in the Decembrist uprising.

After returning to Russia in 1826, Chaadayev wrote eight

"philosophical letters" in which he reviewed Russia's past and raised the question of what should be her future. The circle of friends who gathered in his and other homes discussed the letters in the early 1830s, when he completed them, but no censor would approve them for publication. In 1836, however, a negligent censor passed and a Moscow periodical, the *Telescope*, published the first "Philosophical Letter." Its appearance produced the "effect of a pistol shot in the night."

The letter purported to be written from "Necropolis"—the city of the dead—the name Chaadayev gave Moscow. The author argued that Russia had lived a geographical but not a historical existence, and charged that the nation's ideas and institutions had been forcibly imposed upon her from outside. He condemned Russia's backwardness, the poverty of her church ties, the cultural pollution she had acquired from Byzantium, and her failure to contribute anything to the progress and welfare of mankind. Russia was part of the West, he insisted, but she gave no indication of it, as though she had suffered "banishment outside the times." From the modern, advanced, progressive West she still had much to learn, and she should strengthen her affiliation with the civilization of which she rightfully was a part. The future was bright, however, for Russia's destiny demanded that she step forward as the leader and savior of Western civilization.

When the letter somehow slipped past the censor and appeared in print, an alert churchman caught it and called the tsar's attention to this "libel against the fatherland, the faith, and the government." The emperor suspended the *Telescope*, banished its editor into exile, and dismissed the censor who had let the letter pass. Chaadayev was officially declared insane, was confined to his home, and had to suffer the indignity of a physician's examination every day for a year.

Chaadayev's harsh treatment came almost at the precise moment of the birth of the Russian intelligentsia, on the eve of "the marvellous decade," the ten years preceding the revolutionary year 1848. This was the decade when the early giants of literary and social criticism—Belinsky, Herzen, Bakunin—were hurling their defiance at the regime, and when those who would become their disciples were just emerging from the universities. The intelligentsia—the very word is Russian—meant something more than the intellectuals, although as a group it revealed characteristics and performed functions similar to those revealed and performed by intellectuals in England, France, Germany, or Italy. In Russia the intelligentsia made up a class of writers and thinkers, educated occasionally by tutors but increasingly in the universities, many or most of whom had traveled or studied in the West. Some were sons and daughters of the gentry, but after mid-century many came from the families of merchants, priests, or government officials. An abiding sense of social responsibility, of dedication to the improvement of society, set them apart from the Philistinism around them.

The origin of the conditions that produced the intelligentsia lies back at the dawn of the eighteenth century. Peter the Great, by creating a new class of bureaucrats educated in the West or in the ways of the West and equipped with its skills, created a social schism between the dark masses of his feudal land and the educated men who governed them. The bureaucracy, half Russian and half Western, was from Peter's time on a managerial elite, set above and apart from the rest of society. Peter even took his new managerial class off the land and forced it into state service, thus denying it roots. There developed, in consequence, a gulf between the mass of Russians and those who ruled.

There was little change in the situation even after the beginning of the nineteenth century. The masses at the bottom of the social pyramid still lived in ignorance and squalor, the bestiality of their existence little relieved by a priesthood so stupid, so slothful, and so corrupt that it enjoyed no moral authority and provided no moral leadership. At the top a bureaucratic army, faithful to the system and thoroughly corrupted by it, tried ever more desperately to suppress and to hold in subjection the sullen and restless masses. Yet Catherine's time had witnessed the emergence, between oppressors and oppressed, of a cultivated segment of society, tutored in the works of the Enlightenment, whose members felt a growing uneasiness over the chasm that divided the classes in Russia.

Only a relative few of this emergent segment had traveled in the West before the nineteenth century, and their knowledge of the West, and of how great was the gulf between life for West-erners and life for the "dark folk" in Russia, came from Western writings. During the Napoleonic Wars, however, many saw the West at first hand, and their seeing produced in them a sense of guilt, and then a sense of responsibility to relieve the squalor, the poverty, the brutishness, the corruption, and the backward-ness of Russian life. The idealistic young men who returned to Petersburg in 1815, to discuss with others of like mind what could be done, met with complete frustration in December, 1825.

The crushing of the Decembrist movement, however, only briefly stilled the voices of those who would raise the "accursed questions" of what could be done to correct matters and how it could be done. In the 1830s the voices were those of men too young to have joined with Pestel or Muravev. Some were just emerging from Russian universities or returning home from study in Germany. The government was not willing to let its subjects travel and study in France, breeding ground of revolu-tion and violence in 1789 and again in 1830. But German univer-sities, so Nicholas supposed, must be safely conservative for in this age of Metternich the governments of most German states sternly regulated students and professors.

The young Russians who studied at German universities came home infected with far more dangerous ideas than they would have acquired in France or anywhere else in the West at the time. The infection they had succumbed to was a new romanticism, a new idealism. They lent their enthusiasm to the anti-Enlightenment, for they like their German teachers at-tributed the political and social ills of the Europe of their time to the eighteenth-century skepticism and materialism that had ended in the excesses of the revolutionary age. They became followers of Schelling, Kant, Fichte, and Hegel, moving from one to another as their understanding deepened and matured. Hegel more than any other influenced the young men of the marveleous decade. He offered them a philosophy of history, and of a historical process applicable to the present and future, that led many of them ultimately to reflect upon the inevitability of a new and different sort of revolution.

Along with the teachings and writings of the new German

philosophers the Russian students returned home with a knowledge of and a fascination with the works of such French writers as Fourier, Saint-Simon, Proudhon, and Blanc. As they came home from the West they smuggled in forbidden books, or they later bought them from Russian booksellers who specialized in such gems. They discussed these newly discovered ideas interminably in the circles where the intelligentsia gathered in each others' homes in Moscow and St. Petersburg. Chaadayev's Moscow home was one such meeting place until he went mad by royal order.

The great disputation that raged among young Russians through the reign of Nicholas was that between Westernizers and Slavophiles. The Westernizers were perhaps less dedicated to the imposition of Western institutions upon Russia than of lifting Russia out of the quagmire of her Slavic past and ways of thought to a universal or European cultural level. In a sense they wanted the nation to escape from or avoid both kinds of parochialism—Westernism on the one hand and Slavicism on the other. For Russia to cling to her ancient Slavic-Byzantine darkness, and to resist the progress and modernization that becoming European would make possible, was to fly in the face of reason and to work against the nation's best interest. No detailed creed held them together, although Chaadayev had pointed the way. The Westernizers in general applauded Western science, constitutional government, freedom of expression, and the rule of law; they opposed bondage, autocracy, and the gulf that isolated the illiterate and oppressed masses from the educated and favored few.

One of the outstanding Westernizers was a historian, Timothy Granovsky, appointed professor of history at the University of Moscow at the age of twenty-six after years of study in Germany. His immensely popular lectures on the laws and liberties of the medieval West implicitly criticized Russian law and lack of liberty. But Granovsky was a moderate man, sympathetic to Western liberalism and opposed to political radicalism and socialism.

Another great Westernizer was Alexander Herzen, illegitimate son of a wealthy landowner. Herzen was only thirteen at the time of the Decembrist revolt, but he was old enough to hear and remember sympathetic reports of that noble enterprise. While attending the University of Moscow, he and a friend, standing on the Sparrow Hills looking down upon the city, took an oath to carry on the work of the Decembrists. As a student he joined a discussion circle that held sessions on the works of Saint-Simon and Fourier, but the political police disbanded the group and the university officials expelled Herzen. By the 1830s he was one of those who visited from circle to circle in Moscow, debating the ideas of Schelling and Kant and above all Hegel. In his own words these young Russians were united "by a profound feeling of alienation from official Russia." The secret police file on Herzen described him as "not dangerous but could be dangerous." He never became a Marxist, although he strongly favored non-Marxian socialism.

Herzen discovered America through Alexis de Tocqueville's *Democracy in America*, which he read and reread as a young man long before going into voluntary exile in Western Europe. He studied the works of James Fenimore Cooper, Washington Irving, and Harriet Beecher Stowe. He found relief from the depression that overwhelmed him after the failures of the 1848–1849 revolutions in long visits with Europeans who had crossed the Atlantic. He urged anyone who could rid himself of the fetters of European civilization and "be reborn" to board the first ship to America and "then to migrate to some place in Wisconsin or Kansas." He was not indifferent to American weaknesses; he abhorred slavery and was shocked at the lynchings. But he praised the American federal system, its development of local self-government, and the absence of a centralized bureaucracy.

It is noteworthy that whatever of social and political thought young Russians embraced, then and later in the century, was a Western importation. The nation contributed no original political or social idea to nineteenth-century thought, unless it be the nonviolence of Leo Tolstoy. Herzen later earned the title of father of Russian populism, but its conception came only years after he had left his native land to take up residence abroad. Early in the next reign he started in London a Russian language newspaper, *Kolokol (The Bell)* which worked first for emancipation and then openly for revolution.

A third Westernizer of tremendous influence was Vissarion Belinsky, the greatest of all Russian literary critics. Grandson of a priest and son of a poor physician, Belinsky earned his expulsion from the University of Moscow by writing an essay critical of serfdom. He spent his short life—he died in 1848 at the age of thirty-seven—earning a poor existence as an editor and critic. He sympathized with socialism of the French variety and leaned toward political radicalism.

Perhaps the most powerful expression of the position of the Westernizers appeared in Belinsky's immortal letter to Gogol, which attacked tsardom so fiercely that it was not allowed in print until 1905. Written in 1847, it circulated in manuscript and was committed to memory by young idealists all over Russia. Nicholas Gogol, the literary giant of the reign of Nicholas I, was the author of superbly sarcastic criticisms of serfdom and the bureaucracy in *Dead Souls* and *Inspector General.* For those masterpieces Belinsky had greatly admired Gogol. In 1847, however, Gogol wrote a collection of sermons, *Select Passages from Correspondence with Friends,* in which he praised the conservative regime of Nicholas, defending bondage, and approved the autocracy. Belinsky's long letter was a furious and brilliant indictment of his former friend's recantation for his earlier attacks upon the very conditions Gogol now condoned.

The famous letter denounced the corruption of officialdom, the moral poverty of the Orthodox Church in Russia as contrasted with the Catholic Church in the West, the impossibility of finding justice in the nation's courts and the practice of flogging innocent and guilty alike, the utter lack of human dignity, and the legality of traffic in men "without even having the excuse so insidiously exploited by the American plantation owners who claim the Negro is not a man." Belinsky mercilessly attacked Gogol's religious convictions, his integrity as a writer, and his very decency as a person, and crowned it all with the insulting charge that Gogol had written the contemptible piece in order to win royal favor and a court appointment of some kind. The police moved to arrest Belinsky, but he cheated them by dying before they could carry out their orders.

Not all members of the intelligentsia were leftists. There were distinguished conservatives among them, although they were perhaps neither as numerous nor ultimately as influential as the liberals. There were some on each side of the political and philosophical spectrum; there was no one in the middle. The government was suspicious of both Slavophiles and Westernizers, at least during the reign of Nicholas, although Slavophiles had some success in the latter half of the century in winning official support. In the 1830s and 1840s, however, both were critical of government policy, although they did not want the same things. And at the beginning the two groups disagreed amicably in the same circles, invited into the same homes perhaps to enliven the debate. In later years the friendships cooled and the debate became vitriolic.

The leading Slavophiles were the brothers Ivan and Constantine Aksakov, the brothers Ivan and Peter Kireyevsky, and Alexis Khomiakov. They all agreed that Peter the Great had done the nation a disservice in turning it firmly toward the West. They all hated the thought of constitutional government, although the Aksakovs favored a consultative national assembly with no power to legislate. Democratic or representative institutions, however, they regarded as foreign to Russian experience or preference and therefore subversive. They looked upon the nation's development, at least down to the eighteenth century, as harmonious and serene, and argued that importation of Western ideas and institutions had brought only social unrest. They regarded the West as decadent and insisted that Christianity was to be found only in Orthodoxy. So strongly did most Slavophiles believe in the pristine nature of Eastern Christianity that they looked upon the Poles, Czechs, Croats, and others who had embraced Catholicism as guilty of apostasy. Khomiakov, however, hoped for a universal spiritual Christian brotherhood that would include the Lutheran and Catholic friends he visited on his western travels.

There were some things about the government of Nicholas

I that the Slavophiles did not approve, and the tsar was impatient and resentful of their disapproval. They did not condone the domination of the church by the state. They resented the bureaucracy and the Prussian militarism that so pleased the tsar. And many of them worked as conscientiously as any Westernizer for the emancipation of the serfs. Later in the nineteenth century, however, the Slavophiles' opposition to the autocracy almost completely disappeared. The fact that many of the highest officials of the state, as well as members of the royal family, were Slavophiles gave Slavophilism the name of being uncompromisingly reactionary.

The Policeman of Europe

Nicholas hated revolutionaries but for all the wrong reasons. He resented any disturbance of the calm and the order he so much admired. He subjected his own life and that of his household to a Procrustean discipline, and he expected all people everywhere to submit to regimentation without demur. He regarded any defiance of established order as a personal challenge that he must personally meet. His reign was a time of dedication to the prevention or suppression of revolution at home and abroad.

Soon after his accession Nicholas undertook to settle outstanding issues with Turkey in a way far less subtle than had been Alexander's wont. Although the new emperor had little patience with the Greeks who were striving for their independence, he did not want their revolt to get out of hand. Yet in taking necessary action he chose to work in the context of the alliance born at the Vienna Congress. So Russia, France, and Great Britain agreed to cooperate in pressing the sultan for a recognition of Greek autonomy. For the moment Russia was working closely with the West to parry a threat to peace. When the sultan spurned the pressure, a combined fleet of the three allies destroyed the Turkish fleet at Navarino Bay in 1827. That ended British and French participation in the disciplining of the Turkish government. During the following spring and summer

Russian armies attacked Turkey across the Caucasus into Asia and down through the Balkans to Adrianople and the vicinity of Constantinople. A Russian fleet sailed to the Bosporus and the sultan sued for peace.

The Treaty of Adrianople in 1829 granted Greece her independence, recognized the autonomy of Serbia and of the Danubian Principalities of Moldavia and Wallachia, guaranteed free access to the Black Sea through the Dardanelles for the shipping of all nations, and contained a promise by the sultan to abide by his earlier treaties with Russia, which the Turkish government was forever breaking.

Because Russia had fought the war with Turkey alone, only Nicholas and the sultan were parties to the Treaty of Adrianople. The emperor was either naïve or presumptuous in ignoring the stake of the West in settling affairs in the Near East. The other powers were not happy with the peace treaty, which the tsar had dictated, but the implicit settlement, which the others could only guess at, constituted a tremendous diplomatic triumph for Russia. Since the emperor had settled matters inside the Turkish Empire pretty much to his own liking, and without having to share the disposition with any other European state, he became momentarily the arbiter of Turkish affairs.

The powers of Europe had given some thought to the partition of Turkey, and Napoleon and Alexander had discussed it at Tilsit. Nicholas preferred that there be no partition, even though it might give him Constantinople, a goal of his grandmother's ambition. To defend an outpost so far away from the center of Russian power would be costly and difficult. "The advantages of the maintenance of the Ottoman Empire are superior to the inconveniences which it presents," he insisted. "Its fall, therefore, would be contrary to the true interests of Russia." After the Treaty of Adrianople, consequently, the tsar undertook to defend the integrity of Turkey.

Great Britain and France were not anxious to see Russia dominate the Ottoman Empire. Even during the war, when a Russian army advanced to within sight of Constantinople and a Russian flotilla had sailed out of the Black Sea into the Bosporus, Great Britain and France moved naval forces to the Dardanelles, a tacit warning to the tsar that the Straits were an area of international concern.

Two years after the Peace of Adrianople the sultan called upon Nicholas to rescue him from a threatened attack by one of his own vassals, Mehemet Ali, governor of Egypt. The fact that the Egyptian governor had strong French backing put Russia and France on opposite sides of the approaching explosion in the Near East. The tsar warned Mehemet Ali off, and the Egyptian crisis subsided. But in 1833, Russia and Turkey agreed in the Treaty of Unkiar-Skelessi to join in common defense if either should come under attack. Turkey might meet her commitment, however, not with troops or ships but simply by closing the Dardanelles to hostile warships. Russia would defend the Ottoman Empire against any attack.

The Treaty of Unkiar-Skelessi, however defensive it might appear, was a challenge to British and French influence in the Near East. The French government of Louis Philippe encouraged Mehemet Ali in his defiance of the sultan. Napoleon earlier had campaigned in Egypt, although French policy had supported Ottoman rulers since the sixteenth century. Britain's interest in the area was less manifest, and her policy tended to shift as the tide of great-power domination of Turkey shifted. For the most part Britain seemed to favor either a Turkey strong enough to maintain herself or a weak one under British guarantee. But the treaty of 1833 could not have been aimed more deliberately at France and Great Britain if its terms had spelled it all out. No one else had the power to put a fleet through the Straits to endanger Russia.

Mehemet Ali was up again in 1839 threatening, with French encouragement, to attack Constantinople. Still convinced that Turkish survival was in Russia's best interest, Nicholas arranged a multipower guarantee of Turkish integrity, and the Pacification of the Levant in 1840 pledged Russia, Prussia, Austria, and Great Britain to defend the sultan against his ambitious vassal Mehemet Ali. A year later France joined the others in the Straits Convention which pledged the signatories to re-

spect Turkish closure of the Straits to all warships except when
Turkey herself was at war. All this maneuvering brought Nicholas little reward in 1854 when the Western powers joined the
sultan against him in the Crimean War.

It was less the danger of great-power pressure in the Near
East than the frequent recurrence of revolutionary violence in
the West that Nicholas found most threatening. In July 1830
the Paris mob turned out the reactionary Charles X and en-
throned his cousin, Louis Philippe, a man who cultivated an
image as a "Citizen King." The revolutionary infection spread
quickly to Brussels, where the Belgians declared their independence from Holland. There were uprisings in Italy, but Austrian
troops managed to quell them. The rumble of revolution rolled
over Germany, and several princes granted their people constitutions in frantic efforts to keep their thrones.

The tsar considered marching Russian troops into Western
Europe to restore his friend Charles X and to put the Dutch
back in control of Belgium. But he could not persuade his
Eastern allies, the rulers of Austria and Prussia, to join him
in taking the initiative against the revolutionary tide. The three
sovereigns only took the mild step of announcing their adher-
ence to the principles of the Holy Alliance and invited any ruler
to ask their assistance in putting down any popular challenge
to his authority. As the ruler of the strongest land power in
Europe, and as the one who repeatedly urged the reactionary
governments of the East to threaten counterrevolutionary action,
it was Nicholas who was the scourge of liberalism everywhere,
and not Metternich who received the credit.

In 1830 the tsar did not need to look far to the West for
a source of provocation. The Poles seized Warsaw only a few
months after the Paris outbreak called revolutionaries everywhere to arms. Nicholas had put off his coronation as king of
Poland until June 1830, and the fact that the uprising followed
so soon upon his official appearance in the capital was hardly
flattering. While a conspiracy to declare Polish independence
had been gathering support among Polish army officers for a
year before the coronation, Warsaw remained calm until news

came of the revolutions in Paris and Brussels. The Poles had always looked to the West and had always regarded themselves as Westerners; their defiance of a Russian ruler proclaimed it anew.

When a number of workers, students, and junior officers broke into the royal palace in Warsaw in November 1830, they were hoping to seize the tsar's brother Constantine who had served for years as viceroy. But Constantine fled to the suburbs, vainly urging Nicholas to be patient of his impetuous subjects. The Polish Diet, which had repeatedly defied the orders of the tsar and the viceroy, now proclaimed the nation independent, created a provisional government, ordered the army into action, and called upon the Lithuanians to join in a revival of pre-Partition Poland-Lithuania.

Nicholas took up the challenge with the greatest vigor and relish. While leaders in the Diet called for a free and independent Poland, they made a strong appeal for Western support when they proudly claimed to be fighting the cause of freedom for all Europe. To the cries of "down with Nicholas" they formally deposed him as their king. They failed to quicken the interest of the peasants, however, for the new national government would not seriously consider a land settlement that would have given the rural masses some sense of stake in the revolution.

Through the spring and summer of 1831, Polish forces fought, occasionally with some success, pitched battles against the Russian troops that invaded the country. At the head of 100,000 men Marshal Ivan Paskevich, the tsar's favorite general, moved grimly across the land into Warsaw, and Polish resistance collapsed. Nicholas replaced the liberal constitution of 1815 with an "Organic Statute" that ended the existence of the Kingdom of Poland. It abolished the Polish army, which Alexander I had generously created, and swept away the Diet where defiance had found a platform.

The Poles had stirred the sympathy of Britons and Frenchmen, but there was never any possibility of intervention. The French were digesting their own recent revolution, and the British government had more at stake in Brussels than in Warsaw. The Poles might claim some credit for the success of the French and Belgian revolutions, for they had focused the attention of the tsar upon matters on his own doorstep.

The emperor took stern measures against his Polish subjects. He uprooted many Polish families and moved them elsewhere in the empire. He closed down the universities of Warsaw and Vilna. The restrictions upon foreign travel were extended from Russia to include Poland. This measure availed little, however. Over 5,000 Poles emigrated, most of them moving to France. Prince Adam Czartorysky, who had served as a member of Alexander's Unofficial Committee but who had supported the Polish revolution, settled down in Paris. His home provided hospitality to his fellow exiles who never gave up hope of Western intervention to revive Poland as an independent outpost of Western civilization.

Paris again became the stage for the opening scene of revolution in February 1848 when the so-called July monarchy gave way to a republic. Nicholas shed no tears over the misfortune of Louis Philippe, whom the tsar had never forgiven for accepting the French crown from revolutionaries back in 1830. However, neither was revolution ever forgivable to him, no matter how personally pleasing its consequences might seem.

With ominous implications the revolutionary fever again spread quickly over Europe. Three weeks after the barricades went up in the streets of Paris there were revolutions in Milan and Venice, and soon the entire Italian peninsula was in flames. A revolution in Rome upset the pope's temporal authority until a French army some time later restored it. Revolution broke out in Vienna, and Metternich, who had dominated the Austrian government for forty years, had to leave the capital in disguise to avoid bodily harm. Demonstrations in Prague demanded home rule for Bohemia. Hungary severed all ties with Austria except the personal one of her ruler, and that would later end. The mob in Berlin demanded a constitution, and Frederick William IV promised to grant one. A pre-Parliament of German liberals gathered at Frankfurt to seek a united democratic Germany, and among other defiant measures passed a resolution of support for an independent Poland. Prussian Poles and Austrian Poles were restless. Revolution broke out in the Romanian province of Wallachia. Germans in Schleswig and Holstein rebelled against their ruler, the king of Denmark. Englishmen marched in thousands through the streets of London demanding Parliamentary reform.

Word of all this defiance of authority infuriated the tsar. The forces of liberalism and nationalism—the two were inextricably interwoven in 1848, and liberalism meant not only constitutional government but proletarian gain and even socialism—threatened the established order and everything Nicholas stood for. It was not only that he found such "rebellion and lawlessness" distasteful and reprehensible in others; liberal and radical circles in his own country made it downright indecent by applauding every revolutionary triumph.

Nicholas severed diplomatic relations with France and assembled 400,000 troops along the Polish border ready to march into France to sweep away the revolutionary republic. But the revolution in Vienna and the violence in Berlin made Nicholas give up all thought of saving the French. He could only threaten revolutionaries everywhere by a pontifical warning. Calling upon his own subjects to defend "our Holy Russia" against the lawlessness of the times, and appealing for a rededication to "faith, tsar, and homeland," the emperor closed the manifesto with a sweeping pronouncement: "God is with us! Take heed, ye peoples, and submit, for God is with us!"

When his brother-in-law Frederick William IV sent a Prussian army into Denmark to rescue the German-speaking Schleswigers and Holsteiners, the tsar warned him that unless the Prussians withdrew immediately Russia must regard it as an act of war. As close personally as Nicholas was to the Prussian royal family, he could have shown in no more forceful way his inflexible opposition to any disturbance of the established order.

The emperor's greatest concern was the possibility of a revival of revolutionary fervor in Poland. If the restlessness that soon emerged among the Austrian and Prussian Poles in response to the revolutionary outbreaks in Vienna and Berlin were to spread to Warsaw and Russian Poland, the tsar would face further embarrassment. He did not question the ability of his troops to stamp out any Polish conflagration, but this would produce reaction in Western Europe. French and German intellectuals supported the Poles in their laudable ambition to be free of Muscovite repression. There was talk in Berlin of German-Polish friendship, and even of unofficial German support for a Polish war of liberation from Russian rule.

The tsar's fear of a rising in his own Polish and Lithuanian provinces was so strong that he put a Russian army into Moldavia to warn Romanian revolutionaries against challenging their prince, who was a vassal of the Turkish sultan. Nicholas even advised the sultan to send troops of his own into Romania when the Ottoman government hesitated to risk European displeasure.

Aside from his personal resentment at any defiance of authority, Nicholas reacted most sternly to the revolutions in the Austrian Empire because of possible repercussions among his Polish subjects. He watched through the autumn of 1848 and through the following spring as the Hungarian rebels successfully fought off Austrian efforts to quell the uprising. He heard in dismay the news that in April 1849 a national assembly of Magyars formally deposed their Hapsburg ruler and named the revolutionary leader Louis Kossuth to head an independent Hungary. A free and hostile Magyar state would be a constant threat to the tranquillity of Poland, for it would offer sanctuary to Polish firebrands. This had been precisely how the independent republic of Krakow, created at the Congress of Vienna, had served the Poles until Russian troops had destroyed it in 1846.

Nicholas resented the fact that many Poles had enlisted in the Hungarian freedom army. This proved, at least to his satisfaction, that there was an international revolutionary conspiracy behind the uprisings that were shaking the continent from Paris to Bucharest. The tsar believed that the center of this conspiracy lay in Hungary, a land bordering his own Polish provinces. He even convinced himself that "at the head of the rebellion, and acting as the main instrument of it, are our eternal enemies, the Poles."

When Francis Joseph, the young emperor of Austria,

found himself unable to put down the Hungarian revolt with his own forces, he called upon the tsar for assistance. Paskevich, victor over the Poles in 1831, invaded Hungary with 170,000 men and nearly 600 pieces of artillery to join an Austrian force of about the same size. The Magyars fought fiercely but succumbed to overwhelming numbers, and Kossuth finally resigned and escaped to the United States. Nicholas took no reprisals against even the Polish elements in the Hungarian army that had faced his troops. In fact, he expressed disgust at the savage punishments meted out by the Austrian government.

By his intervention in Hungary, Nicholas earned immortality as a counterrevolutionary, as the defender of the established order, and as the unrelenting foe of nationalism. He probably deserves much of the credit for the fact that, in Central and Eastern Europe at least, the revolutions ended in tragedy. Indeed, his own generation recognized him as the chief bulwark against the tide of liberalism, nationalism, and revolution. Liberals everywhere hated him; their animosity toward him was perhaps the only thing upon which they could agree. Conservatives everywhere were grateful for his steadfastness, particularly after Metternich's departure for England removed that longtime defender of the status quo.

Although the revolutions of 1848–1849 may have seemed a failure throughout much of Europe, and although Nicholas may have found reason to congratulate himself for the contribution he had made to that failure, the revolution in France began a chain of circumstances that led ultimately to Russian defeat and humiliation in the Crimean War. That defeat, in turn, made clear to the tsar—not to Nicholas but to his son—that the system of autocracy and bondage that Nicholas had personified and perfected made Russia weak, not strong, against the West.

When the French republic born of the 1848 revolution elected its president, the man it chose was Louis Napoleon Bonaparte, nephew of the emperor Napoleon. Four years later, in defiance of the tsar's warning that he was violating the terms of the 1815 settlement, the colorless little man scrapped the constitution under which he had won election and proclaimed himself Emperor Napoleon III. Nicholas immediately insulted him by refusing to call him "brother."

In an effort to emulate the heroic deeds of his great uncle, the new French emperor demanded that the Turkish sultan restore to French Catholic priests their historic right to maintain the Christian holy places in Palestine. Frenchmen had shown no interest in their treasured rights for generations, and the maintenance of the holy places had been left to Greek Orthodox clergymen. When the sultan gave in to French pressure, the tsar warned him that there must be no change in policy, insisting that Orthodox right of maintenance had been granted in Catherine's time by treaty and had long been exercised. Napoleon threatened naval attack upon the Ottoman Empire unless his demands were met, and Nicholas threatened to invade the sultan's vassal states of Moldavia and Wallachia if there were any change. The French won their point, and Russian troops crossed the border into Moldavia. The sultan, with British and French support, declared war upon Russia. The ensuing conflict, the Crimean War, lasted from midsummer 1853 until the year after Nicholas's death in 1855.

The Crimean War was not the result of "a churchwardens' quarrel" over who should have custody of the key to the Church of the Nativity in Jerusalem. What determined the Western powers to support the sultan, whose conduct was always capricious and whose solemn word was wholly unreliable, was the tsar's invasion of Moldavia—a province of the Ottoman Empire—and the fear it confirmed that Nicholas would interfere in Turkish domestic affairs whenever he could not otherwise have his way.

The tsar had so naïvely revealed to the British ambassador his ambitions in Eastern Europe that statesmen in London may be forgiven for having been suspicious about every Russian move in the Near and Middle East. In a series of conversations with Sir Hamilton Seymour early in 1853, Nicholas repeated a familiar refrain of his that Turkey, "the sick man of Europe," was at the point of death. He bluntly suggested that Great Britain and Russia should agree on the future disposition of certain territory: Bulgaria, Wallachia, Moldavia, and Serbia would be independent but under Russian protection; Great Britain might have Egypt and Crete; Austria would receive the eastern coast of the Adriatic and the offshore islands. England must not have Constantinople. Nicholas protested that Russia did not want it, but that it might be necessary for a time to occupy the city with Russian troops. Seymour reported the talks to London, with the observation that they indicated to him the tsar's ambition to force Turkey into a position of vassalage to Russia. The London government answered that plans to dispose of the dying Turkish Empire were premature, and added that France should also have a voice in the disposition when the time came. On the morrow of the outbreak of the Crimean War, the British government published the Seymour communications on the tsar's suggestions as evidence of "the dark ambitions of a foreign despot."

That London's fears were not entirely groundless is apparent from the demand Nicholas made of the sultan in the spring of 1853 that all Orthodox residents in the Ottoman Empire—they numbered 12,000,000—be guaranteed religious freedom. Implicitly the tsar was asking recognition of his right to protect that religious freedom and to interfere in Turkish affairs if necessary to do so. The sultan regarded the demand as an infringement upon his sovereignty, and the Western powers supported that view.

Turkey declared war upon Russia in October 1853 when Nicholas refused to pull his army out of Moldavia. The tsar countered with the solemn avowal that he had had to take up arms to defend "the sacred rights of the Orthodox Church." If the religious quarrel over the holy places had been the only point at issue, there probably would have been no European war, even taking into consideration the French emperor's play for attention.

The Crimean War was the result of Western refusal to accept Russian domination of the Ottoman Empire. The threat that the tsar in effect would make the sultan his vassal was a threat to overturn the balance of power, not only in the eastern Mediterranean but over all of Europe.

The war found Nicholas standing alone against a coalition of Turkey, Great Britain, France, and Sardinia. Sweden threatened to attack but did not do so. Austria stayed out of the war but kept up pressure upon the tsar to give in to Western demands and even threatened to enter the war unless Nicholas accepted allied terms. This ingratitude for his rescue of the Hapsburg dynasty in 1849 disgusted the emperor. Even Prussia, whose king the tsar had roughly handled on occasion but whose support Nicholas was certain he could count on, was at best neutral in the involved diplomatic wranglings that went on throughout the course of the war.

Allied naval forces attacked Russian defenses in the White Sea, the Black Sea, the Baltic, and the Pacific. Allied armies landed in the Crimea for a protracted campaign against the great naval base at Sevastopol, which for a year resisted the "Charge of the Light Brigade" and other stupid military ventures. The Russians captured the Turkish fortress of Kars south of the Caucasus. But Russian leadership proved even less effective than British and French, and after the fall of Sevastopol the tsar was ready for peace.

The Treaty of Paris of 1856 provided for mutual restoration of the Crimean bases the Allies had taken and the Turkish forts the Russians had captured. All the signatories agreed to protect all Christians in the Ottoman Empire, promised to respect Turkish integrity, and accepted responsibility to guarantee the autonomy of Serbia and the Danubian Principalities. Russia's position as sole guarantor of Orthodox Christians and of Serbian and Romanian autonomy thus came to an end. The crowning humiliation was the provision that Russia might no longer maintain naval installations or a war fleet on the Black Sea. The same limitation applied to Turkey, but it obviously was aimed at Russia. Within fifteen years, however, Russia had thrown off the limitation and had returned to the Black Sea as a naval power. British officials in 1856 had expected that such would be the eventuality.

Russia stood foremost among the continental powers from 1815 to 1856. As late as 1853, Russia maintained that position, for in the years after the revolutionary fiascos of 1848–1849 the tsar enjoyed the respect—whether in the form of admiration by the conservative or hatred by the liberal—of all Europe. The Crimean War destroyed all that. The humiliating military defeat—the emperor had mobilized over a million men, but the poverty of equipment, supplies, and leadership gave the victory to an enemy a small fraction as large—and the mortification of the peace terms put an end to Russian prestige for a generation to come.

The nation regained some of its self-respect during the Franco-German War of 1870 when it scrapped the Treaty of Paris limitations upon its naval presence on the Black Sea. Militarily and politically the nation recovered its pride when it defeated Turkey decisively in a war in 1877. But after the Crimean War, France and even Austria-Hungary, and after 1871 imperial Germany, were Russia's equals on the continent. Never again in tsarist times would the nation recover the position of primacy among continental powers that it had held in 1815.

The consequences of the Crimean War to Russia were salutary in a quite unexpected way. The war proved, as perhaps nothing else could have done so dramatically, the utter failure of Nicholas's "system" of preventing unrest and revolution by fostering reaction at home and abroad. The contemptible performance of Russian armies, the restlessness of the masses during the war and their obvious unwillingness to wait longer for emancipation, and the indifference of the nation to the outcome of the war, were so dissillusioning to Nicholas that he seemed almost to prefer death over having to face the consequences of the imminent defeat. Indeed, the rumor soon spread that the emperor had taken poison.

CHAPTER FIVE

Reforms,
Protests,
and Revolutions

PRESSURE to end bondage had been mounting for nearly a century. Sometimes that pressure came from a lonely writer or journalist, from a Novikov or a Radishchev. In Pugachev's time it had come from the surly masses, and the execution of the popular hero had reduced the pressure only momentarily. Toward the close of the eighteenth century and through the early years of the nineteenth, exposure of thousands of serfs to Western civilization increased the potential for unrest. Serfs had filled the ranks of the huge Russian armies that had fought in the West in the wars of the French Revolution, and those wars had subjected the serf-soldier to long periods of contact with the free peasant-soldier or citizen-soldier of Western armies. The Russian soldier had returned to his native land and to the bondage that still held him in thrall. To expect him to submit passively was unrealistic. The rural unrest that marked the last decade of the reign of Alexander I and that mounted in severity throughout the next reign should have surprised no one.

Emancipation

Less than a fortnight after the end of the Crimean War, Alexander II called upon the gentry to suggest terms of emancipation, warning his listeners that unless the abolition of serfdom came from above it might come from below. Western pressure had done much to force an end to bondage upon a slow-moving administration. Both the victory over Napoleon's European empire in 1814 and the defeat at the hands of a Western coalition in 1856 had contributed substantially to the pressures that made emancipation ineluctable. By 1860 no one in Russia any longer approved of bondage, and from an economic point of view it had become increasingly anachronistic. Politically and morally it was indefensible. Liberals and conservatives, Westernizers and Slavophiles alike, called for an end to serfdom.

After four years of deliberation a committee of bureaucrats and gentry serfowners put together the terms by which the emperor would carry out the emancipation. By the Law of February 19 bondage came to an end in 1861 for all 20,000,000 privately owned serfs. The peasant was no longer a chattel to be sold or given or gambled away, or flogged or exiled to Siberia or "sent for a soldier" at his master's whim. Now he was free to marry when and whom he pleased, to purchase and dispose of real and personal property, and to appear even as principal in a court of law.

As the last nation in Europe to strike off the shackles of her bondsmen, Russia now in a very real sense became a part of Western civilization. When two years later slavery ended in the United States, bondage distinguished only non-Western cultures—those in Africa, in parts of Asia, and in the Arab world.

The government faced the real problem of freeing slaves, the overwhelming majority of whom were illiterate, who had never traveled outside the village of their birth, and who knew no skill except tilling the soil. It met the problem by ordering conditions under which the emancipated peasants might work out with the state owner an agreement to purchase a portion—on the average a little less than half—of the arable land on the estate. Once villagers and landowner agreed upon a price and upon the amount of land to change hands, the peasants undertook to pay a fifth of the purchase figure and the government paid the nobleman the remainder in government bonds. The peasants were then to pay into the imperial treasury over a period of forty-nine years the sum the crown had advanced to the landowner plus interest. These annual payments, the so-called redemption dues or redemption payments, were excessively high because the price settled between peasants and landlord represented either a highly inflated value for the land or a figure that covered both land value and labor service formerly rendered by the serf.

The land the peasants received must be sufficient to provide each male with from three to thirty acres, the amount varying from district to district according to ancient local custom or fertility of the soil. No individual peasant, however, received anything. The land went to the village whose corporate responsibility it would be to collect each man's share of the annual redemption payment and forward the sum to the proper official. Some villages allowed their members to occupy their "allotments" permanently, although title could not pass to the individual until the government had received the last of the redemption dues. Other villages assigned to each head of family a number of strips of land in the village fields, reassigning the strips from time to time and varying the amount to meet changing needs as family size rose or shrank. Here, too, when the village had made the last redemption payment, there could be a permanent division of the land among the peasants, each to receive his portion in fee simple.

The terms of the emancipation were so disappointing that they remained the fundamental cause of rural unrest well into the twentieth century. The peasants resented the amount of land left to the gentry. In times of violence they would break down fences to sickle grain in the broad fields of the neighboring landowner, or let their animals graze in his pasture. When revolution ended the old regime, the peasants moved quickly to divide among themselves that portion of each estate they had not received under the Law of February 19.

The redemption dues were so high that frequently they could not be met and became deliquent. Then the government would announce a new schedule of payments stretching still longer into the future. The last rescheduling of payments due the government was announced in 1896. It provided that the peasants finally would work off the obligation some time after 1950.

The peasants were not alone in resenting the terms of the emancipation. From 1861 to 1917 revolutionaries and reformers, individuals and organizations alike, called both for an end to the redemption dues and a breaking up and distribution of gentry estates. Land reform was the nation's most persistent need, and the stubborn refusal of the government to provide it was surely one of the most important factors contributing to the ultimate overthrow of the monarchy.

Nearly a million peasants belonging to members of the royal family obtained their freedom in 1863 and received more generous allotments at a lower cost than did the private landowners' former serfs. In 1866 the 13,000,000 state peasants— those living on lands belonging to the state, as distinct from the imperial family—were freed with a choice of remaining tenants on state land for a modest rent or of purchasing their land on terms similar to those applicable to former serfs.

The Other Great Reforms

The emancipation touched off a succession of political and social changes that together made up what came to be called the Great Reforms. Indeed, the greatest of all the Great Reforms, the emancipation itself, forced some changes by freeing millions of serfs from the authority of the gentry who had owned them. The Law of February 19 shifted to the corporate village and its elected elder the police and administrative responsibilities the serfowner had formerly exercised. The Emancipation Act further combined several adjoining villages into a township, where heads of peasant families met in assembly to elect a township elder, an executive committee, and a court to handle civil and minor criminal offenses of local concern. In the face of massive peasant indifference, village and township government became the burden of the elders, who in turn were responsible to national authorities in matters affecting police, taxation, and military recruitment.

In 1864 the emperor signed the Zemstvo Law that established in each county and province a zemstvo or institution of local self-government. Three elements voting separately in each county chose delegates to an assembly: individual landowners of whatever class or "estate," townsmen meeting a property or business-turnover qualification, and villages. The right to vote in rural areas rested upon land ownership: each 3,000 peasant allotments and any individual or group of individuals owning an equal amount of land sent a delegate to the county assembly. Each assembly, meeting annually, chose its executive board, levied taxes to meet local needs, encouraged industry and agriculture, and dealt with the maintenance of bridges and roads, prisons and asylums, hospitals and schools, and poor relief. Each county assembly chose from among its members delegates to the provincial assembly whose concern it was to deal on the provincial level with the same sort of problems handled by the county zemstvo on the county level.

The Zemstvo Law of 1864 simply put into operation in county and province the plan proposed by Speransky back in 1809. There was no national Duma as Speransky had urged, however, and there would be none until 1905. The halfway nature of the reform created widespread disappointment and provided liberals with another point of complaint against the regime. Even Lenin noted that, denied the Western means of correcting abuse through a national forum and legislative machinery, Russians had no alternative to revolution.

Earlier attempts by Peter the Great and Catherine II to establish machinery of municipal government had accomplished little. After a review of German and Austrian practice Alexander II in 1870 created a pattern of city government in which citizens, arranged in three groups of small, medium, and large taxpayers, elected delegates to a city council or duma. The duma chose a mayor and administrative board, levied taxes to meet municipal needs, and dealt with such problems as street paving and lighting, public health, education, poor relief, and local crime.

The most Western of all the Great Reforms was the Judiciary Act of 1864. The committee charged with making a proposal to the emperor made a deliberate study of the British and French judicial systems but based its recommendations chiefly upon French practice. The Act created district courts, each presided over by a judge appointed by the Ministry of Justice from a list nominated by the judiciary itself. All criminal and some civil cases handled in district court were subject to jury trial. Jury service was limited to property owners; this qualification was modest in the early years and so high in later years as to exclude all but the moderately wealthy. There was an appeal from the district court to a provincial court and a final appeal to the Senate, whose members appointed by the tsar served as a supreme court.

The new judicial system went into operation slowly, appearing first in Moscow and Petersburg and not reaching Kiev until 1881. Jury trials never extended to Poland or the Caucasus. Many types of cases did not come within the purview of the district and provincial courts. Cases involving only peasants in noncapital crimes were handled in township courts; in effect, the new court system ignored the rural masses. Church courts handled divorce cases; courts-martial dealt with the soldiery and even with the citizenry in areas subject to martial law, which was frequently applied in peace time; crimes against the state came under the jurisdiction of administrative courts; police courts dealt with infractions of the peace; violations of censorship codes were dealt with administratively; and an ever lengthening list of offenses was removed by administrative fiat from the jurisdiction of the district court system.

In spite of the deliberate efforts of the government to hamstring the new system of justice, the reform of the judiciary had a salutary effect upon Russian society. The law assured judges of tenure except for malfeasance. Trials were open to the public, and in the fetid atmosphere of later years there was freedom of speech only in the courtroom. The law forbade cruel punishments, except for flogging that was a frequent sentence for common soldiers and peasants.

Not the least of the beneficent consequences of the Judiciary Act was the mature growth of the legal profession. The judges in the new court system did their best to maintain the dignity and independence of the judiciary and particularly to protect the right of the accused to counsel. In fact, many a revolutionary won a public platform in court where he could have found it nowhere else, and the public admitted to his trial often cheered him on in his defiance of the police and the prosecution. Lawyers became leaders in the zemstvo assemblies and stood out later in the national Duma as men who dared call the administration to account for its mismanagement and intolerance. When political parties appeared early in the twentieth century, men trained in the law distinguished themselves from one end to the other of the broad spectrum of political thought and action.

The spirit of reform manifested itself momentarily in the field of education. Women gained admission to Moscow University in 1872 and to the other universities soon after. By1881, 2,000 women were attending Russian universities. Within months of his accession Alexander II relaxed some of the restrictions on institutions of higher learning. There was an end to limitations on enrollment, and some of the curbs of the previous reign slowly fell away. The Ministry of Education permitted lectures on European governments and philosophy; teaching in both these areas had suffered proscription during the censorship blight under Nicholas. The relaxation made possible the use of university quarters for discussion of the terms of emancipation in the months before the promulgation of the Law of February 19. But the refusal of the government to allow student organizations, and the opposition of liberal student opinion to the unsatisfactory terms of the emancipation, led quickly after 1861 to protests at the universities and to open confrontation with the police.

While the Ministry of Education wavered between mildness

and severity in its dealings with university students, some sub-ordinate officials in the Ministry approached in a surprisingly liberal way the problems posed for education by the emancipation of the serfs. Nicholas Pirogov led a group of young Russians into Western Europe to prepare them for university teaching and returned impatient to overturn the class nature of Russian education. Constantine Ushinsky, the organizer of the modern primary school system in Russia, spent five years on official assignment studying European systems of education. His concern when he finished his travels was to make education available to all Russian children, to make citizens of former serfs, now that bondage had come to an end.

The shameful performance of the army in the Crimean War—over 2,000,000 men had been mustered, but only a small fraction had seen service—made reform of the military imperative. The disaster had resulted in part because of the breakdown of communication and the faulty transportation system that handicapped the service of supply. Hospital services were even worse than in the Western armies. Equipment was far out of date, and the troops fought with the same weapons they had carried against Napoleon. Russia, although on the defensive in the Crimea, suffered three times as many casualties as did the Allies.

Dmitry Miliutin, minister of war for twenty years under Alexander II, carried through a number of army reforms calculated to bring the Russian military machine abreast of the West. The enlistment period was reduced from the twenty-five-year enlistment that had been in force since the time of Peter the Great to six years, after which the discharged soldier must serve nine years in the reserves and then five in the militia. The aim of the practice, generally followed throughout the continent, was to reduce the cost of military preparedness by maintaining a small force backed by a seasoned and trained reserve available in wartime.

There were generous reductions of the enlistment period and exemptions. Breadwinners and only sons need not serve. All other males, regardless of social class, were subject to recruitment upon reaching the age of twenty. But the six-year enlistment term was cut to four years for graduates of elementary schools, to three years for secondary school graduates, and to six months for university graduates. Volunteers need serve only half as long; a university graduate, for example, served only three months. Illiterate recruits learned to read and write, an innovation that did much to augment the elementary education program.

There was an improvement of officer schools, and the admission of commoners was encouraged. The achievement of commissioned rank was no longer a monopoly of the gentry. In keeping with Western practice, the smaller division replaced the unmanageable corps as the standard unit of organization. Rifles replaced smoothbores. The army sought out improved artillery from such Western arms makers as the German Krupp, the British Armstrong, and the French Schneider. There was an improvement in medical and supply services. The technical and organizational changes followed German practice, for the war minister was much impressed by decisive Prussian victories over Denmark and Austria and the German triumph over France in 1870. The cruelest punishments—for example, running the gauntlet between files of men armed with birch rods or rifle butts—were discontinued. Men no longer looked upon military service as penal servitude, and courts stopped the demeaning practice of condemning convicts to the army.

The era of the Great Reforms witnessed a tremendous surge in business activity; some of it was inspired or even financed by the government. When Alexander II succeeded his father, Russia had only a few hundred miles of railway; at the end of the reign there were over 15,000 miles of track. Western firms did some of the building, but most of the railroad construction was the work of Russian companies financed by the treasury with funds borrowed from British, Dutch, and German investors. The effect of the railway expansion was to turn the nation into a single market and to stimulate the export trade, particularly in grain.

The phenomenal increase in the number of corporations and the size of their capital reflected an increased domestic and foreign demand for the output of Russian industry. A state bank and many private banks and lending agencies gathered idle capital and directed it into domestic investment. The post-emancipation boom in production, made possible by the expansion of the industrial labor force, brought great profits to management. Working conditions, hours, and wages improved very slowly, however, a situation that stirred sullen resentment among the workers whose organization into unions the government forbade.

Russia was moving slowly toward industrial capitalism during the first half of the nineteenth century. The emancipation tended to speed up the process. By midway in the last half of the century the nation had become a part of the capitalist system of the Western world. Her economy began to respond quickly to the business cycles in which the Western world was caught up. She prospered as the foreign demand for her goods, particularly her raw materials, held firm. Her industries and transportation facilities expanded when the Berlin Bourse or the London Stock Exchange bid strongly for her securities. And when her labor force was restless, or when revolution threatened, the market for her securities weakened, the foreign sources of capital dried up, and the entire economy suffered.

The conditions under which the emancipation came about contributed to a radical change in the economic status of the gentry. Roughly half the arable land of European Russia came under the ownership of peasant communes during the reign of Alexander II. The peasants, sometimes as individuals and frequently as village corporations, bought or leased much of the remainder of the land. Some of the gentry made careers of farming their land as a capitalist venture, concentrating upon a cash crop, usually wheat or flax, for export. A majority of the gentry, however, surrendered their position as landowners. They sold their estates and went into the professions—law, medicine, or teaching—or into the bureaucracy, or the military, or occasionally into business.

The Great Reforms were extremely costly to the imperial government. The advance of government bonds to the gentry in payment for the land purchased by the peasant villages created no great burden. Although the gross compensation due the landlords was about 600,000,000 rubles, the nobles over the previous forty years had borrowed over two thirds that amount from the government, and the treasury simply deducted the debts and paid out the difference. But railroad construction was needlessly expensive, the more so since the government did nothing to discourage speculation, overcapitalization, mismanagement, and faulty workmanship. A great number of primary and secondary school buildings went up, and that was costly. The army reforms imposed a sustained burden upon the treasury. The considerable increase in the size of the bureaucracy raised payroll requirements.

The new responsibilities that the Great Reforms settled upon the Russian government and the financial burden they imposed made the finance minister a key figure in the administration. The emperor sent Count Michael Reutern to Western Europe and the United States to study improved budget techniques, for Russian financial administration was a quagmire of mismanagement, confusion, and corruption. Reutern concentrated his study upon the Prussian and American systems, reformed budget procedures when he returned to Russia, and became minister of finance in 1862.

Reutern's first concern as finance minister was the creation of a single treasury, for theretofore a dozen administrative departments had gathered revenue and arranged their own expenditures. Centralization of income and disbursement in a single office, the application of Western audit techniques, and the publication of a single budget, were designed to promote public confidence, both Russian and foreign, and to facilitate government borrowing.

Other needs, if Russian and Western bankers were to subscribe with confidence to government loans, were the regularization of tax revenues, the stabilization of the currency, and the avoidance of costly wars. Reutern's successes in these areas were extremely modest. He halted the farming out of the tax on alcoholic beverages and levied a simple excise tax upon their sale. When he left office in 1878, a third of all revenue came from the liquor tax. Direct taxes yielded another third, and nearly half the income from direct taxes came from the poll or "soul" tax first levied by Peter the Great.

The budget was almost perennially out of balance, and the government customarily fell back upon the easy way of meeting the deficit by issuing paper rubles. The annual resort to the printing press drove the value of the paper ruble down steadily until it settled at about two thirds the value of silver in the last year of Alexander's reign. War costs made any approach to budget stability impossible. The Russo-Turkish War of 1877–1878 cost the treasury a billion rubles, and the likelihood that a war would undo whatever benefits his administration had brought about made Reutern vigorously protest the outbreak of hostilities. When the emperor ignored his advice, the count resigned. The financial havoc produced by the insatiable appetite of army planners is apparent from the fact that in 1881, a year of peace, the War Ministry received thirteen times the appropriation granted to the Ministry of Education.

Tensions with the West

The accession of Alexander II brought some relaxation of the harsh rule that Nicholas had imposed upon the Poles after their revolution in 1830. There was a general amnesty for those who had languished in prison or in Siberian exile and a pardon for those who had settled in Paris and London. The emperor allowed a medical college to open in Warsaw and granted permission for the founding of an agricultural society whose members might discuss land reform. He permitted the use of the Polish language in the schools and appointed a committee to arrange the reopening of the University of Warsaw. There was an emancipation of the Jews. Polish peasants received use of their land for a modest rent and no longer had to render a labor obligation to the landowner. The effect of easing the burden upon the peasants, of course, brought the tsar few friends among the Polish gentry.

Alexander's gloved-hand treatment of the Poles, or at least of the masses, won him little support. Members of the agricultural society resented the fact that the land reform favored the peasants. Students, most of them sons of landowners, marched in defiance of the Russian troops stationed in Warsaw. Polish army officers demanded a revival of an independent Poland. The Catholic Church supported anti-Russian sentiment. Ardent Polish nationalists attempted the assassination of the tsar's brother Constantine who was serving as viceroy in Warsaw. When the civil administration of Poland, appointed by Alexander II, threatened to execute would-be assassins and draft rebellious students into the Russian army, an uprising followed in January 1863.

Large and very active émigré groups in the West had kept alive the dream of a free Poland ever since Nicholas I had snuffed out the revolt of 1830. A conservative and aristocratic segment of the Polish freedom movement in exile maintained headquarters at the Paris residence of its leader, Prince Adam Czartorysky. This group, counting upon French and British intervention in support of the Poles, wanted a restoration of the 1791 constitution and a constitutional monarchy. The radical wing of the Polish exile movement was the Polish Democratic Society, which organized in France in 1832 but later moved to London. Its aim was an independent Polish republic. One of its leaders, General Ludwig Mieroslawski, fought with revolutionaries in Germany and Sicily in 1849. He founded a Polish military school in Italy in 1861 to train leaders for the coming war of liberation. Young Poles in Italy found inspiration in the successes of the Risorgimento. All Polish exiles expected support from Russian revolutionaries when the strike for freedom should take place. No such support was forthcoming, however.

Polish commoners and particularly the peasants for the most part remained indifferent to the 1863 uprising. The revolt was less a popular nationwide affair than an uprising of the gentry, who sensed in the gentler policies of Alexander II, particularly in the land settlement, a Machiavellian scheme to pit peasants against landowners. A huge Russian army scattered a small Polish force that had hastily gathered to proclaim and defend independence, but guerrilla forces fought on desperately in isolated instances for another year.

There were strong public expressions in England and France of support for the Polish rebels. The French emperor, Napoleon III, wrote a tactless letter to Alexander II asking him to grant the Poles autonomy. The British Foreign Office asked the Russian government to revive the Polish Kingdom of 1815— Congress Poland—and grant amnesty to the rebels. Great Britain, France, and Austria joined in a request that Alexander call a national assembly of Poles, free the Catholic Church from the persecution it had suffered at Russian hands, and restore use of the Polish language in schools and government offices.

St. Petersburg treated the Western pressure with thinly veiled contempt. Count Otto von Bismarck, ambassador to Russia before he became minister president of Prussia, staunchly supported Russian action in Poland and promised military support to the tsar against his Polish subjects if that should become necessary. In a formal convention Berlin granted Russia permission to send Russian troops into Prussian territory in pursuit of Polish rebels. The effect was to deflate the Western powers and leave them to no more serious action than the hurling of threats and insults. Diplomatic protests from London, Paris, and Vienna only raised vain hopes among the Poles and led them to fight on long after any prospect of victory had disappeared.

Russian foreign policy immediately after the Crimean War rested upon friendly relations with France, for Napoleon III had pressed Great Britain most vigorously to accept a peace treaty in 1856. St. Petersburg was most resentful of Austria's perfidy in repaying Russian support during the Hungarian revolt of 1849 with diplomatic hostility during the Crimean War. As the Christian peoples in the Balkan peninsula moved toward independence from Turkey, Austrian and Russian interests in the peninsula must sooner or later conflict.

France and Russia worked together in support of the union of Moldavia and Wallachia as the principality of Romania, although both Great Britain and Austria opposed the union lest it come under Russian domination. When a *coup d'état* in Belgrade replaced a pro-Austrian ruler with a pro-Russian one, the change won French as well as Russian approval. Outside the Balkans, France in 1859 joined Sardinia in a war against Austria to reduce Austrian influence in northern Italy and assist Italian unification in the process. Russia weakened the Austrian war effort by marching an army to the Austro-Russian frontier and threatening Vienna.

Franco-Russian cordiality ended abruptly with Napoleon III's ill-advised encouragement of Warsaw in the Polish insurrection of 1863. For nearly thirty years thereafter Prussia and later imperial Germany would replace France as Russia's most sympathetic friend and ally. Bismarck's support of Alexander II during the Polish crisis and his constant expression of sympathy for the tsar's impatience to abrogate the exclusion of Russian warships from the Black Sea—the prohibition had been part of the Peace of Paris that in 1856 ended the Crimean War—proved to be wise investments.

In all the wars that Bismarck managed to provoke in Prussia's march to unify Germany, the Russian Foreign Office was either benevolently neutral or actively sympathetic. When, in 1864, Austria and Prussia went to war with Denmark over the duchies of Schleswig and Holstein, St. Petersburg warned Sweden not to interfere in support of Denmark. When Bismarck insisted upon keeping both duchies for Prussia and fought Austria for the fine prize, the tsar raised no objection that his uncle, the Prussian King William I, should profit so richly from the enterprise. As Bismarck schemed to provoke France into a war with the German states in 1870, Russia agreed to bring military pressure to prevent Austria from succoring France. The German chancellor obviously won handsome repayment for his support of the tsar against his rebellious Polish subjects in 1863.

Bismarck's astuteness—his calculated cultivation of Russian backing and his care to offer Austria generous peace terms after defeating her in the Six Weeks War of 1867—earned its reward in 1873 when Francis Joseph of Austria, William I of Germany, and Alexander II of Russia joined in the League of the Three Emperors. The vaguely worded arrangement committed the three powers to no specific joint action, but it seemed to Western observers to join the conservative rulers of Eastern Europe in the sort of understanding that had united them in the generation after the Congress of Vienna. The conclusion of the arrangement eased Bismarck's fear of possible Russian and Austrian support of France—Austria because of her recent defeat by Prussia, and Russia as a reaction to the exalted strength of the new Germany and the weakness of the defeated and isolated France.

The League of the Three Emperors remained in force until 1878, when the Russian Foreign Office announced that German perfidy at the Congress of Berlin had abrogated it. Bismarck found himself with no alternative but to arrange an alliance with Vienna, by which Germany and Austria pledged a common defense in case Russia attacked either power.

Shortly before his death in 1881, Alexander II approved the revival of the League of the Three Emperors in more positive terms than the earlier arrangement had provided. The new treaty carried the commitment of the three cosigners to remain neutral if any one went to war with another power not a party to the agreement. They promised to confer before accepting any alteration of Turkish borders, and all agreed to support the closure of the Dardanelles when Russia was at war, thus assuring St. Petersburg that there would be no repetition of the Crimean War.

By 1887 it had become patent to all that the interests of Russia and Austria-Hungary clashed so hotly in the Balkans that the two were not comfortable in the same alliance. Bismarck, who could not surrender Germany's close ties with Vienna, worked out a Reinsurance Treaty by which Russia and Germany promised neutrality if either went to war against a third power; this would not hold, however, if Russia attacked Austria or Germany attacked France. When Bismarck went into retirement in 1890, the Reinsurance Treaty lapsed, leaving Russia diplomatically isolated.

There were revolts in Bosnia and Herzegovina in 1875 against Ottoman persecution and corruption, and the possibility threatened that Balkan Christians throughout the Turkish Empire would rise against the sultan. Austria, Russia, and Germany joined, with French and Italian backing, in a demand that the Turkish government grant equal treatment to Christians and Moslems, halt its discriminatory taxation, end police corruption, and permit Christian representation in local government. The sultan was deaf to the request, and Serbia and Montenegro declared war upon the Ottoman Empire. The Bulgars then rose against their Turkish masters, only to be slaughtered in a massacre that provoked indignation throughout the world.

The Serbs, whose army was led by a Russian general acting without the tsar's approval, were overwhelmed and their country was threatened with vicious reprisals. To prevent such a catastrophe, a strong Russian army crossed the Danube in the summer of 1877, drove through Bulgaria, and early the following year advanced to the Sea of Marmara west of Constantinople. But a British fleet warned that it would move to the Bosporus if necessary to defend the capital against Russian seizure, and Russia and Turkey agreed to the Treaty of San Stefano.

By the San Stefano settlement of March 1878, the sultan granted independence to Serbia, Romania, and Montenegro, and ceded to Russia small bits of territory along the Danube and south of the Caucasus. He promised administrative reforms in Bosnia and Herzegovina. And he agreed that a huge Bulgaria, stretching from the Danube to the Aegean and from the Black Sea to the Serbian border, should be autonomous under a Christian prince who nominally would be a vassal of the sultan. A Russian army of 50,000 would occupy Bulgaria for two years to oversee the emergence of the new state. Had the terms of San Stefano been allowed to stand, only Thrace and Albania would have remained of the sultan's European possessions.

The old Western fear that Russia would dominate Turkey as she had done under Nicholas I, and the still greater alarm that the Balkan segment of the Turkish Empire was already falling under Russian domination, became manifest immediately. The British government moved troops from India to Malta in preparation for any war that might be necessary to stem the Russian advance to the shores of the Mediterranean. Austria prepared to move an army into action against any Russian presence in the Balkans. Then Bismarck, insisting that Germany had no vital interests at stake, asked the great powers to a meeting in Berlin to find a solution to the problems that were threatening the peace.

The Congress of Berlin drastically altered the terms of the San Stefano settlement in two ways. Austria received authority to occupy and administer Bosnia and Herzegovina, although technically the provinces would still belong to Turkey. Thirty years later Austria annexed them outright, a move that strained Austro-Serb and Austro-Russian relations on the eve of World War I. More irritating to Russia at the moment, however, was the disposition of the inflated Bulgarian state that San Stefano had provided for. The new Bulgaria, one third the size of the earlier creation, would consist only of the land between the Danube and the Balkan Mountains. Another third, to be known as Eastern Rumelia, would be autonomous under a Christian prince responsible to the sultan. The last third of the Bulgaria of San Stefano would become once again part of the Ottoman Empire.

The Russian foreign minister, Prince Michael Gorchakov, blamed Bismarck, whom he hated violently, for the Russian diplomatic defeat over Bulgaria. It is true that Bismarck had supported the British prime minister Disraeli and the Austrian foreign minister Andrassy, both of whom had refused to accept a huge Balkan Slav state that would be beholden to Russia for its creation and that would almost inevitably permit Russian control of the entire Balkan peninsula. Such an eventuality, Disraeli at least felt, would have returned the situation in the Near East to the anxious years of Nicholas I, when the specter of Russian domination of Turkey had brought about the Crimean War. So bitter was Gorchakov over what he chose to regard as a Russian humiliation, condoned if not engineered by Bismarck whose construction of the German Empire Russia had supported at every step, that he declared the League of the Three Emperors to be no longer in force. He soon went into retirement, however, and his successor Nicholas Giers worked much more smoothly with the German Foreign Office.

Russian involvement in the restless Balkans was in part a reflection of government policy traceable back at least to the reign of Peter the Great, whose hope that the Balkan Christians would rise to greet his march against Turkey proved forlorn. It was a product, also, of Pan-Slavism as it ripened both in the Balkans and in Russia.

The Slavophilism of the reign of Nicholas lost much of its fire after the Great Reforms. Many of the early Slavophiles had died or had retired or had seen their publications wither for lack of support. Others had focused their energies upon land reforms in Russia and Poland. For many the emancipation of the serfs had satisfied their most cherished wish. After the 1860s some conservative and nationalist elements tended to reflect earlier Slavophile political goals—a consultative national assembly and the exaltation of the ancient Slavic village community, the *mir,* with its assembly of elders. But for the most part Slavophilism in the late nineteenth century was almost synonymous with reaction, with support of the autocracy, with a glorification of Orthodoxy, with a suspicion of the West, and with a passionate resentment of liberals and leftists for their fascination with Europe.

The Pan-Slavism that emerged in Russia after mid-century was both an expression of extreme nationalism and a clamor for Russian expansion to gather small Slav groups into a great Slav empire. It was suspicious of the West and of "Europe," which it regarded as fundamentally hostile to Slavdom's welfare and prosperity. It held to the view that Russia and all Slavic peoples had a common origin and a common destiny, that they shared common sentiments and common interests. Russia must bring all Slavs together, even at the expense of war against the West if that proved necessary. The three pillars upon which the Pan-Slav empire must rest were Orthodox Christianity, the Romanov dynasty, and the Russian state. Nicholas's minister of education, Uvarov, would have smiled content that his trinity—Orthodoxy, Autocracy, Nationality—still found favor years after his death.

Pan-Slavism was an emotion that inspired many non-Russian Slavs all over eastern and southeastern Europe. Here it preached a brotherhood of all Slavs, not only Orthodox but also Catholic and Protestant, although most Russian Pan-Slavs looked upon Catholic and Protestant Slavs as apostates or as having become so Westernized as to be beyond redemption.

Non-Russian Pan-Slavs believed that Balkan Slavs and those who had lost their identity in the Austro-Hungarian Empire should join together, after their Russian brothers had rescued them, into a superstate that would be a confederation of equal partners.

If the government in St. Petersburg was not officially Pan-Slav, many of its office holders were. One outstanding example was Count Nicholas Ignatiev, ambassador to Turkey prior to the Russo-Turkish War of 1877, who dictated the terms of the Treaty of San Stefano. Another was General Michael Cherniaev, who left Russia to lead the Serbian Army to defeat against the Turks in 1876. Pan-Slavs then, both in the Balkans and in Russia, were responsible in considerable measure for the Bosnian revolt, the Serbian war against Turkey, the Bulgarian uprising, the Russo-Turkish War, the glorious diplomatic triumph of San Stefano, and the distasteful Congress of Berlin that Pan-Slavs everywhere so bitterly resented.

Pan-Slavism gathered strength, both in Russia and in other Slavic lands, after the Congress of Berlin. The diplomatic defeat of Russia made it apparent that Slavs had friends only among themselves. That Bosnia and Herzegovina should come under Austrian protection rather than under that of either Russia or Serbia was manifestly unreasonable and unfair. That the Slavs of Bulgaria should be denied unification was a grave injustice. The Congress of Berlin did much, if more were needed, to crystallize the bitter anti-Western sentiment of Pan-Slavs everywhere.

Revolutionary Movements

The death of Nicholas brought a sense of relief to the Russian people and the hope that the pall of censorship and oppression might fall away. The severest critics of the late tsar were willing to believe the best of his successor. The announcement by Alexander II of the end of the Crimean War carried with it an expression of hope for an improvement in the "internal organization" of the country, for "equal justice to all." Those who hated the father and wished the son well were willing to accept these vague references as pledge of a liberal domestic policy. The prospect that autocracy would end and that bondage would give way to complete freedom soon proved illusory. Reform and revolutionary thought and action burgeoned from the disappointment and resentment that the disillusionment produced.

Resistance to the government's modest and halfhearted approach to the reform needs of the nation found expression in a variety of programs, some put forward by individuals and others by organizations. Some were mild, others extreme. Some aimed at reform, others at revolution. Some operated from bases in Western Europe; others chose to fight it out inside Russia with officialdom and the security police. The relentless battle went on for twenty years and ended only with the assassination of the "Tsar Liberator" whose compromise between bondage and freedom, autocracy and representative government, failed to satisfy any significant segment of Russian society.

The revolutionary movement of the 1860s and 1870s rested upon a primarily Western philosophical base. It rested also upon a Russian experience and tradition of violence that ripened and grew sharper as the revolutionary activity over twenty years expanded and survived official determination to stamp it out. Popular defiance of government went back at least to the peasant revolts of the seventeenth century, and Pugachev's uprising in Catherine's time was still fresh in the memory of officials and landlords. The Decembrist movement had ended only in a more sophisticated threat of violence.

Those who fought for reform or revolution during the reign of Alexander II, however, owed far more to the West for nurture and sustenance than did any of those who had preceded them. Their debt was great to the Russians in exile in the West— Herzen, Bakunin, and others—who could speak freely where no one inside Russian could do so. To the very moment of the revolutions of 1917 the West would continue to provide sanctuary for Russians who defied their government. From Herzen to Lenin there would be substantial, active, and highly vocal colonies of revolutionaries in Paris, Geneva, Lausanne, Zurich, London, Brussels, Nice, Turin, Vienna, and other Western cities.

The revolutionary émigrés, although frequently under

surveillance from the local police, received considerable financial support from Western sympathizers. They wrote and published their revolutionary tracts and sold them in quantity all
over the West. They maintained their own revolutionary press;
Herzen's *The Bell* was only one of scores of newspapers and
periodicals that appeared, sometimes in Russian and also in
French or English translation, sometimes originally in French
with a Russian translation to be smuggled into Russia.

There were people other than Russians in such voluntary
exile, of course—Germans, Frenchmen, Poles, Italians, and various refugees from Austria, Turkey, and elsewhere. There came
to be something of an international set of revolutionaries. They
attended international meetings and set up international organizations. Bakunin joined Karl Marx in 1864 in founding the
socialist International Workingmen's Association, commonly
called the First International, although Marx later forced
Bakunin's expulsion. A Russian branch of the First International
appeared in Geneva in 1870.

The First International, which transferred its headquarters
to the United States, died out in the 1870s. A federation of
Marxist Social Democratic parties assembled in Paris in 1889,
however, in the so-called Second International. It met from time
to time in congresses of delegates from many countries, and also
maintained a permanent secretariat. It fell apart at the outbreak
of World War I when some Social Democratic parties—notably
the German—supported their homeland, and others—notably
the Russian—did not. Lenin organized a Communist International or Comintern in Moscow, posing as the Third International, in 1919.

The Russian revolutionary movement of the 1860s and
1870s was dependent upon the West for its philosophical sustenance as for its physical sanctuary. The French socialists—
Fourier, Saint-Simon, Proudhon, and Blanc—strongly influenced Herzen and Bakunin, and either directly or through the
writings of these early Russian exiles also influenced the younger
generation of revolutionaries who defied Alexander II. The
greatest influence of all in the late nineteenth and early twentieth centuries came from the writings of Karl Marx and Fried-

rich Engels, the German team of socialists whose voluminous writings gathered together and applied, or distorted, the ideas of German, French, and English philosophers and social reformers and especially the English classical economists—Adam Smith, Thomas Malthus, and David Ricardo—of the late eighteenth and early nineteenth centuries. Marx himself, of course, put together the seminal work *Das Kapital* in the recesses of the British Museum, for he lived out the last thirty years of his life in exile from his native Germany. The first volume of *Das Kapital* appeared in 1867, and a Russian translation, the first into any language, was published in 1872.

Marx's influence upon Russian revolutionaries was both positive and negative. Many accepted his teachings as gospel, and the principles he proclaimed became, with some modification by Lenin, the creed of the Bolsheviks, the left wing of the Russian Social Democratic Labor Party. Yet Marx's preachments also met a challenge among Russian revolutionaries, some of whom regarded his approach to the problems of Western industrial society as unacceptable or as inapplicable to the backward agricultural society of Russia. Indeed, Marx himself came only late in his career to regard Russia as worthy of his attention or capable of profiting from his doctrines.

Whatever the course of Western thought that would attract the support of Russian reformers and revolutionaries in the second half of the nineteenth century, the death of Nicholas I found a substantial number of young men poised for action. There was a disposition to wait for the new emperor to disclose what his policy would be, and an inclination to suppose that the nation would move forward as soon as the Crimean War came to an end. If the reforms long overdue were not soon forthcoming from above, however, there would be mounting pressure from below to force them in the interest of, and in the name of, the Russian people.

The accession of Alexander II and the mounting evidence of his determination to end bondage brought a chorus of approval from Westernizers at home and abroad. Herzen, who had chosen exile in France and then England rather than live under the oppressive rule of Nicholas I, was ecstatic in his praise of the new emperor. When the tsar prodded the obdurate nobles to accept the inevitability of emancipation, Herzen wrote in his London newspaper, *The Bell,* "Thou hast triumphed, O Galilean." A socialist, a revolutionary, the father of Russian populism—Herzen was all of these—could hardly have been more enthusiastic.

Nicholas Chernyshevsky, a priest's son who used literary criticism in the publication *The Contemporary* to preach the gospel of revolutionary socialism, compared the tsar with Peter the Great. "The blessing, promised to the peacemakers and the meek, crowns Alexander II with a happiness with which as yet none of the sovereigns of Europe has been crowned—the happiness of alone beginning and completing the liberation of his subjects."

Praise soon turned to censure, however. Chernyshevsky lost patience as the planning and wording of the emancipation document stretched over years while government censorship forbade public discussion of serfdom and its abolition. He denounced as wholly inadequate the terms of emancipation when the Law of February 19 finally appeared. His opposition and his connection with revolutionaries were sufficient excuse for the secret police to seize him. After two years in a Petersburg dungeon, he spent twenty years in Siberian exile.

From the safety of his London home Herzen launched a sustained attack upon tsardom soon after the promulgation of the Act of February 19. An editorial in *The Bell* posed the question "What Do the People Need?" His answer, "land and freedom," became a rallying cry for revolutionaries from that day forward. He denounced the terms of the emancipation as fraudulent and called for more generous land allotments to the peasants without any increase in redemption payments. He demanded a broad extension of local self-government to reduce the influence of parasitic officials responsible to the St. Petersburg bureaucracy. He urged the creation of a national legislature elected by universal suffrage.

Herzen did not stop with his demands for reform. He called for an underground opposition press and for the organization of secret societies to promote unrest among the peasants and in the armed forces. He encouraged the Poles in their struggle for independence. When in the autumn of 1861 the government closed the universities in answer to student riots inspired in part by local grievances and in part by the resentment of liberals at the ungenerous terms of emancipation, Herzen editorialized in *The Bell* that the students should go "to the people." The "going-to-the-people movement," or the Populist movement, grew out of that inspirational appeal.

If Herzen was a humanitarian and reforming journalist who had little patience with anarchy and terrorism, his sometime friend Michael Bakunin was in every sense a man of action. Son of a wealthy landowner, as was Herzen, Bakunin left Russia at the age of twenty-five to wander over the face of Europe, America, and Asia urging and participating in revolutions wherever he could find one or start one. He was, along with Karl Marx, one of the founders of the First International in 1864, but he disagreed so violently with Marx over the place of the state in the proletarian revolution that the International expelled him in 1872. The Russian, who regarded the state as the source of all social ill and evil and the cause of human corruption and criminality, called for the abolition of the state, the family, organized religion, and private property. He was one of the founders of modern anarchism.

Bakunin's ideas were not original with him, of course. He picked out bits and pieces here and there from Western thought —from Rousseau, from the classical economists, and most especially from Pierre Proudhon. Bakunin and Marx agreed in their resounding denunciation of religion and private property. And scorn of the family and of marriage was popular at the time among the liberals of Western Europe and the "romantic exiles" from Russia who settled in France, Italy, Switzerland, and England.

The Great Reforms of the 1860s were a disappointment to the older generation of reformers, to the "fathers" the novelist Ivan Turgenev identified in his immensely popular *Fathers and Sons.* Turgenev, himself one of the "fathers," was a Western liberal in attitude who spent much of his life in Germany and France. He had no sympathy for revolution but advocated mod-

eration and patience while popular education and economic
progress smoothed the way for reform.

The "fathers" had grown up as heirs of the Decembrists,
who had put much faith in political reform, some even expecting royal cooperation. Herzen himself had urged a popularly
elected national assembly. Earlier he had gone into voluntary
exile because the stifling air of the Russia of Nicholas I denied
him the civil and political freedom he found necessary for an
unfettered expression of his views.

The new generation, the "men of the sixties," the "sons"
of Turgenev's novel, showed no interest in the political democracy that Herzen had so treasured. Indeed, they regarded political democracy or parliamentarianism as a British and French
trick to beguile the masses and to mask the rule of an aristocracy
of landed or industrial wealth. And so they cast off the liberalism
of the fathers and embraced the principle of social revolution
in which the form of political institutions was a matter of indifference. Nor had the young generation the patience of the old.
There was none of the gradualism that Turgenev approved and
that even Herzen and Chernyshevsky, who had applauded Alexander II on the eve of emancipation, seemed all too ready to
condone.

The concern of these men of the sixties lay with the *narod,*
the people, the Russian masses. Since Russia was an agricultural
country hardly on the threshold of industrialization, the masses
meant the rural masses. In the countryside there was to be found
a peculiarly Russian, non-Western institution that bespoke a
homely sort of social equality—the peasant village commune.
In the village assembly of heads of peasant families lay the only
sort of democracy that mattered. The village commune came,
even for Herzen and Chernyshevsky, to symbolize the kind of
socialism that might make possible the avoidance of the evils of
the Industrial Revolution that Herzen saw all about him in nineteenth-century London.

These iconoclastic "sons," many of whom were students
coming out of the universities in the mid-century years, constituted a new element in the intelligentsia. They were "men of various ranks," sons of priests, professional men, minor officials,

and only occasionally sons of the gentry. In spurning the values of the older generation, they came to embrace nihilism, which to them signified the rejection of the humanities, the acceptance of materialistic values, and the need to press for technological knowledge and industrial progress. They would approve nothing—hence the title nihilism—that did not square with the principles of modern science. In this much they were as Western as their contemporary Charles Darwin.

Later Russian revolutionaries were amazed to find themselves called "Nihilists" in the British, French, American, and Italian press. The term became popular in the West as a means of identifying Russian terrorists and Populists of all sorts, moderates and extremists alike. It catered to the air of mystery that surrounded the Russian revolutionary movement. And it served to cloak the ignorance of men of the Western press who were so quick to write about the various reform and revolutionary groups without distinguishing among them or seeking to understand their problems or aims. Among Russians, particularly in official circles, "Nihilism" became a simplified slogan presumably proclaimed by all enemies of the regime, by all who rejected established authority. In this sense the name was as appropriate for Narodniks as for assassins, for Herzen or Chernyshevsky as for Dmitry Karakozov who in 1866 fired a pistol at the tsar at close range and missed.

Turgenev used the word nihilism in a deprecatory way in his novel *Fathers and Sons.* Dmitry Pisarev, who spent the early 1860s in prison as a dangerous radical and who did much of his writing there, welcomed the title of nihilist. He urged young members of the intelligentsia, or at least the "critical realists" among them, to prepare themselves to be leaders of the people in the creation of a new society. As part of that preparation they must cast off the traditions and the prejudices they had inherited and must not waste their time upon such socially useless distractions as art and even history. The only worthwhile goal was to find a solution to the problem of "nakedness and hunger," of poverty and misery.

Pisarev reasoned that Russia's greatest need was to learn the most modern technological skills that the West could teach and become, in a tangible and material way, a part of European civilization. Russia must become a modern industrial economy, led by an enlightened and dedicated elite using the methods of modern science. Although he had been exposed to the thought of Saint-Simon, Fourier, Proudhon, Herzen, and Chernyshevsky, he preached no violent revolution. He had none of Herzen's sentimental affection for the *mir,* the agricultural commune. He had little patience with the capitalist system but encouraged a sort of individual and group initiative, free of competition, which he deplored.

The Western European coloration of reform and revolutionary thought and action in Russia is nowhere more striking than in the work of P. G. Zaichnevsky, son of a small landowner who owned only a few hundred serfs. At the age of seventeen he entered the University of Moscow, ostensibly to study mathematics, but his fascination with the writings of French socialists and with the youth movements of Central Europe led him to concentrate upon the promotion of "socialism and democracy." Mazzini's Young Italy particularly intrigued him, and he titled his revolutionary manifesto *Young Russia.* It was written in a prison cell and published in 1862 by the underground press in Moscow.

Zaichnevsky proposed to capitalize upon the indignation and resentment generated by the disappointing terms of the emancipation of the peasants. He called upon young "natural proletarians"—educated people who were willing to work for a free and wholesome society—to prepare the ground for revolt by working among the villagers of rural Russia.

Young Russia sounded the call for an immediate revolution that inevitably would be as violent as the French Revolution to which Zaichnevsky made frequent reference. The new society would be socialist and democratic, rid of such restrictive institutions as marriage, the family, and private property. The nation would govern itself through a federal arrangement of regional and central assemblies whose members would be elected by universal adult suffrage. Each village *mir* would assign, for a few years only, a piece of land to anyone who asked for it. Public shops would market goods and "social factories" under the direction of popularly elected managers would be responsible for industrial production. The emancipation of women and the elimination of class would make the new Russia a completely egalitarian society. Education would be free.

Democracy could not, of course, come to birth at the moment of the revolutionary triumph. Zaichnevsky foresaw a period of indeterminate length during which "the revolutionary party" would retain centralized authority. It would end the "despotism" of the old regime and "take the dictatorship into its own hands" in order to establish the new institutions as quickly and firmly as possible.

Nicholas Chernyshevsky, a priest's son, completed four years of historical and literary studies at the University of St. Petersburg in 1854. After a short career as a teacher of Russian literature in a secondary school, he joined the editorial staff of the influential journal, *The Contemporary*. As a successor to Belinsky in the field of literary criticism, Chernyshevsky continued to insist upon the responsibility of the artist to concern himself with the social needs of the day. He studied Hegel, Feuerbach, Proudhon, Fourier, Saint-Simon, the English classical economists, and the American writers Hawthorne, Emerson, Cooper, and Stowe. To the readers of *The Contemporary* he held up the knightly image of American society, or at least that of the northern states on the eve of the Civil War—a society that would set Europe the example of ending slavery and ridding the young republic of the only serious stain upon its fabric. No Russian reformer of any influence was as fascinated with, and indeed as knowledgeable about, the United States as Chernyshevsky. On the eve of emancipation of the Russian serfs, he lost all patience with the tsar whose earlier support for reform had won his confidence. Even before the Manifesto of February 19 proclaimed the end of bondage for privately owned serfs, Chernyshevsky warned his readers that Alexander II was no more deserving of trust than his father had been.

For his defiance of the emperor, Chernyshevsky was imprisoned for two years before suffering the public humiliation of a mock execution and exile in chains to Siberia. While in prison awaiting trial and sentence, he wrote the novel *What Is To*

Be Done? that proved to be irresistably inspiring to the revolutionary youth of the next generation and even into the twentieth century. The hero of the novel was a revolutionary socialist who symbolized the need for young Russian men and women to organize circles, or bands, to advance the revolutionary cause.

One of the circles that grew out of the promptings of the novel *What Is To Be Done?* appeared among the students at the University of St. Petersburg. The student who offered his room as a meeting place decorated it with portraits of leaders of the French Revolution—Robespierre and Saint-Just—and with magazine pictures of Herzen, Bakunin, and Chernyshevsky. When the meeting convened, members read out revolutionary proclamations they had composed. Then they read and discussed books smuggled in from the West—Louis Blanc's *History of the French Revolution* or F. M. Buonarotti's *Conspiracy of Babeuf.*

The society Chernyshevsky advocated was not one with a powerful state authority, for he was suspicious of the state. It would consist rather of phalansteries—voluntarily associated self-governing communities each practicing agriculture and industry on a cooperative basis. The state would continue to exist only long enough to finance the phalansteries through their infant years and then would wither away. Chernyshevsky drew heavily upon the Frenchmen Charles Fourier and Louis Blanc. The Russian ingredient in the system was the peasant village, which already functioned as an agricultural community, governing itself democratically or at least capable of doing so.

Serge Nechaev, a twenty-year-old teacher and part-time university student, visited Bakunin in Geneva in 1869. Together they worked out a revolutionary catechism, setting forth rules of conduct for those who would organize to overthrow the government. Nechaev proposed that the members of the revolutionary movement must dedicate themselves without reservation to the goals agreed upon by the leaders. Sacrificing relatives, friends, or fellow revolutionaries might be necessary; murder, robbing, or spying on other members must be done on order from above; all thought of honor or moral scruple must give way to the needs of the organization.

Nechaev, whom contemporaries called "the Jacobin," was

an avowed disciple of Babeuf, the French revolutionary who proposed to replace the Directory with a dictatorship that would abolish private property. Nechaev proposed a nationwide organization of five-man cells; local cells would be responsible to a district cell that in turn would receive orders from a provincial or national cell. Men in each group would know their fellows in that cell but no one else in the organization, so as to prevent the revelation of contacts to the security police. Each cell, upon orders from superiors, would carry out assassinations or acts of terror, incite strikes and riots, and engage in such disruptive and paralyzing activities that tsardom might fall from an inability to function. His organization attracted only a few members, and he died after years in prison. The conspiratorial methods and jesuitical conduct that he advocated later found favor with the Bolsheviks and with communists everywhere.

If Lenin confessed no obligation to Nechaev, he readily admitted his debt to Nechaev's friend, Peter Tkachev, editor of a journal *Nabat,* or *The Tocsin.* Tkachev, who died insane in 1886, had less influence during his lifetime than he did later. The similarity between Lenin's revolutionary tactics and those recommended by Tkachev is striking, and Russian historians after 1917 candidly acknowledged as much. Tkachev insisted upon the need for a small, dedicated, conspiratorial elite of intellectuals to lead the revolution and seize power, the dictatorial centralization of the revolutionary party, the maintenance for an indefinite period of a postrevolutionary "socialist dictatorship" under the authority of the intellectual elite who had prosecuted the revolution, the reorganization of the economy along modified Marxist lines, the liquidation of all political opposition during and after the revolution, and the protection of the new regime by a committee of public security, or secret police force.

A Soviet magazine in 1923 carried an officially endorsed article granting Tkachev's enormous contribution both to revolutionary tactics and to postrevolutionary policy. Calling Tkachev "the first Bolshevik," the article continued: "It is an irrefutable fact that the Russian Revolution proceeded to a significant degree according to the ideas of Tkachev, with the seizure of power made at a time determined in advance by a revolutionary party, which was organized on the principles of strict centralization and discipline. And this party, having seized power, is working in many respects as Tkachev advised."

The admission that Leninism did not originate with Lenin came while he was still alive and before his apotheosis. His successors would be less candid.

The Bolshevism of Tkachev was a blend of Western and Russian revolutionary thought and practice, as indeed was the later Bolshevism of Lenin. The inspiration for Tkachev's elitist organizational approach came from the Frenchman Auguste Blanqui. It is less easy to identify the other sources upon which he drew, because his education in revolutionary goals and methods came with a rush. At the age of seventeen Tkachev enrolled in the University of St. Petersburg, and three weeks later was one of 300 students arrested by the police for attending a forbidden meeting and demonstrating against recently issued punitive regulations affecting students—compulsory attendance at lectures, the wearing of a distinctive uniform for easy identification, and proscription of all student associations and gatherings.

Tkachev spent two months in a St. Petersburg prison where scores of revolutionaries were awaiting trial or exile to Siberia. From them he quickly absorbed the jumbled philosophies of Western and Russian thinkers, and from them, too, he caught an infectious enthusiasm for action. After his release he became the editor of a succession of radical journals published in the 1860s. Involvement in the Nechaev affair in 1869 put him in prison, but he escaped four years later and fled to the West. He published his journal *The Tocsin* in Geneva in the mid-seventies and died in Paris in 1886.

A nobleman, Peter Lavrov, colonel and professor of mathematics at the Artillery Academy in St. Petersburg, supported students as they demonstrated against the government in 1861 and joined a short-lived subversive society, Land and Freedom. Four years later a court-martial dismissed him from the army and banished him to a remote province for "disrespect" for the emperor, for "sympathy and intimacy with persons known for their criminal inclinations," and for "an intention" to publish "pernicious ideas." Such was the administration of justice in the Russia of the reform era that supposed attitudes and intentions were quite sufficient grounds for denying a man his freedom. Lavrov later escaped to the West.

As Lavrov developed intellectually in the late forties and fifties of the nineteenth century, he became an enthusiastic admirer of Herzen. He was a friend of Chernyshevsky. As a student of the German philosophers Kant and Hegel he published articles and delivered public lectures on Hegelianism. He was also influenced by the writings of Saint-Simon, Fourier, Feuerbach, Owen, Proudhon, and John Stuart Mill. By 1870 he had accepted many of the teachings of Marx.

Lavrov emphasized the importance of the individual, his sense of dignity, and "an inner sense of justice," which he assumed all men free of persecution to possess. He denounced the evil social structure of his time for its enslavement of the masses for the advantage of the few. Those few had a heavy moral responsibility to work for the creation of a new society in whose advantages and progress all would share.

While under police surveillance and house arrest in a small town in central Russia, Lavrov wrote and serially published a number of revolutionary tracts. Later suppressed by the official censor, they were reprinted abroad in a collection entitled *Historical Letters*. The year of publication, 1870, was the year of Herzen's death and Lenin's birth.

In 1861, Herzen had urged that students, "exiled from knowledge" when the government closed down the universities in an effort to halt student demonstrations, should "go to the people," to the *narod* or masses, with their protest against tsardom. Those who joined in the "going-to-the-people" movement, or *Narodnichestvo*, came to be called Narodniks or Populists.

Another wave of student uprisings broke out in 1869. They were the result in part of the revolutionary propaganda of the 1860s and in part of the repressive policies of the minister of education, Dmitry Tolstoy. But now there was a strong sense of focus and direction, which had been lacking in 1861. It was

Lavrov's *Historical Letters,* perhaps "the most important single document of social protest in the Russian evolution from Herzen to Lenin," that sharpened the focus of the Narodnik movement.

Lavrov called upon students to meet their debt to the people, to whose heavy toil they owed their privileged position and education, by going into the industrial centers and most especially into the countryside to educate the masses politically. They must teach the people the meaning of democracy and socialism and promote in them a willingness to fight for a democratic and socialist society. This was not Tkachev's elitism, in which a small disciplined vanguard would direct and lead the revolution. Lavrov's educated elite would go among the people not to lead them in revolt, for only the people could liberate themselves and launch and prosecute their own revolution. It was the task of the educated elite to propagandize and to educate the masses, to bring them along to the point of understanding the need for revolution and for carrying it out.

In the early 1870s the followers of Lavrov organized themselves into circles whose members, with exuberant confidence in the wisdom and goodness of the masses, went into city schools and factories and into the villages to distribute socialist literature, to teach night classes, and to preach the revolutionary gospel wherever they could assemble an audience. Perhaps the most famous of these Narodnik groups was the Chaikovsky Circle in St. Petersburg. One of its founders was Nicholas Chaikovsky, who some years later sailed with friends to America to organize a communist agricultural community in Kansas that quickly failed, leaving its disillusioned members to return to their homeland.

Another founder of the Chaikovsky Circle was Mark Natanson, a medical student at the University of St. Petersburg. When not in prison or Siberian exile, he and his wife Olga were forever joining or organizing socialist and revolutionary groups. Their favorite authors were François Fourier and Robert Owen until they discovered Marx. Other notables in the Chaikovsky Circle were Sophia Perovsky, daughter of St. Petersburg's governor-general, and the anarchist Prince Peter Kropotkin, of ancient and respected lineage. His *Memoirs of a Revolutionist* reveals the inclination of the young socialists to join not one but several organizations at once in an effort to satisfy their ardor for reform and to provide multiple expression of their defiance of the autocracy.

In the Populist or Narodnik movement of the 1870s, hundreds of young men and women went into the villages of rural Russia to live among the peasants, to share their lives and burdens, to serve as teachers, midwives, veterinarians, and social workers. Some peasants listened patiently to these dedicated young people, but many others were suspicious and occasionally villagers turned the Narodniks over to the police. Hundreds were arrested and tried in open court. Their candid avowals of their beliefs and goals were allowed by the judges and applauded by the crowds who attended. Vera Zasulich, daughter of a nobleman, shot the military governor of St. Petersburg, but the jury acquitted her to the wild cheers of a crowded courtroom. Many Narodniks made no effort to avoid arrest in order to declaim and to popularize their creed during the course of the trials to which the public flocked.

The police moved relentlessly against the Chaikovsky Circle and others like it. Between 1873 and 1877 they rounded up 1,600 young men and women, many of whom came from socially prominent and wealthy families. Then there were mass trials—"The Trial of the Fifty" and "The Trial of the 193"—that became public spectacles, where sympathizers in the audience took notes of the testimony and later published them abroad. Of the 900 young people who were imprisoned or exiled to Siberia, nearly one third were sons or daughters of the gentry, 100 were children of nonnoble officials, and 200 were children of Orthodox priests.

The revolutionary movement did not die out in the face of stern government pressure. Many avoided the police net, and others escaped from Siberian exile to disappear among the urban crowds of Petersburg, Moscow, Kiev, and Odessa. But there was widespread disenchantment with the peasantry. Lavrov's insistence that the people must make their own revolution, and that the intelligentsia should confine themselves to awakening the popular conscience, lost favor. When the Populists lost faith in the people, or at least in the people's willingness to mount their own attack upon the social institutions that held them in thralldom, the old tactics changed. Now the conviction grew that the dedicated young intelligentsia themselves must fight autocracy in the name of socialism and the people.

Under the leadership of Mark Natanson the Narodniks gathered in St. Petersburg in the autumn of 1876 and organized a secret society to which two years later they gave the name Land and Freedom, the name of a sentimentally revered earlier association that had foundered. It was not a political party, for it had no plans for the development of postrevolutionary society except that it had to be socialist. Its concern was to overturn the prerevolutionary society in all its manifestations.

The new Land and Freedom proposed to enlist the support and the talents of all intellectuals who opposed tsardom and so to avoid the splintering of the reform movement that had turned some into Lavrovists and others into Bakuninists and still others into Nechaevists. There were five sections, each with a different goal and requiring a different role, which a volunteer might join. One was the administrative section, where handwriting experts forged passports and documents that would ease travel at home and also abroad, for the secret police had agents in every European nation. A second section worked in secondary schools and universities to provoke student unrest and enlist new members for the society. A third section went among factory workers to stir up strikes and city riots. A fourth sought once more to win peasant confidence and stir revolt in a second "going-to-the-people" movement that proved no more successful than the first. This fourth section won a more sympathetic hearing among the religious dissenters whose millions suffered often vicious persecution by armed forces sent amongst them from time to time. The fifth or "disorganizing" section assassinated public officials as punishment for maltreatment of Populist prisoners, rescued fellows from the police, and ferreted out and liquidated traitors and spies.

The drastic increase in police brutality and execution of revolutionaries that greeted the appearance of Land and Freedom and the achievements of its disorganizing section only brought sterner vengeance and mounting terrorism from the secret society. When assassins from Land and Freedom killed the head of the political police—the infamous Third Section, the very name of which recalled the dark days of Nicholas I—the government published an appeal to the public to help put an end to revolutionary terrorism. Some moderate liberals in the zemstvos discussed with Land and Freedom leaders the possibility of halting the terror in return for a government grant of such civil liberties as freedom of speech, press, and assembly. The discussions achieved nothing, however, for the zemstvoists could promise nothing and the revolutionaries were skeptical of such bourgeois tokenism.

The disorganizing section of Land and Freedom, whose spectacular accomplishments thrilled many members of the parent organization and alarmed others, came round to the view that the assassination of public officials in large numbers might paralyze the government and bring it tumbling down. The grandest prize of all, of course, would be the emperor. In the spring of 1879 a member of Land and Freedom fired five shots at Alexander II but missed.

The attempt upon the tsar brought to a head a growing cleavage in the society. After less than three years of existence Land and Freedom split into two new organizations. One, called Black Partition, would work among the peasants rather than in cities, would seek land reform through division of great estates to the peasants, and would renounce the use of terror. The other new society, called People's Will, would devote its energy to the assassination of public officials, and particularly would concentrate upon the emperor. After several ingenious attempts upon the tsar's life, members of the People's Will killed him with a bomb hurled on signal by Sophia Perovsky, daughter of a former governor-general of St. Petersburg. She and a few others paid for the assassination on the gallows.

The revolutionary movement of the 1860s and 1870s was remarkable in many ways. Its derivation was Western in the socialism that was its goal and in the Jacobinism of its tactics. Marxism became increasingly popular among the intelligentsia.

The movement was Western, too, in that many of its leaders found sanctuary in Italy, Switzerland, France, Belgium, and England, and the revolutionary press poured forth a stream of propaganda that was smuggled into Russia to be read avidly by students, peasants, workers, and even officials. Herzen's various homes—in London, Nice, Paris, Geneva—were gathering places for touring Russians of all classes. Daughters of the gentry took their education in Zurich in such numbers that Alexander II ordered them home and ended the ban on their enrollment in universities. They returned, after sitting at the feet of Bakunin and others, to pass along their learning to the *narod* to whom, as Lavrov had insisted, they owed their education.

Yet there was much that was anti-Western in the revolutionary movement of the 1860s and 1870s. Most of the intelligentsia doubted that the constitutionalism toward which Western liberals worked, and which had appealed to some of the Decembrists, was either attainable or desirable for Russia. And capitalism, the socioeconomic system of the West, had little appeal for Russian revolutionaries, as, of course, it had little appeal to the most radical reformers in the West. It was the radical social critics of the West—Proudhon, Blanc, Fourier, Saint-Simon, Blanqui, Marx, and Engels—and not the moderates or liberals, who held a fascination for the Russians.

Some Russian reformers devoutly believed that the nation might become socialist without passing through Marx's intermediate stage of capitalism. The village commune, a native Slavic institution, might serve as the agency by which Russia should vault over capitalism into a system in which society, rather than the individual, would own and operate the nation's means of production.

The Approaching Crisis of Autocracy

The assassination of Alexander II brought to the throne his son Alexander III, a man of small mind and small deeds. The outward serenity of the reign was the product of the sternest police repression. Censorship of the press and tight control of university students and faculty were as much in evidence as in the reign of Nicholas I. Trial by administrative courts and by courts-martial meant the suspension of much of the judicial reform of 1864. Arbitrary arrest, imprisonment, and exile were commonplace.

The People's Will party almost completely succumbed to the reaction that followed upon the death of its most famous victim, and revolutionary terrorism disappeared except for a single manifestation. In 1886 a handful of university students that included Alexander Ulianov, Lenin's older brother, plotted the assassination of Alexander III. The scheme misfired, and the plotters went to the gallows. Aside from this feeble protest, the graveyard quiet of the reign went undisturbed. It was a period of industrial progress and urban growth, but of rural poverty and seething unrest.

The chief adviser of Alexander III was his former tutor, the archpriest of reaction, Constantine Pobedonostsev. A former professor of law and one of the architects of the Judicial Reform of 1864, he became director-general of the Holy Synod a year before the assassination of Alexander II. Later he became tutor to the future Nicholas II, and his sinister influence lay heavy upon the last two Romanovs until 1905 when revolutionary pressure drove him into retirement.

Pobedonostsev's *Reflections of a Russian Statesman,* an English translation of which first appeared in 1898, became the credo of the reactionary, the Slavophile, the Pan-Slav, the anti-Semite, the defender of autocracy, and the opponent of progress. The book was a detailed attack upon Western liberalism in every manifestation and a solemn warning to the people not to follow those who would destroy Holy Russia with such radicalism.

He never wavered in his attack upon those who urged the tsar to establish a constitutional regime, referring to the parliamentary system of the West as "that basic evil" and "the great lie of our time." He denounced the very word constitution as "deceitful and accursed," and warned Nicholas II to resist "the insane longing for a constitution" that would herald "the ruin of Russia." He urged Alexander III to rid the judicial system of the jury, imported from the West, as completely disruptive to

Russian justice. He derided the "fiction" of a free press, and regarded freedom of expression as license to abuse the autocracy that he held in such veneration.

Pobedonostsev was viciously anti-Sematic. But he dealt no more gently with Old Believers, Protestants, Catholics, or the various sects that had drifted away from the state church than he did with the Jews. He upheld Orthodoxy as a bulwark against contamination from the West, and he left no room in Russian society for any faith but Orthodoxy. He was a relentless enemy of secular education, and he repeatedly insisted that the Church, of which he was the lay head, must control all schools. He fought against the national identity of subject peoples—the Finns and the Poles most particularly—for he regarded, rightly perhaps, every manifestation of separatism as a threat of desertion to the West.

Alexander III died quietly in his bed in 1894, and his gentle, weak-willed son succeeded him. Nicholas II, last of the dynasty, had had his father's own tutor, Pobedonostsev, and continued his father's wrong-headed reactionary policies through the first decade of his reign. When a delegation from the Zemstvo assembly of Tver province congratulated the new tsar upon his accession, it expressed the hope that zemstvo representatives might take part in national affairs. Nicholas curtly referred to such thoughts as "senseless dreams." Then, lest anyone misunderstand him, he went on with the warning: "I shall defend the principles of autocracy as firmly and unswervingly as did my father." This amounted to a declaration of war upon those of his subjects who had looked forward to some moderation in the repressive rule of Alexander III and Pobedonostsev. Indeed, Pobedonostsev remained for a decade as the new emperor's chief adviser.

The years from 1880 to 1900 were years of marked industrial progress for Russia. Foreign capital came in apace, and finance ministers fought valiantly to stabilize or expand revenue and so encourage investments from the West. The severity with which Alexander III clamped down upon potential sources of unrest—universities, the press, zemstvo assemblies—was in some measure an attempt to reassure potential foreign investors that the monarchy was secure. On the other hand, the confidence of Western bankers and individual investors was shaken by the heartless anti-Semitism and the ruthless Russification practiced upon Poles, Ukrainians, Georgians, religious dissenters, Catholics, and even Moslems. French government loans to St. Petersburg to expand the Russian railway net were the product more of France's search for a strong ally against Germany than of any affection French republicans felt for the authoritarian rule of the Romanovs.

By 1881 the emancipation had done its work of ending bondage and of transferring roughly half the gentry-owned land to the former serfs. Many great landowners sold the remainder of their estates to village corporations or individual peasants or merchants and sought careers in the army, the judiciary, or the bureaucracy. Some invested in business the money they received from the terms of the emancipation and from later land sales.

Whatever the source of its capital — whether from foreign or from domestic investors — business enterprise prospered mightily and expanded dramatically. There was enormous growth in the last quarter of the nineteenth century in the manufacture of textiles, beet sugar, chemicals, steel, and some machinery and in the mining of coal, iron, and oil. In this rapid industrialization Russia imported Western techniques and Western equipment, thus appropriating ready-made what it had taken the West generations to develop. If the nation avoided some of the slow and costly experimentation necessary to invent and perfect her own industrial tools and plant, she blindly repeated many of the social mistakes that the West had committed a century earlier. Working conditions were foul, wages were low, fines were high, hours were long, accidents were numerous, and the proscription of unionization left workers at the mercy of employers. The government forbade strikes, although extremely violent ones occasionally broke out in desperate defiance even of the Cossacks who galloped with slashing sabers against the strikers.

Some conditions that characterized this emergent industrialization boded ill for the future. The size of the typical industrial enterprise was far larger than in the West. Over half of all Russian plants employed more than 500 workers each, and many had a labor force of over 1,000. This was particularly so in Petersburg and Moscow, the politically sensitive cities of the empire. The massing of workers in large firms made them readily conscious of the economic insecurity they shared, and they were easier to organize, politically as well as economically, than smaller work units would have been. Only a small percentage of the population made up the work force—3,000,000 of 170,000,000 in 1914—but the concentration of the workers in large bodies made the proletariat an extremely volatile element in restless times. In the six months preceding the outbreak of World War I, 1,500,000 Russian workers were out on strike.

Russia's exports rose considerably in the last quarter of the nineteenth century, although her share of world trade remained steady and insignificant. Her exports consisted chiefly of raw materials and foodstuffs—oil, iron, lumber, furs, sugar, and wheat. She sold textiles in Asian markets. Her sales of raw materials to the West offset her purchase of machinery and other manufactures, an exchange that provoked Lenin's charge that Russia occupied a colonial status in the global capitalist economy.

At the end of the nineteenth century there was a worldwide depression from which Russia could not escape, for her economy was becoming sensitive to business fluctuations in the capitalist world beyond her borders. As the foreign demand for Russian exports dried up or the world price fell, many factories closed down or employers cut wages. Unemployed and underemployed filled the streets by the thousands, and there were huge strikes, not only in Petersburg and Moscow but in distant cities such as Kiev, Odessa, Astrakhan, Tiflis, Baku, and Batum. There was widespread unrest, too, in the countryside, as the resentment of urban workers overflowed into the hungry villages where city laborers had lived and worked only a generation earlier, and where many still must return to live with relatives in times of slack work in the factory towns.

Growth of Political Opposition

The reign of Alexander III had witnessed no attempt to organize political parties or movements inside Russia. There was some contact, however, between isolated intellectual circles and a Marxist social-democratic organization, the Emancipation of Labor, founded in Geneva in 1883 by the émigré George Plekhanov. The former student of mining engineering had been active in Lavrovist circles, in the Land and Freedom movement and, when that organization fell apart, a founder of the Black Partition group. Disillusioned as were many others at peasant indifference to the Populist movement, Plekhanov went into exile in 1880 and soon thereafter became a convert to Marxism.

The Emancipation of Labor printed a number of socialist tracts and smuggled them to discussion circles of students and intellectuals inside Russia. Some were the writings of Marx and Engels; others Plekhanov himself wrote. The program of the party assumed that Russia must pass through a capitalist stage before entering the higher socialist stage of historical development; that the revolutionary class, the only class capable of carrying out the revolution, was the industrial proletariat, not the peasantry; and that leaders of the movement must not indulge in terror, for this would divert attention from the ultimate goal, the creation of a new socialist society. Since the Emancipation of Labor made no effort to establish itself as a working-class movement and took no part in promoting the strikes of the 1880s and early 1890s, it devoted its energy to debating with non-Marxists the nature and goals of the coming socialist revolution.

The first Marxist group to organize inside Russia was the creation in 1895 of Vladimir Ulianov, who had taken the revolutionary name of Lenin. The group took the defiant title of the Fighting Union for the Emancipation of the Working Class. The organization brought together a number of Marxist circles in the St. Petersburg neighborhood. Its agitation among workers, in which it exploited dissatisfaction with wages and hours to promote labor's ultimate interest in revolution, rested upon the assumption that the urban proletariat must fight for and win its own emancipation.

The Fighting Union established branches in Moscow and other industrial cities and took credit for an outbreak of major strikes in 1896 that forced the government to limit the work day to eleven hours. There were many more Marxists outside the

Fighting Union than inside, however. Here and there, groups of Marxists operated presses, both underground and openly. The St. Petersburg periodical *The New World* fell under Marxist control and carried the writings of Lenin and Plekhanov as well as essays by the brilliant Marxist economists Peter Struve and Michael Tugan-Baranovsky. As long as there was no political attack upon the monarchy, the censors passed the vaporous theorizings of the intellectuals, satisfied perhaps to keep their activities from going underground.

Marxist leaders, aware that the continued existence of a number of groups and organizations weakened the movement, met in Minsk in March 1898 to bring the splinters together into one parent Marxist party. The result was the birth of the Russian Social Democratic Labor Party, the RSDLP. The nine delegates to the Minsk conference represented five Russian groups and the Bund, a Marxist association of Jewish workers created a year earlier. Lenin did not attend, for he had been living in Siberian exile for two years. The new party chose a central committee, but the secret police soon arrested all its members. There was no carefully considered program, but only a manifesto that Peter Struve drafted in terms too mild to please most of the others.

The RSDLP gathered for the second time in Brussels in 1903, but the Belgian police forced the party to move on to London. The forty-three delegates agreed on a maximal program in which they aimed at a socialist revolution, the overthrow of capitalism, and the creation of a dictatorship of the proletariat. It also accepted a minimal or short-run program which aimed at an end to autocracy, the emergence of a democratic republic, the eight-hour work day, and the transfer to the peasants of that land on each estate they had not received in 1861. The maximal and minimal goals approved by the second congress in 1903 remained the program of the Social Democrats until after the Bolshevik Revolution of 1917.

The delegates to the London meetings also agreed upon the party's organization: there would be a central committee to set policy and an editorial board of control for the party's newspaper, *Iskra,* or *The Spark*. Elections to fill the top spots provoked violent debate and recrimination. Lenin and his followers won a victory in naming the editorial board of *Iskra;* he called his majority on this single issue Bolsheviks, or men of the majority. To those who lost Lenin gave the name Mensheviks, or men of the minority. The names stuck, although within a year the Mensheviks, Plekhanov among them, had won control of the central committee. Then Lenin withdrew from the editorial board of *Iskra* and within months was bringing out a Bolshevik newspaper, *Vpered,* or *Forward.*

The Bolsheviks called a third meeting of the Social Democrats in London in the spring of 1905, but the Mensheviks preferred to meet by themselves in Geneva. At a Prague congress in 1912 the Bolsheviks formally expelled the Mensheviks from the Social Democratic Party. Later that year the Mensheviks met in Vienna and pledged themselves to continue working for social democracy as they understood it.

The divergence of Bolsheviks and Mensheviks bespoke in part a personality clash between the ruthless Lenin, something of an upstart who was less than thirty years of age when the Social Democratic Party came into existence, and the professorial Plekhanov, "dean" of Russian Marxists who was senior to Lenin by fifteen years. Plekhanov, more strictly Marxist than Lenin ever was, insisted that the revolution to overthrow the autocracy would usher in a democratic republic, and that capitalism and democracy "bourgeois democracy" to the Marxist—would operate side by side in Russia for a lengthy and indeterminate period. The immediate concern was the overthrow of tsardom, and Plekhanov and the Mensheviks would cooperate fully with bourgeois liberals to bring that about.

Lenin and his Bolsheviks would have none of such gradualism. The fall of the monarchy must lead immediately to socialism under the dictatorship of the proletariat. And Lenin held to the view that the Social Democratic Party—the Bolshevik variety of social democracy—must not only lead the revolution but in turn must submit without question to the dictates and authority of its own small central committee. Plekhanov insisted that the party must operate democratically; all members would take part in reaching policy decisions and implicitly would be free to criticize such decisions after their adoption. Both Bolsheviks and Mensheviks placed their reliance upon urban labor to launch the revolution, and both would come belatedly to seek peasant cooperation.

Not all revolutionaries were willing to leave the Russian countryside and place their reliance solely upon the urban proletariat. Populism had so caught the fancy of the post-reforms generation that in the 1880s and 1890s there were still many groups, usually centering around a vigorous personality, at work in the villages or interested in a socialist society primarily for what it would win for the peasants. Mark Natanson, one of the founders of Land and Freedom, had his followers. So, too, did Catherine Breshko-Breshkovskaya, affectionately called "the little grandmother of the Revolution" for her indefatigable labors for a new society. Victor Chernov, later one of Lenin's chief rivals for the leadership of revolutionary Russia, had a small following of peasants and intellectuals who embraced the peasant cause.

In 1900 a number of these peasant leaders met at Kharkov and organized the Party of Socialist Revolutionaries. Although there was much of Marxism in their creed—belief in the inevitability of capitalism's collapse, for example—there was even more of Russian revolutionary tradition. The SRs, or Socialist Revolutionaries, demanded the downfall of autocracy as enthusiastically as did the SDs, the Social Democrats. Their primary concern, however, was land reform—breaking up the great estates, turning over all agricultural land to the village communities, and establishing a socialism resting upon rural communalism.

The most flamboyant activity of the Socialist Revolutionary Party centered in its "Battle Section," a group of its members who specialized in terrorism and assassination in the tradition of the People's Will. Its victims in later years included cabinet ministers, provincial governors, generals, a prime minister, and even a member of the royal family. The secret police managed to plant agents in the Battle Section, the very head of which later was Yevno Azev, a double agent who ordered fellow SRs to assassinate some "enemy of the people," and then reported to the political police where, when, and by whom the deed would be done.

Although the orientation of the Social Democrats was Western—its Marxist dogma was wholly an importation—and although there was an element of Westernism in the creed of the Socialist Revolutionaries, a third group was wholeheartedly and enthusiastically Western in a much more recognizable way. These were the liberals, those reformers—they were only mildly revolutionary—whose goals for Russia were the goals not of Western revolutionaries but of moderate Western reformers. They would have Russia adopt Western institutions as they then existed, with only slight modification to make them perhaps more democratic. Western liberalism, Western constitutionalism, Western civil rights, the Western view of the dignity of man—these were the goals of the early twentieth-century Russian liberals.

Liberalism covered a spectrum of political thought from the conservative to the mildly non-Marxist socialist. It included men like Peter Struve, the economist and sometime Marxist whom Lenin's extremism drove from the ranks of the Social Democrats. At the other extreme it included the conservative landowner Dmitry Shipov, zemstvo leader in Moscow province, who wanted a consultative parliament with no real power to legislate.

At the turn of the century Russian liberalism found its strength among professional people and the associations they organized to represent them, among zemstvo delegates, and among the so-called third element of clerks, veterinarians, teachers, and other professional and semiprofessional people employed by the zemstvo boards to work in the villages. In general, the liberals stood for equality of all classes before the law, free speech, free press, freedom of assembly, freedom of conscience, freedom from arbitrary arrest, and a parliament of some sort with either consultative or legislative powers. They wanted for Russia the civilities and the decencies of Western civilization. One typical liberal was Paul Miliukov, an internationally respected historian who lectured on several occasions at American universities and who was at home in the West and wanted his native land to become part of it.

Liberals began after the death of Alexander III to organize for professional and political strength. Members of zemstvos elected delegates to a zemstvo congress but were warned after the first meeting not to hold another such "unconstitutional" assembly. There soon sprang up unions of teachers, doctors, lawyers, engineers, and others, each ostensibly concentrating upon professional problems of mutual concern but quickly interesting itself in politics. In the early twentieth century a Union of Unions would speak powerfully for all professional associations.

A number of liberals formed an underground association, the Union of Liberation, in 1903. A newspaper, *Liberation,* was published in Stuttgart under the editorship of Peter Struve and smuggled into Russia along with the illegal publications of the Marxists. Early in 1904 members of the Union of Liberation assembled in St. Petersburg and agreed to work for an end to autocracy and the creation of a constitutional regime. A later effort to cooperate with the government faced such stubborn opposition from reactionary bureaucrats that the liberals found themselves forced into a revolutionary stance.

A Constitutional Regime

The early years of the twentieth century were years of growing unrest in the countryside, among urban workers, and among university students. In 1902 there were 200 peasant uprisings of sufficient size to require the calling in of troops, which was four times as many outbreaks as the administration regarded as normal and acceptable. When a government investigator asked an old villager whether the revolts were not the result of Socialist Revolutionary propaganda pamphlets, the peasant replied: "It is not the little books, but the fact that there is nothing to eat." Semistarvation and undernourishment were endemic in rural Russia. Strikes in railway yards, ironworks, textile mills, and even bakeries in the autumn of 1902 indicated that the discontent was not limited to the countryside. Student unrest, as always, reflected the smoldering resentment of peasant and proletarian.

The minister of interior, Vyacheslav Plehve, suggested to Nicholas II that what the nation needed to put an end to internal unrest and unite the people behind the government was "a little victorious war." This was one cause of the Russo-Japanese War of 1904–1905, the willingness of the bureaucracy to launch a war in order to turn the nation's attention away from its plight. The underlying cause of the war was the clash of Russian and Japanese interests in Korea and Manchuria.

The war went badly for Russia, and the lengthening casualty lists, added to the depressed economic conditions in town and country, precipitated a crisis. In January 1905, after the war had dragged on a year, a mob of 200,000 strikers and demonstrators marched on the Winter Palace to petition the tsar. The leader was an Orthodox priest, Father George Gapon. The written plea, which the demonstrators proposed to lay before the tsar, reviewed all the ills from which the nation suffered—despotism, an irresponsible bureaucracy, high taxes, war, land shortage, unemployment, low wages, and other oppressive conditions. It asked the emperor to end the war, stop redemption payments, legalize labor unions, grant freedom of speech, assembly, press and conscience, put an end to arbitrary arrest, and convene a national legislature.

The petitioners marched in a quiet and orderly way, some carrying icons and pictures of Nicholas II. Troops advanced against the huge throng and ordered it to disperse. When it refused to do so, the soldiers fired into the unarmed mob, and hundreds fell. The authorities admitted to the killing of over a hundred and the wounding of hundreds more. This was Bloody Sunday, January 9, and the day marked the opening of the 1905 Revolution. Before the month was out, over 400,000 workers were on strike, adding political to economic demands. There were peasant revolts all over South Russia. The defiance of authority reached the point of touching even the royal family. A university student, son of a police official, killed the tsar's uncle, the Grand Duke Serge, on orders of the Battle Section of the Socialist Revolutionaries.

Slowly and reluctantly the autocracy gave ground. While appealing to all loyal subjects to defend the throne, the minister of interior, Alexander Bulygin, announced that the tsar would assemble elected representatives of the people "to participate in the discussion of legislation." This cautiously worded pronouncement promised the assembly power only to discuss, and said nothing of the manner of its election. An imperial order granted religious toleration and ended discrimination against dissenters, while another proclaimed the right of any subject or group to petition the sovereign.

The Union of Liberation spurned such halfway measures, and called for the direct election by secret ballot and universal manhood suffrage of a constituent assembly. This positive approach won the endorsement of the Union of Unions, a newly formed confederation of the unions of various professional groups—teachers, lawyers, engineers, pharmacists, journalists, doctors, zemstvo members, university professors, and others—whose president was the historian Paul Miliukov. A Peasants' Union, organized by intellectuals who presumed to speak for rural Russia, took similar action. Zemstvo leaders gathered in Moscow in July 1905 and approved the draft of a constitution calling for a Western democratic type of government for the nation.

The first six months of 1905 proved disastrous in the war against Japan. A huge Russian army lost the three-week battle of Mukden, but the Baltic fleet was on the way to rescue the Russian cause, steaming three fourths of the way round the world to do so. The Russian and Japanese fleets met on equal terms in the Tsushima Straits. The Japanese sank over half the Russian warships, including most of the capital ships, and captured nearly all the rest in the worst naval disaster of modern times. The tsar asked for a peace conference, and delegates of the combatant powers met in early August in Portsmouth, New Hampshire, at the invitation of President Theodore Roosevelt.

The Japanese victory was in effect a defeat for Russia at the hands of a Western power. The new Asian power was advancing toward modern industrialized Western civilization at a far more rapid pace than was Russia. The ships of her fleet were more modern and better equipped and her crews were better trained than were those of the Russian Baltic fleet. Her naval officers had gone to school in England, and at this time the British navy was without a peer. The same was true of the army, whose officers were trained in Germany. Japan's troops were better equipped and better led than the Russians they fought against. Only the threat of being overwhelmed eventually by vastly superior forces moved the Japanese government to accept peace overtures.

Meanwhile the domestic situation grew progressively more critical. Peasant uprisings mounted in number and intensity. Army expeditions became necessary to bring industrial strikes under control. The Battle Section of the SRs kept up the terrorist pressure and managed to assassinate the military governor of Moscow. There was mutiny in the Black Sea fleet, and the battleship *Potemkin* hoisted the red flag and then sailed to a Romanian port to surrender.

In the early autumn of 1905 a wave of strikes swept over the industrial centers of European Russia, reaching a climax in a St. Petersburg general strike. There were widespread strikes in Moscow, where indeed printers and bakers had started it all. Defiant workers threw up barricades in the streets of Kharkov and Odessa. In cities all over Russia railways, telegraph and telephone lines, banks, schools, hospitals, electric and gas works, food shops, and even some government offices closed down. The nation's economy ground to a halt. When crowds joined strikers to march in the streets, carrying revolutionary banners and shouting "down with autocracy," public order gave way to governmental paralysis. From the beginning the strikers were insisting upon a democratic republic, a constituent assembly, civil rights, and amnesty for political prisoners. Request for the eight-hour day seemed almost an afterthought; their program was essentially political and revolutionary.

On October 13 perhaps forty delegates, elected to represent the workers in various factories, gathered to form the St. Petersburg Soviet of Workers' Deputies. From that moment on the number of delegates steadily increased, as additional work forces sent their representatives to speak for them in the soviet. By the end of November there were nearly 600 deputies, each purporting to speak for 500 workers.

The soviet, or council, was simply a representative assembly where the deputies sat for constituencies identified not by geography but by profession, work force, or social group. For example, 1,000 telegraphers in the capital would select two deputies and 500 cabbies would choose another. The revolutionary parties—Mensheviks, Bolsheviks, and Socialist Revolutionaries—were the driving force behind the elections, and the overwhelming majority of delegates were members of one or the other, the Mensheviks being the most numerous of all. The St. Petersburg Soviet published the first issue of its newspaper, *Izvestiia,* or *The News,* on October 17. Responding quickly to the example set by the capital, there was soon a soviet in every city in the land.

The emperor sought advice from his chief minister, Count Serge Witte, former finance minister and builder of the Trans-Siberian Railway, who had just returned from heading the Russian delegation to the Portsmouth peace conference. Witte advised Nicholas that there were two choices: he must grant his people a constitution or proclaim a military dictatorship to restore order. When the Grand Duke Nicholas, the emperor's uncle, refused to accept appointment as dictator, the tsar agreed to sign Witte's constitutional proclamation.

The October Manifesto put an end to the autocracy and created a parliamentary regime. It provided for the election, implicitly on the basis of universal male suffrage, of a national legislature, the Duma, with power to approve official appointments and to pass laws. The tsar even promised that no enactment of any kind should become law without the approval of the Duma. The manifesto also guaranteed freedom of conscience, speech, press, assembly, and association, and an end to arrest without cause.

Most liberals greeted the October Manifesto with wild applause, for it heralded Russia's donning the political raiment worn by every civilized nation not only in the West but throughout the civilized world. Now Russia had a parliament, or at least the promise of one. Now, at least in this one respect, she was as far advanced as Japan, Spain, Greece, Bulgaria, and the Latin American states. Before 1905 she found herself, in this one regard, in the company of such backward and uncivilized states as those in the Arab world or in Central and East Asia where monarchy still was absolute. Miliukov and other realists among the liberals realized, however, that the birth of the Duma was only the first step toward achieving a parliamentary democracy. His caution and skepticism proved later to be fully justified.

The reaction of the moderates, the liberals, to the October Manifesto was not that of others to right or left. Conservatives heard the imperial pronouncement with alarm that the tsar was surrendering to the mob. And the cynical revolutionaries warned against putting any faith in the promises of "the liberal financial shark Witte" as long as "the police thug" General Dmitry Trepov remained military governor of Petersburg.

With the publication of the October Manifesto the St. Petersburg Soviet called off the general strike, but the deputies planned another in case the government reneged on its promise to convene the Duma. Still stunned perhaps by the awesome popular strength that had shown itself in the general strike, the government made no effort to break up the meetings of the soviet. In fact, it announced an amnesty for political criminals, and many of the revolutionaries who had escaped to the West from Siberian exile or prison returned to join the action. Leon Trotsky, a Social Democrat who could not accept Lenin's position in the quarrel with Plekhanov but who also felt uncomfortable with the Mensheviks, had already returned to St. Petersburg from abroad. Trotsky won election to the soviet and became its vice chairman. Lenin, now back in the capital, took no part in soviet affairs, but directed the thoughts and actions of his own party. He quickly sensed, from the violence that was ravaging the countryside, that the natural ally of the proletariat in launching the Russian revolution was the peasantry. The party must serve as the vanguard of both.

If the fever of popular uprising tended momentarily to subside in Petersburg after the appearance of the October Manifesto, the government action had no such quieting effect upon rural Russia. The land hunger that had mounted with the population increase in the countryside after emancipation made the peasants always surly and perennially defiant, but the violence of the 1905 revolts was the worst since Pugachev. All over European Russia, from the Baltic provinces to the Crimea and the lower Volga, the gentry were driven from their homes or slain in their beds and their homes pillaged and burned. Those who spoke for rural Russia in the Peasants' Union met in Moscow in November to demand that all arable land go to the peasants, and that a constituent assembly meet within three months.

For a month after the October general strike in the capital the government moved cautiously or not at all, as though hypnotized by the frightening display of power that the revolutionary forces could muster. When in early November workers remained indifferent to a call by the St. Petersburg Soviet for a second general strike, Witte decided to reassert administrative authority. The Moscow police arrested the leaders of the Peasants' Union. Then police in the capital seized the chairman of the St. Petersburg Soviet. When this provoked no mass violence, government troops moved against the soviet and took prisoner all its members. After a trial for conspiracy to overthrow the government, Trotsky and a few others received life sentences to Siberian exile, but he escaped to the West and ultimately took up residence in New York.

Troops in the capital and at military bases from the Baltic to the Black Sea had defied their officers during the revolution, and there was a serious mutiny at the naval base of Sevastopol. Thousands of troops in the Far East, awaiting shipment home after the war with Japan, became mutinous and tried to capture the Trans-Siberian Railway. Loyal troops finally restored order in the military by seizing thousands of soldiers and sailors. Other troops savagely put down a December general strike in Moscow. Still others marched into the countryside in regular punitive expeditions to flog villagers and burn the huts of those who had taken part in the recent revolts. By the end of January 1906 officialdom had recovered control of the domestic scene.

The Revolution of 1905 was the product of forces at work inside and outside the nation. The deepening misery of the rural and urban masses, and the stubborn reluctance of officialdom to relieve it, made an explosion certain to come in time. The emasculation of the Great Reforms seemed to indicate that what the government would extend with one hand it would withdraw with the other. The refusal of the emperors to consider the creation of a national legislature, or indeed to hear of any popular check upon the autocracy, assured the survival of an oriental despotism unique in the Western world. The stifling of the freedoms of speech, press, association, and conscience meant the denial of the decencies of civilized society.

The external pressures that helped to produce the Revolution of 1905 had been building for three generations. The Decembrists, with their exposure to the infectious liberalism of the West, had mounted a pitifully weak protest. But they had inspired Herzen to a lifetime of war against the tyranny they had fought, and he in turn had inspired a generation of "sons" and indirectly a generation of "grandsons" to carry on the struggle. The debt of those nineteenth-century Russian reformers and revolutionaries to Western thought was enormous and was one they readily acknowledged. And the obligation was one that continued to grow down into the twentieth century.

German philosophers made a strong impression upon the youth of the nineteenth century—Kant, Fichte, Feuerbach, Schelling, Hegel, and Marx. So, too, did German artists. Herzen insisted that "a knowledge of Goethe, especially his *Faust,* was as obligatory as wearing clothes." The students of Herzen's generation even "made philosophical investigations into every chord of Beethoven and Schubert."

French writers had a profound influence upon the Russian intelligentsia. Voltaire, Montesquieu, the *philosophes,* Saint-Simon, Fourier, Blanc, Blanqui, and the French economists all had enthusiastic followers. De Tocqueville's *Democracy in America* was popular even among bureaucrats. In fact, the American system of government and the free air that seemed so uniquely to characterize American society, at least from a distance, exerted a strong attraction for young Russians.

British influence, although perhaps less pronounced than either French or German influence, was not inconsiderable, most particularly in the late nineteenth century. Although an interest in Adam Smith was apparent even in the reign of Catherine the Great, the classical economists of the Manchester School had little to say to Russians, to whom socialism of one variety or another seemed to offer more dramatic solutions to the problems that plagued the nation. Yet many were devoted readers of John Stuart Mill and of Thomas Buckle's *History of Civilization,* with its confidence that the story of the past, and implicitly that of the future, was one of material progress.

The Russian intelligentsia, and even those in official and court circles who fought reform, spoke several European languages with ease. No one had to wait for Western works to find a Russian translator. Even Pobedonostsev regularly read several English newspapers. D. M. Wallace, who spent many years in Russia and was one of a pioneer group that introduced Russia to the English people, noted in the early twentieth century that "in St. Petersburg and Moscow society everyone speaks French, most people speak English, and nearly everyone knows German." A fellow pioneer, Sir Maurice Baring, observed that most educated Russians were familiar with the works of Herbert Spencer, John Morley, Dickens, Wells, Shaw, Wilde, Galsworthy, and the American Jack London.

The immediate foreign impact that precipitated the Revolution of 1905 was, of course, the humiliating defeat by Japan. Given the seething unrest that threatened social upheaval at the time, however, it is hardly likely that a Russian victory would even have postponed the revolution. In very fact, the nation remained shockingly indifferent to the war and to its outcome. The defeat was all the more shameful for coming at the hands of a nation only recently emerged from feudal darkness and isolation. Japan, however, had gone to school to the West, had sent her best young men to England, France, Germany, and the United States, and then had welcomed them home to build a new modern industrial society frankly imitative of the West. The victory was unmistakably a victory of modern Western civilization over a backward nation whose ruling clique resisted Western influence. The progressive elements among the intelligentsia had been saying for nearly a century that Russia must take her position among the nations of the civilized West. Surely the defeat by Japan seemed to confirm it.

The 1905 revolution had accomplished much, even though

it did not reach the goals that any of its supporting groups hoped for it. There was an end to the autocracy, and try as they might the reactionaries who surrounded the tsar could never revive it. There was finally a Western type parliament popularly elected to represent all the peoples of the empire, and the institution successfully resisted the efforts of the tsar, who still called himself "Autocrat," to destroy it. Surely the greatest gain of 1905, however, was the experience it provided to those who in 1917 would successfully apply its lessons.

If the constitutional experiment soon proved a disappointment, the reason lay in the fact that the autocracy had denied the masses any preparation for their role in constitutional government. They knew nothing of the decencies of civilized Western society, of the freedoms of expression and association that would have made possible the existence of a public opinion. The bureaucracy learned of public opinion only through strikes, riots, demonstrations, assassinations, or *jacqueries*, or through the writings of its exiles that were smuggled into the country. There was no platform from which a Russian might protest or seek redress.

The emperor's subjects had had by 1905 only very brief and very modest experience in local self-government. The bureaucrats were a professional class apart, who with few exceptions were enemies rather than servants of the people. The zemstvo assemblies had given their members some slight practice in parliamentary procedures, and those who served on zemstvo boards had gained some administrative experience. But men stood for election as zemstvoists not on any platform or as members of any party. And the selfless men who would serve without pay in a position the bureaucracy regarded with suspicion were so few in number that there were never any hotly contested elections.

From the moment of its birth the constitutional experiment suffered the resentment of the imperial family and the calculated efforts of the tsar's chief ministers to make it unproductive. Nicholas II never questioned the divine origin of his unlimited authority and regarded any attempt to curb it as somehow sacrilegious. The empress incessantly insisted to the point of hysteria that the tsar must pass on to the tsarevich the autocratic power undiluted. The royal couple never forgave Witte for drafting the October Manifesto.

Yet Witte himself preferred abolutism to other types of government and suggested granting a constitution in 1905 only because he saw no other way to save the monarchy. He confessed also that the autocracy that he most admired could only work with an autocrat on the throne, and Nicholas surely was no autocrat. But Witte was not alone in opposing a constitutional regime. Ivan Goremykin, his successor as prime minister, regarded representative government as "nonsense" and referred to public opinion as "idle talk." Goremykin's successor, Peter Stolypin, spoke contemptuously of the third Duma in 1908: "Thank God! We still have no parliament." These were the words of men whose responsibility it was to win Duma support for imperial policies. Small wonder that in the short ten years of its existence, the Duma exerted little influence upon imperial affairs, foreign or domestic.

While the suffrage for election of delegates to the Duma was so broad as to include nearly all male heads of families, the election machinery was cumbersome and illiberal. The imperial fiat that set forth the rules divided urban voters into two groups—the wealthy few made up one group and all the rest made up the other. Each group voted for delegates to a provincial college, and the college then chose the deputies to sit in the Duma. The rural voters were still more distant from the final selection. Peasant householders elected voters to sit in a district college to choose delegates to a provincial college to select deputies to the Duma. This indirect method of voting, similar to what Speransky had recommended to Alexander I back in 1809, became part of the communist constitution of 1918. No other parliamentary system in the world followed such devious practices.

Political parties could not legally exist before the October Manifesto. With the official call for elections to the first State Duma, several parties stepped forward to solicit support. The Socialist Revolutionaries, declaring their primary concern to be socialization of the land, decided to boycott the elections and to continue the terrorist work of the Battle Section. A rightist splinter group opposed to terror broke away, formed the People's Socialist Party, and put forward candidates for election to the Duma. The Mensheviks and Bolsheviks formally and coolly arranged a truce and met together in the Fourth Congress of the Social Democratic Party at Stockholm in April 1906. The party voted against participation in Duma elections but chose not to interfere with the few SDs who had already entered the contest.

Those who welcomed the October Manifesto, even though many of them found it less than satisfactory, were the liberals who had worked so long for a Western type of parliamentary regime. They had found their voice in the zemstvo assemblies and most recently in the zemstvo congresses, some of which had to meet privately in Petersburg or Moscow homes. After 1905 the liberals spoke to the nation not through the zemstvos but through two formal parties, the Kadets and the Octobrists.

Zemstvo liberals assembled in Moscow in October 1905 to determine what their course should be. Left-wing and right-wing points of view immediately appeared, and the splintering that would cripple constitutionalists from that moment forward became painfully manifest. While the program to which moderates and extremists agreed was a compromise, at least it bespoke the fascination with Western political institutions that was the hallmark of Russian liberalism, as contrasted with extremism, of all hues. The left wing members of this October conference preferred a democratic republic and the immediate convocation of a constituent convention directly elected by universal suffrage. The compromise that came out of the conference, however, called for a constitutional monarchy with a parliament—the Duma—drafting the constitution. The emphasis upon a constitution—a fetish of Western liberals that had fascinated Russian liberals for at least a century—gave the new party its name Constitutional Democrats, or Kadets for short.* At a meeting three months later the Kadets endorsed health insur-

*The party's name in Russian was *Konstitutsionno-demokraticheskaya.* The popular name *Kadets* is from the initial letters, *K* and *D,* pronounced *Kah* and *Deh.*

ance for workers, a progressive income tax, and expropriation of large estates with compensation for their owners. The brilliant historian Paul Miliukov became the party's irrepressible leader.

The conservative zemstvoists, to whom the Kadet program was unacceptable, formed the Union of October 17, or Octobrist Party, choosing to stand on the October Manifesto and to oppose any further democratization of the government. It favored agricultural experimentation and modernization rather than expropriation of great estates, and supported the interests of business rather than those of labor. Its chief spokesman, the talented Alexander Guchkov, was the son of a wealthy Moscow businessman.

Extremists on the right coagulated into several groups differing from each other primarily in the emphasis they gave to anti-Semitism, autocracy, Orthodoxy, Russification, and Pan-Slavism. The Union of Russian Men, which enjoyed the backing of the metropolitan bishop of Moscow, uncompromisingly opposed all reform and every manifestation of Western influence. The Union of the Russian People made the widest appeal and enlisted the largest membership of any right-wing group. It sought the support of all classes, even workers and peasants, for a reactionary and anti-intellectual program. It praised the monarchy and condemned the bureaucracy for shutting off the "little father" tsar from his people. It was viciously anti-Semitic and applauded the pogroms—the organized beatings and killings of Jews and the burning of their homes—that took hundreds of lives in mass assaults on the ghettos in which the police often cooperated. It was narrowly nationalistic, casting suspicion upon all foreigners and upon non-Russian, non-Orthodox peoples of the empire. The leader of this proto-fascist party was Vladimir Purishkevich, a Bessarabian landowner who sought election to the Duma primarily to seek its abolition and the return to autocracy.

Over a period of months before the convocation of the first State Duma, the Ministry of Interior completed the framework of the constitution introduced by the October Manifesto and laid down precise rules for its operation. The pronouncement of October 17 had promised that no enactment might become law without the consent of the Duma. Now the new "Fundamental Laws," which passed for a constitution to the end of the monarchy, created a second house, the Council of State, half of whose members the emperor would name, the other half to be elected by various groups—nobility, clergy, provincial zemstvos, business organizations, and university faculties.

The creation of a coequal legislative chamber, with a built-in majority voting the dictates of the tsar, would effectively still the popular voice of the State Duma. The Council of Ministers, with its president Witte, wanted to make sure that the parliament would not get out of hand. There could be no amendment of the Fundamental Laws without the tsar's approval. The emperor's veto of all legislation was absolute. A vote of censure, requiring a two-thirds majority of both houses, might be passed along to the tsar, but it would accomplish nothing. All ministers, military officers, and bureaucratic officials owed their appointment and their tenure to the sovereign. A third of the items in the budget, including military expenditures and foreign loans, were not subject to legislative review. The Duma was to have no control over censorship, police, the military, religion, or foreign affairs. Some of these it might discuss, although it was not free to discuss its own power or the terms of its own election. The emperor could summon and dismiss the Duma at will and could issue laws or decrees between sessions that the two houses, by law at least, should approve when they met again. Frequently, however, the government flagrantly and callously ignored the law requiring approval.

The Fundamental Laws, and the cabinet rulings for implementing them, were a deliberate attempt by the government to avoid Western democracy. In the October Manifesto the tsar had seemed to bow to pressure for a Western parliamentary system. The creation of a constitutional monarchy of the British type, or at least of the German, was implicit in the promise that no enactment should become law without Duma consent. Once the administration had recovered control of the streets, however, it moved relentlessly to make impossible the birth of Western democracy on Russian soil.

Although more than forty parties and groups elected

deputies to the first Duma, one third of the 524 members were Kadets. More than a hundred Laborites—their group or party was a coalition of ten splinters—voted with the Kadets. So, too, did many of the 200 peasants, most of whom came to the first session unaligned. There were eighteen Social Democrats, all of them Menshevik in outlook. No reactionary won election. Nearly forty Octobrists represented the conservative point of view, but almost every other member favored a far more liberal stance than the Council of Ministers and Witte's successor, the aging reactionary Goremykin, would allow.

From the very first session of the Duma it was obvious that the people's representatives and the government would deadlock hopelessly on any important issue. The Kadets and their allies wasted little time in putting together an appeal to the tsar, which the Duma passed unanimously with a few abstentions. The resolution called for true parliamentary government, ministerial responsibility, an end to the Council of State, universal suffrage, abolition of indirect voting, amnesty for political prisoners, and expropriation of great estates to provide more land for the peasants. Goremykin came down to the chamber to read in a low monotone the government's decision that the Duma's address to the throne was not acceptable. The house passed a vote of censure and called for the resignation of the Council of Ministers, but the government took no notice of the Duma's action.

In the resolution they put before the house, the Kadets under Miliukov's vigorous leadership proposed to leave no doubt, either in officialdom or among the people, that they would settle for nothing less than a parliamentary democracy that was unmistakably Western in inspiration. Miliukov and many others of his party were fully acquainted with the British system. Many Russians spent summers in England; even Pobedonostsev had visited London on three occasions for stays of several months. Many Kadets were familiar at first hand with the French parliamentary system with its figurehead president. And many had seen the constitutional monarchy at work in Italy. The intentions of Kadets, as they drafted the resolution for Duma consideration, could have been no clearer had they prefaced it with a statement insisting upon the adoption of the British or Italian system of democracy.

Ten weeks after convening the Duma, the tsar dissolved it and kept its members from assembling on their own by surrounding their meeting place with troops. The nation's first parliament had passed one measure, to which both houses and the tsar gave their approval—it provided relief for famine victims in the drought-stricken valley of the lower Volga.

The second Duma was no more reasonable than the first, in spite of the government's efforts to assure a docile membership by purging the worst firebrands of the first Duma, disqualifying "undesirable" candidates on technical grounds, ordering priests to tell the faithful how to vote, and sending hoodlum gangs into the streets to break up leftist meetings. The session lasted a hundred days and accomplished nothing. When the Duma defied a government order to expel its SD members, dissolution followed.

Before the election of the third Duma Peter Stolypin, Goremykin's successor as president of the Council of Ministers, rewrote the electoral laws so that the electors, whom the voters chose to select the Duma deputies, would reflect more "satisfactory" views: over half of the electors would represent rural landowners, a fifth would represent the peasants, a fourth would represent property-owning townsmen, and two percent would represent industrial workers. The alteration of the electoral laws proved eminently satisfactory to the tsar. Octobrists and even more conservative groups won a strong majority of seats in the third Duma, while Kadet and Laborite representation was helplessly small. The third Duma lasted out its legal limit of five years, but the fourth, which showed about the same political complexion as the third, was swept away by the March Revolution that ended the monarchy.

When it became apparent to moderates and liberals alike that there was no parliamentary way of forcing tsardom to proceed with much-needed political and economic reforms, the parties in the Duma accepted the need for restraint and patience. They came to realize that their first obligation to the nation was getting the tsar to accept the fact of the Duma's existence and survival. The Octobrists met their responsibilities as the majority party. They even supported the government to the point where the very conservative prime minister Stolypin, detested in some court circles as being dangerously liberal, sought Duma support. In turn the Octobrists, and even the Kadets, preferred Stolypin to some reactionary whom they might get if they hounded the prime minister into resignation or imperial disapproval and dismissal. The Kadets accepted their role of the opposition with remarkable poise and occasional cooperation. Miliukov, fascinated as he was with Western political institutions, chose to work with reasonable patience for a constitutional monarchy of the British type, if that were conceivable with a Romanov.

War and Republican Government

The parliamentary quiet that settled over the third Duma in 1908 continued well into the life of the fourth Duma elected in 1912. Guchkov and other Octobrist leaders refused offers of cabinet appointments unless the emperor accepted the British principle of ministerial responsibility to the legislature. The Stolypin regime spanned several years of economic prosperity and slow modification of the worst elements of the autocracy. The redemption dues were canceled, and the peasants received the right to claim full ownership of their individual plots. Labor won the right to organize but not to strike. Newspaper censorship relaxed to the point where a number of new dailies and periodicals appeared, and they expressed every conceivable point of view. The publication of rightist papers and journals was hardly surprising, but even the Bolshevik daily *Pravda* circulated freely.

Whether Russia might ultimately have produced a thoroughgoing democracy of the British type, with a constitutional monarchy under which a responsible ministry and a freely elected Duma exercised complete authority, no one can say. The possibility of such a development rapidly faded under the impact of a costly war that neither the monarchy, nor the free republic that momentarily followed it, managed to survive.

In some measure the opportunity to develop a Western

type of democracy never came to Russia because of the tremendous sacrifice the nation made from 1914 to 1917 in defense of its Western allies and, avowedly, in defense of Western
civilization and Western values. So exhausting was the German
pressure upon the Russian war machine, the Russian economy,
the Russian land, and the Russian people, that the nation
reached the very limit of its endurance. Russia did not leave the
war by choice; there was none.

    With astonishing ease a revolution in March 1917 over-
turned a monarchy that had responded too late and too slowly
to the need for progress and so had been unable to avoid its
own destruction. The new government, whose premier months
after its birth declared it to be a republic, sought power not to
end the war but to prosecute it more effectively and so fulfill
Russia's contractual obligation to her Western allies. The overthrow of the Romanovs had the approval, all for different
reasons of course, of workers and businessmen, peasants and
landlords, soldiers and generals, Russians and non-Russians,
political moderates, liberals, and revolutionaries, and Christians, Moslems, and Jews. It even had the support of some members of the royal family.

    What the new Provisional Government did not realize, and
never came to understand, was that the Russian people had had
enough of war. The premier, Alexander Kerensky, promised the
allies one more offensive for the summer of 1917 to relieve
pressure on the Western front. The offensive began in a promising way and then quickly collapsed. The desperation born of the
military defeat, added to deepening economic chaos, the successful propaganda of the revolutionaries, and widespread resentment that the war still dragged on, led ultimately to the downfall
of the Provisional Government and the emergence of a Bolshevik regime.

    The revolutions of 1917 were to some extent the product
of a persistent, centuries-long struggle—by the best minds
among rulers and laymen alike—to win Russian admission into
the civilization of the West. The course of that long struggle
was never a smooth one. Of all the capricious turns of fate, however, surely one of the most striking in Russian history appeared
in the fact that the communist regime, bitterly anti-Western

from the beginning, triumphed at the moment when the nation lay prostrate from its efforts to save Western civilization.

The centuries of Western impact upon tsarist Russia drastically altered the civilization that Lenin and his successors took it upon themselves, after 1917, to cast in a new mold. Indeed, it is inconceivable that there could have been a Lenin had it not been for that Western impact. Had the nation managed to seal itself off from contact with the outside world, as Japan succeeded so remarkably in doing over a period of centuries, the course of its development surely would have been quite different from what it actually came to be.

Russia's interest in the West began almost as a flirtation and grew at a slow pace for two centuries before there came that flood of influence that Peter the Great loosed upon the land. For more than two centuries after Peter stepped up the pace of borrowing from the West, Russia became steadily more Western, more European, in spite of the reluctance of some of her rulers to accept the fact and the resentment of a segment of her people against the changes forced upon Russian society.

The Western impact upon tsarist Russia, sustained though it was over a period spanning more than four centuries, did not succeed in destroying the cultural identity of the nation. Russia became European or Western in many ways, but not in the sense that the nations of Central and Western Europe were European and Western. The Westernization of Russians, in fact, was nowhere near as complete as was that of Poles or Czechs or even some of the South Slavs.

The government of the Soviet Union after 1917 managed with far more success than had the tsarist government to control the impact of the West upon its people and its institutions. Western influence continued after 1917, to be sure, but it did so under effective limitation, encouraged or discouraged, turned on or turned off, as the leaders in their whimsical way might dictate. It was improbable, however, that Western influence could contribute substantially to a thoroughgoing revolution in the Soviet Union, as the Western impact had contributed so mightily to the revolution that swept away the tsarist regime.

Bibliographical Note

Russia and the West, in one form or another, is a topic that has long fascinated both Russians and Westerners. For a provocative discussion of this topic by a Russian émigré, see Wladimir Weidlé, *Russia: Absent and Present,* New York, 1961, and particularly the introduction by Richard Hare. The March 1964 issue of *Slavic Review* carried three essays on the subject: "Russia and the West: A Comparison and Contrast," by H. L. Roberts; "Russia's Perception of Her Relationship with the West," by Marc Raeff; and "The Historical Limits of the Question of Russia and the West," by Marc Szeftel. See also Serge Pushkarev's article, "Russia and the West: Ideology and Personal Contacts before 1917," in the April 1965 issue of the *Russian Review.* A list of the great and timeless histories of Russia must begin with Vasily Osipovich Kliuchevsky's *Kurs russkoi istorii* (A Course in Russian History) published between 1904 and 1921. A stiff and clumsy translation by C. J. Hogarth appeared in English as *A History of Russia* between 1911, the year of Kliuchevsky's death, and 1931. Fortunately, a highly readable and accurate translation by Liliana Archibald of the fourth volume became available in 1959 under the title *Peter the Great.* In 1968 the third volume appeared in a new and excellent translation by Natalie Duddington entitled *A Course in Russian History: The Seventeenth Century.* Kliuchevsky, greatest of all Russian historians, interested himself hardly at all in foreign affairs. His concern was the people and the domestic scene, which he approached from a sociological and institutional point of view.

Kliuchevsky's student, Pavel Nikolaievich Miliukov, was both a brilliant historian and a quite remarkable statesman. His *Ocherki po istorii russkoi kultury* (Essays on the History of Russian Culture), published between 1930 and 1937, appeared in a three-volume English translation entitled *Outlines of Russian Culture*, Philadelphia, 1942. The first volume of the translation bore the subtitle *Religion and the Church in Russia*, the second *Literature in Russia*, and the third *Architecture, Painting, and Music in Russia*.

Another Russian historical giant, S. S. Platonov, concentrated his research upon the sixteenth and seventeenth centuries, particularly upon Ivan the Terrible and the turbulent times that followed his death. Platonov's *Lektsii po russkoi istorii* (Lectures on Russian History) carried the title in English translation, *History of Russia*, New York, 1925.

M. N. Pokrovsky, the dean of Soviet historians until his death in 1932, published among many other works a five-volume *Russkaia istoriia s drevneishikh vremen* (Russian History from the Earliest Time), which was translated into an abbreviated two-volume edition entitled *History of Russia from the Earliest Times to the Rise of Commercial Capitalism*, New York, 1931.

One of the few great general studies of Russian history to appear in a Western language was Karl Stählin's four-volume *Geschichte Russlands von den Anfängen bis zur Gegenwart*, published between 1923 and 1939 and reprinted in 1961. Another, written by P. N. Miliukov, C. Seignobos, and L. Eisenmann, was *Histoire de Russie* in three volumes, published in 1932–1933; the first two volumes appeared in an English translation as *History of Russia*, New York, 1969.

The most thorough, detailed, and challenging account of Russian history in any language other than Russian is the multivolume study by George Vernadsky, also a student of Kliuchevsky. While the monumental work carries the title *A History of Russia*, New Haven, Conn., 1943–1969, each volume bears its own title and, in fact, stands independent of the others. The first, *Ancient Russia*, appeared in 1943; the second, *Kievan Russia*, in 1948; the third, *The Mongols and Russia*, in 1953; the fourth, *Russia at the Dawn of the Modern Age*, in 1959; and the fifth, *The Tsardom of Moscow, 1547–1682*, in 1969. A work of some merit and puzzling judgments is M. T. Florinsky's two-volume *Russia: A History and an Interpretation*, New York, 1953.

Several studies of certain aspects of Russian history deserve attention. Among economic histories there is the *History of the National Economy of Russia to the 1917 Revolution* by the Soviet scholar P. I. Lyashchenko, Ann Arbor, Mich., 1949, a translation of *Istoriia russ-*

kago narodnago khoziaistva (History of the Russian National Economy). The work is notable not least of all for the fact that the several editions through which it has passed reflect doctrinal agility and shifting official attitudes toward the nation's past. An older work by James Mavor, *An Economic History of Russia,* two volumes, New York, 1925, has not lost all its value, although new research techniques and new materials suggest a fresh approach to the subject. Jerome Blum's *Lord and Peasant in Russia from the Ninth to the Nineteenth Century,* Princeton, N. J., 1961, is the first complete history of the Russian peasant, as well as a rich account of the landowning gentry, over such a long expanse of time.

V. V. Zenkovsky's *A History of Russian Philosophy,* translated by G. L. Kline, two volumes, New York, 1953, is the best in its field. A shorter work, *History of Russian Philosophy* by N. O. Lossky, New York, 1951, is sound. A thoughtful and challenging study of certain topics in Russian intellectual and cultural history is *The Icon and the Axe* by James H. Billington, New York, 1966. An older work, a classic, is Thomas Masaryk's *The Spirit of Russia,* 2 volumes, New York, 1919; reprinted 1961. The standard histories of education are W. H. E. Johnson's *Russia's Educational Heritage,* Pittsburgh, 1950, and Nicholas Hans's *History of Russian Educational Policy,* New York, 1931. P. L. Alston's *Education and the State in Tsarist Russia,* Stanford, Calif., 1969, complements the older works in some respects.

For a study of Russian literature, an indispensable work is Prince D. S. Mirsky's two volumes, *A History of Russian Literature from the Earliest Times to the Death of Dostoyevsky,* New York, 1927, and *Contemporary Russian Literature, 1881–1925,* New York, 1926. The first volume and the first two chapters of the second were combined into *A History of Russian Literature from the Beginnings to 1900,* New York, 1958.

Although the political thought of Russian writers is best examined in their own works, most of which are now available in English and many in inexpensive editions, T. Anderson provides an overview, from Kievan to Soviet times, in his *Russian Political Thought, an Introduction,* Ithaca, N. Y., 1967. Well over half of his coverage deals with the eighteenth and nineteenth centuries.

The sorry plight of Jewry in Eastern Europe is told in *History of the Jews in Russia and Poland* by S. M. Dubnov, three volumes, Philadelphia, 1916–1920. *The Cambridge History of Poland,* edited by W. F. Reddaway, two volumes, Cambridge, 1941, is balanced and judicious. See also W. P. and Z. K. Coates, *Six Centuries of Russo-Polish Relations,* London, 1948.

Chapter 1

The detailed coverage for pre-Petrine Russia is in Vernadsky's five-volume *A History of Russia.* The story of the Russian conversion and the early church is in G. P. Fedotov's *The Russian Religious Mind: Kievan Christianity,* Cambridge, Mass., 1946; reprinted 1966. The second volume is entitled *The Middle Ages, the 13th to the 15th Centuries,* Cambridge, Mass., 1966. The standard Byzantine history is A. A. Vasiliev's *History of the Byzantine Empire,* Madison, Wis., 1929. *The Mongol Empire* by M. Prawdin, New York, 1940, paints Russia under Mongol rule as a province in a huge state.

The best modern biography of Ivan III is J. L. I. Fennell's *Ivan the Great of Moscow,* New York, 1962. Ian Grey's *Ivan III and the Unification of Russia,* New York, 1967, is a well-written account based upon a careful reading of the chief secondary works in Russian and English. *Ivan the Terrible* is the title of three biographies, one by K. Waliszewski, Philadelphia, 1904, another by R. Vipper, Moscow, 1947, and another by Hans Eckhardt, New York, 1949. A recent study of Ivan as a ruler seeking to build a strong monarchy is *The Shaping of Czardom under Ivan Grozny* by B. Nørretranders, Copenhagen, 1964. Contacts with England in the sixteenth century are dealt with in *The Early History of the Muscovy Company, 1553–1603* by T. S. Willan, Manchester, England, 1956, and in *Britain's Discovery of Russia, 1553–1815* by M. S. Anderson, New York, 1958.

The early Romanovs are the subject of Z. Shchakovskoy's *Precursors of Peter the Great,* London, 1964, and *The First Romanovs,* London, 1905, by R. N. Bain, the first British student of the Petrine period. An interesting treatment of Nikon is W. Palmer's *The Patriarch and the Tsar,* London, 1905. See also S. A. Zenkovsky, "The Russian Church Schism: Its Background and Repercussions" *(Russian Review,* 1957). The standard account of the Russian sects is *Russian Dissenters* by F. C. Conybeare, Cambridge, Mass., 1921; reprinted New York, 1962.

In part because of the paucity of surviving sources, accounts by Western travelers to Russia before the middle of the eighteenth century have earned more attention and respect than have later accounts. The Hakluyt Society published a number of such accounts, including S. von Herberstein, *Notes upon Russia,* London, 1852: A. Jenkinson, *Early Voyages and Travels to Russia and Persia,* London, 1886; and E. A. Bond (ed.), *Russia at the Close of the Sixteenth Century,* London, 1856. See also G. Fletcher, *Of the Russe Commonwealth,* Cambridge, Mass., 1966; S. H. Baron (ed.), *The Travels of Olearius in*

Seventeenth-Century Russia, Stanford, Calif., 1967; and L. E. Berry and R. O. Crummey, *Rude and Barbarous Kingdom: Russia in the Accounts of Sixteenth-Century English Voyagers,* Madison, Wis., 1968.

Chapter 2

Reinhard Wittram's superb and scholarly two-volume *Peter I, Czar und Kaiser: Zur Geschichte Peters des Grossen in seiner Zeit,* Göttingen, 1964, supersedes all earlier biographies of Peter the Great. The Soviet scholar M. M. Bogoslovsky gathered an exhaustive collection of sources on Peter in his *Petr I, materialy dlia biografii* (Peter I, Materials for a Biography), five volumes, Leningrad, 1940-1948. Florinsky's treatment of Peter in *Russia: A History and an Interpretation* is one of passionate dislike. *Peter the Great, Emperor of Russia,* two volumes, New York, 1884, by E. Schuyler is quite out of date. B. H. Sumner's *Peter the Great and the Ottoman Empire,* London, 1949, and his *Peter the Great and the Emergence of Russia,* London, 1950, were written for a very wide audience in the "Teach Yourself History Library" series but are thoroughly sound. V. O. Kliuchevsky's fourth volume has finally had a translator equal to the subject. Liliana Archibald's translation appeared as *Peter the Great,* New York, 1958. *Russia in the Era of Peter the Great* by L. J. Oliva, Englewood Cliffs, N.J., 1969, is thoughtful and challenging. Ian Grey's *Peter the Great,* Philadelphia, 1960, is a popular but reasonably accurate treatment. C. de Grunwald's biography by the same title, London, 1956, is also a popular account. The exploits of Peter's navy are dealt with in *The Maritime History of Russia, 848-1948,* London, 1949.

Chapter 3

There is no recent scholarly biography in any language of any of the eighteenth-century successors of Peter the Great. At the turn of the twentieth century R. N. Bain wrote a life of Elizabeth entitled *Daughter of Peter the Great,* London, 1899, and another of the husband of Catherine II entitled *Peter III, Emperor of Russia,* London, 1902. A recounting of the effort by the nobles to impose some sort of constitutional limitation upon Anne appears in a collection of documents assembled and translated by Marc Raeff, *Plans for Polit-*

ical Reform in Imperial Russia, 1730–1905, Englewood Cliffs, N. J., 1966.

The longest biography of Catherine the Great is quite out of date. A. Brückner's *Istoriia Ekateriny Vtoroi* (The History of Catherine II) was published in five volumes in St. Petersburg in 1885. A brief account lacking in depth is *Catherine the Great* by Ian Grey, Philadelphia, 1962. A popular account with the same title is by K. Anthony, Garden City, N.Y., 1925. K. Waliszewski's *Le Roman d'une imperatrice: Catherine II de Russie,* Paris, 1902, appeared in English as *The Romance of an Empress,* New York, 1929. G. S. Thomson's *Catherine the Great and the Expansion of Russia,* London, 1947, written for the "Teach Yourself History Library" series, is for the general public but is not intended to be a full-length biography.

A. N. Pypin edited some of Catherine's works and published them as *Sochineniia Imperatritsy Ekateriny II* (Collected Works of the Empress Catherine II), twelve volumes, St. Petersburg, 1901–1907. There are two editions of Catherine's fascinating memoirs, one edited by K. Anthony, *The Memoirs of Catherine II,* New York, 1927, and the other edited by D. Maroger, *The Memoirs of Catherine the Great,* New York, 1955. Catherine's companion and lady-in-waiting, Princess Dashkov, left her memoirs; see E. Dashkova, *Zapiski Kniagini Dashkovoi* (Notes of the Princess Dashkov), which appeared in English as *The Memoirs of Princess Dashkov,* London, 1908.

W. F. Reddaway edited a volume of sources on the Legislative Commission entitled *Documents of Catherine the Great: The Correspondence with Voltaire and the Instruction of 1767,* Cambridge, 1931. On the Commission see P. Dukes, *Catherine the Great and the Russian Nobility: A Study Based on the Materials of the Legislative Commission of 1767,* Cambridge, 1967, and K. A. Papmehl, "The Problem of Civil Liberties in the Records of the 'Great Commission.'" *(Slavonic and East European Review,* 1964).

There have been several excellent monographs on certain aspects of Catherine's reign. See H. Rogger, *National Consciousness in Eighteenth Century Russia,* Cambridge, Mass., 1960; H. Kaplan, *The First Partition of Poland,* New York, 1962; R. H. Lord, *The Second Partition of Poland,* Cambridge, Mass., 1915; and R. H. Lord, "The Third Partition of Poland" *(Slavonic and East European Review,* 1925). There is a definitive biography of Russia's greatest general in P. Longworth, *The Art of Victory: The Life and Achievements of Field-Marshal Suvorov,* London, 1966. G. Soloveytchik's popular biography, *Potemkin,* New York, 1947, rests upon solid research.

On the intellectuals, see M. Raeff, *Origins of the Russian Intelligentsia: The Eighteenth Century Nobility*, New York, 1966, and the somewhat old-fashioned intellectual survey by S. R. Tompkins, *The Russian Mind from Peter the Great through the Enlightenment*, Norman, Okla., 1953. See also M. S. Anderson, "Some British Influences on Russian Intellectual Life and Society in the Eighteenth Century," *(Slavonic and East European Review*, 1960). Radishchev's *Journey from St. Petersburg to Moscow* has been translated by Leo Wiener, Cambridge, Mass., 1959. There are two modern biographies of of Radischev: D. Lang, *The First Russian Radical: Alexander Radishchev*, London, 1959, and A. McConnell, *A Russian Philosopher, Alexander Radishchev, 1749–1802*, The Hague, 1964. Lang's work is perhaps bolder in interpretation and more sprightly to read. McConnell's study is the more scholarly of the two.

Chapter 4

Several works of a general nature deal with the entire nineteenth century or with the period from the beginning of the nineteenth century to the fall of the monarchy in 1917. The place of honor here goes to the charming little study by M. Karpovich, *Imperial Russia, 1801–1917*, New York, 1932. The most reliable recent work dealing with the nineteenth century is by Serge Pushkarev, *The Emergence of Modern Russia*, New York, 1963. M. V. Nechkina's *Russia in the Nineteenth Century*, two volumes, Ann Arbor, Mich., 1953, is the translation of a standard Soviet treatment. *Years of the Golden Cockerel: The Last Romanov Tsars, 1814–1917* by S. Harcave, New York, 1968, is sound and well written. H. Seton-Watson's *The Russian Empire, 1801–1917*, Oxford, 1967, must be used with caution. An older work written with a strong liberal and anti-Romanov bias is A. A. Kornilov's three-volume *Kurs istorii Rossii v XIX veke* (A Course in Russian History in the Nineteenth Century), Moscow, 1912–1914, translated by A. Kaun as *Modern Russian History*, two volumes, New York, 1917; reprinted 1943. Kornilov's study ended with the death of Alexander III, but Kaun, who had taken part in the 1905 Revolution, added a section on the reign of Nicholas II. Russian foreign policy is the concern of B. Jelavich, *A Century of Russian Foreign Policy, 1814–1914*, Philadelphia, 1964.

Alexander I still awaits a definitive biography. The Grand Duke Nikolai Mikhailovich, a thoroughly respectable craftsman, published several studies of his ancestor, including *Imperator Aleksandr I, opyt istoricheskago izsledovaniia* (Emperor Alexander I, A Historical Study), three volumes, St. Petersburg, 1912; *Perepiska Imperatora Aleksandra I s sestroi Velikoi Kniaginei Ekaterinoi Pavlovnoi* (Correspondence of Emperor Alexander I with His Sister the Grand Duchess Catherine Pavlovna), St. Petersburg, 1910; and *Les Relations diplomatiques de la Russie et de la France d'après les rapports des ambassadeurs d'Alexandre et de Napoleon, 1808–1812,* seven volumes, St. Petersburg, 1905–1914. The court historian during the first half of the nineteenth century, N. K. Shilder, wrote a long biography, *Imperator Aleksandr I, ego zhizan i tsarstvovanie* (Emperor Alexander I, His Life and Reign), four volumes, St. Petersburg, 1904–1905. One of Russia's greatest historians, S. M. Solovev, produced a single volume biography, *Imperator Aleksandr I* (Emperor Alexander I), St. Petersburg, 1877.

The French ambassador to Russia during World War I, M. Paléologue, published a biography of sorts entitled *The Enigmatic Czar: The Life of Alexander I of Russia,* London, 1938. L. I. Strakhovsky's *Alexander I of Russia,* New York, 1947, features the legend that the emperor did not die in 1825 but wandered off into Siberia to live for another forty years the life of a saintly recluse.

The most significant of the memoirs dealing with the reign are those by a member of Alexander's Unofficial Committee, entitled *Memoirs of Prince Adam Czartoryski and His Correspondence with Alexander I,* London, 1888. There is an exciting firsthand account of the campaign of 1812 by Sir Robert Wilson, *Narrative of Events during the Invasion of Russia by Napoleon Bonaparte, 1812,* London, 1860. Another observer of the invasion was the French ambassador to Russia on the eve of the campaign; see A. Caulaincourt, *With Napoleon in Russia,* New York, 1935. The leading modern scholar is the Soviet historian E. Tarle, whose *Napoleon's Invasion of Russia,* New York, 1942, is a colorful narrative, indeed. See also A. Palmer, *Napoleon in Russia,* New York, 1967.

A good number of scholarly studies on particular aspects of Alexander's reign has entered the literature since World War II. On Alexander's interest in peace projects, see O. J. Frederiksen, "Alexander I and His League to End Wars" *(Russian Review,* 1943), and P. K. Grimsted, "Capodistrias and a 'New Order' for Restoration Europe: The 'Liberal Ideas' of a Russian Foreign Minister (Capodistrias), 1814–1822" *(Journal of Modern History,* 1968). See also Mrs. Grimsted's carefully researched *The Foreign Ministers of Alexander I: Polit-*

ical Attitudes and the Conduct of Russian Diplomacy, 1801–1825, Berkeley, Calif., 1969. Studies of the nineteenth-century economy tend to concentrate upon the postreform period. A welcome exception is W. L. Blackwell's *The Beginnings of Russian Industrialization, 1800–1860,* Princeton, N. J., 1968. On the military settlements, see R. E. Pipes, "The Russian Military Colonies, 1810–1831" *(Journal of Modern History,* 1950). G. Vernadsky's "Reforms under Czar Alexander I: French and American Influences" *(Review of Politics,* 1947), deals with the early years of the reign. For a recent essay on the reform interests of Alexander see the article by Allen McConnell, "Alexander I's Hundred Days: The Politics of a Paternalist Reformer" *(Slavic Review,* 1969).

The only full size biography of Speransky to appear in any language in nearly a century is the scholarly *Michael Speransky, Statesman of Imperial Russia, 1772–1839* by M. Raeff, The Hague, 1957. M. Kukiel deals with another of Alexander's advisers in *Czartoryski and European Unity, 1770–1861,* Princeton, N.J., 1955. The emperor's friend and leading adviser in the last half of the reign is the subject of *Arakcheev, Grand Vizier of the Russian Empire: A Biography* by M. Jenkins, New York, 1969. On constitutional schemes, see the documents, most of them dealing with the reign of Alexander I, edited by M. Raeff, *Plans for Political Reform in Imperial Russia, 1730–1905,* Englewood Cliffs, N. J., 1966, together with the excellent long introductory essay by the author. The Grand Duke Nikolai Mikhailovich's three-volume work on Stroganov, *Le comte Paul Stroganov,* St. Petersburg, 1905, consists primarily of documents. The minutes of the meetings of Alexander's Unofficial Committee make up an entire volume. One aspect of the work of the Unofficial Committee is dealt with in O. A. Narkiewicz, "Alexander I and the Senate Reform" *(Slavonic and East European Review,* 1969).

The Decembrist movement has received much attention from American and Soviet scholars. The documents dealing with the uprising have been published from time to time—eleven volumes are now in print—under the editorship of M. N. Pokrovsky and since his death under that of M. V. Nechkina as *Dokumenty po istorii vosstaniia dekabristov* (Documents on the History of the Revolt of the Decembrists), Moscow, 1925 to present. The two-volume account of the Decembrists by M. V. Nechkina, *Dvizhenie dekabristov* (The Decembrist Movement), Moscow, 1955, is the most scholarly and up-to-date in any language.

A. Mazour's *The First Russian Revolution, 1825; Its Origins, Develop-*

ment, and Significance, Stanford, Calif., 1937, was a pioneer effort in English. It was reprinted in 1967 with a supplementary bibliography listing the many works published on the Decembrists in the preceding thirty years. M. Zetlin's *The Decembrists,* New York, 1958, is fascinating reading. A perceptive essay by M. Raeff introduces the documents that make up the bulk of his *The Decembrist Movement,* Englewood Cliffs, N.J., 1966. See also A. E. Adams, "The Character of Pestel's Thought" *(American Slavic and East European Review,* 1953).

The ponderous biography of Nicholas I by the German historian, Theodor Schiemann, *Geschichte Russlands unter Kaiser Nikolaus I,* four volumes, Berlin, 1904–1909, contains much documentary material. So, too, does the work by N. K. Shilder, *Imperator Nikolai I, ego zhizn i tsarstvovanie* (Emperor Nicholas I, His Life and Reign), two volumes, St. Petersburg, 1903. There is a short biography by C. de Grunwald, *Nicholas I,* New York, 1954.

If the tsar himself has proved unattractive to historians, certain aspects of the reign have come in for searching analysis. On domestic policy, see N. V. Riasanovsky, *Nicholas I and Official Nationality in Russia, 1825–1855,* Berkeley, Calif., 1959, which amounts to a history of the reign, and not just a treatment of the doctrine of Official Nationality. W. M. Pintner's *Russian Economic Policy under Nicholas I,* Ithaca, N. Y., 1967, is an analysis of the beginnings of the Industrial Revolution in Russia. There is a good account of the Polish uprising in 1830 by R. F. Leslie in *Polish Politics and the Revolution of 1830,* London, 1956. The army of which the emperor was so fond is the subject of a study by J. S. Curtiss, *The Russian Army under Nicholas I, 1825–1855,* Durham, N. C., 1965. On the political police, see S. Monas, *The Third Section: Police and Society in Russia under Nicholas I,* Cambridge, Mass., 1961, and the definitive study by P. S. Squire, *The Third Department: The Establishment and Practices of the Political Police in the Reign of Nicholas I,* New York, 1968.

The intellectual ferment of the reign of Nicholas has attracted many scholars. A brilliant introduction to the subject is I. Berlin's, "A Marvelous Decade, 1838–1848: The Birth of the Russian Intelligentsia" *(Encounter,* 1955). *The Russian Intelligentsia* by S. R. Tompkins, Norman, Okla., 1957, is a somewhat old-fashioned treatment by a competent scholar. There has been much debate over the meaning of the term intelligentsia. See M. Raeff, *Origins of the Russian Intelligentsia,* New York, 1966 and the collection of essays edited by R. E. Pipes, *The Russian Intelligentsia,* New York, 1961, especially the articles by M. Malia, "What Is the Intelligentsia?" and R. E. Pipes,

"The Historical Evolution of the Russian Intelligentsia." There is
a comparison of various definitions in D. R. Brower, "The Problem
of the Russian Intelligentsia" *(Slavic Review,* 1967).

The early meetings of the intelligentsia that led up to "the marvellous
decade" are analyzed in the scholarly work by E. J. Brown, *Stankevich
and His Moscow Circle, 1830–1840,* Stanford, Calif., 1966. W. L.
Langer's long awaited volume in the Rise of Modern Europe series,
Political and Social Upheaval, 1832–1852, New York, 1969, has proved
a disappointment to students of Russian history. Its attention is almost
exclusively upon Central and Western Europe. The internal affairs
of Russia in these seminal decades, which led the nation to the Great
Reforms and the intellectual revolt of the 1860s and 1870s, receive
scant attention.

On the Westernizers, see M. Malia, *Alexander Herzen and the Birth
of Russian Socialism, 1812–1855,* Cambridge, Mass., 1961; I. Berlin,
"Herzen and Bakunin on Individual Liberty," and M. Malia, "Herzen
and the Peasant Commune," in E. J. Simmons, *Continuity and
Change in Russian and Soviet Thought,* Cambridge, Mass., 1955.
Herzen's memoirs have been translated by C. Garnett and recently
republished as *My Past and My Thoughts,* four volumes, London,
1968. A good biography of Belinsky is H. E. Bowman's *Vissarion
Belinski, 1811–1848: A Study in the Origins of Social Criticism in
Russia,* Cambridge, Mass., 1954. There are excellent treatments of
Belinsky in Masaryk's *Spirit of Russia* and in R. Hare's *Pioneers of
Russian Social Thought,* New York, 1964, which also includes a per-
ceptive essay on Herzen. Chaadayev is the subject of an article by J.
Lavrin, "Chaadayev and the West" *(Russian Review,* 1963).

Several studies deal with the influence of Fourier upon members of the
intelligentsia in Nicholas's time: Georges Sourine, *Le Fourierisme
en Russie,* Paris, 1936; N. V. Riasanovsky, "Fourierism in Russia:
An Estimate of the Petrasevcy (members of the Petrashevsky Circle)"
(American Slavic and East European Review, 1953), and F. K. Kaplan,
"Russian Fourierism of the 1840s" *(American Slavic and East European Review,* 1958).

There are several excellent studies of the Slavophiles, including *Ivan
Aksakov, 1823–1886: A Study in Russian Thought and Politics* by
S. Lukashevich, Cambridge, Mass., 1965; *Tribune of the Slavophiles:
Konstantine Aksakov* by E. Chmielewski, Gainesville, Fla., 1962;
P. K. Christoff's *An Introduction to Nineteenth Century Russian
Slavophilism: A Study in Ideas; Vol. I: A. S. Xomjakov* (Khomiakov),
The Hague, 1961; R. Hare, *Pioneers of Russian Social Thought,*
New York, 1964, much of which deals with leading Slavophiles; and

Russia and the West in the Teaching of the Slavophiles by N. V. Riasanovsky, Cambridge, Mass., 1952. An article By E. Dunn entitled "A Slavophile Looks at the Raskol (Old Believers) and the Sects" *(Slavonic and East European Review,* 1966) considers the fact that both Slavophiles and Old Believers were anti-Western.

Russia and Europe, 1825–1878 by A. A. Lobanov-Rostovsky, Ann Arbor, Mich., 1954, deals primarily with war and diplomacy. There are two scholarly studies of Russia in the Near East: P. W. Mosely, *Russian Diplomacy and the Opening of the Eastern Question in 1838 and 1839,* Cambridge, Mass., 1934, and V. J. Puryear, *England, Russia and the Straits Question, 1844–1856,* Berkeley, Calif., 1931. See also O. J. Hammen's "Free Europe against Russia, 1830–1854" *(American Slavic and East European Review,* 1952). For the Crimean War, see the formidable work by A. W. Kinglake, *The Invasion of the Crimea,* nine volumes, London, 1863–1887.

Chapter 5

For the period between the accession of Alexander II and the outbreak of World War I there is H. Seton-Watson's *The Decline of Imperial Russia, 1855–1914,* New York, 1952, which, however, is not completely reliable. A. E. Adams edited a collection of essays, *Imperial Russia after 1861,* Boston, 1965. There is no scholarly biography of Alexander II in any language. S. Graham's *Tsar of Freedom,* New Haven, Conn., 1935, is a poor substitute. W. E. Mosse's brilliant *Alexander II and the Modernization of Russia,* New York, 1962, is sound on the reforms, the treatment of subject nationalities, and foreign affairs, but there is little on the Populist and revolutionary movements. As in the case of the other Romanovs of the nineteenth century who await serious biographies, however, Alexander II has attracted a host of scholars to the study of particular topics.

On the emanicipation and the conditions among the peasants in the post-reform period, the outstanding work is by G. T. Robinson, *Rural Russia under the Old Regime,* New York, 1932. J. Maynard's *The Russian Peasant and Other Studies,* London, 1942, deals expansively with the position of the peasant after emancipation. Terence Emmons is the author of *The Russian Landed Gentry and the Peasant Emancipation of 1861,* Cambridge, 1968, and the editor of an assortment of essays, *Emancipation of the Russian Serfs,* New York, 1970. L. A. Owen's *The Russian Peasant Movement, 1906–1917,* London, 1937, considers rural Russia in the last decade of the empire. D. W. Treadgold examines various aspects of postemancipation peasantry in *The Great Siberian Migration: Government and Peasant in Resettlement from Emancipation to the First World War*, Princeton, N. J., 1957. For the Judiciary Act see Kucherov, "The Jury as Part of the Russian Judicial Reform of 1864" *(American Slavic and East European Review*, 1950). The author deals in much more detail with the court system in *Courts, Lawyers and Trials under the Last Three Tsars*, New York, 1953. There is a first-rate biography by F. A. Miller, *Dmitry Miliutin and the Reform Era in Russia*, Nashville, 1968.

The monumental study of the Populist and revolutionary movements of the reign of Alexander II is F. Venturi's *Il Popolismo Russo*, two volumes, Turin, 1952, which was translated by F. Haskell as *Roots of Revolution: A History of the Populist and Socialist Movements in Nineteenth Century Russia*, London, 1960. Several less ambitious studies on Narodniks and revolutionaries in the 1860s and 1870s are available: *Sons against Fathers: Studies in Russian Radicalism and Revolution* by E. Lampert, Oxford, 1965; J. H. Billington's *Mikhailovsky and Russian Populism*, London, 1958; *Road to Revolution* by A. Yarmolinsky, New York, 1962; E. H. Carr's *The Romantic Exiles*, London, 1933; and *The Russian Anarchists* by P. Avrich, Princeton, N.J., 1967. See Also A. P. Pollard, "The Russian Intelligentsia: The Mind of Russia" *(California Slavic Studies*, 1964), and M. A. Miller, "Ideological Conflicts in Russian Populism: The Revolutionary Manifestoes of the Chaikovsky Circle, 1869–1874" *(Slavic Review*, 1970). The Western revolutionary tradition to which the revolutionaries and Populists were heir is the subject of the classic *To the Finland Station* by E. Wilson, New York, 1940. The fascination that the United States and the American social and political experiment held for Herzen, Bakunin, Chernyshevsky, Lavrov, and Chaikovsky is the subject of a careful study by David Hecht, *Russian Radicals Look to America, 1825–1894*, Cambridge, Mass., 1947.

For studies of individual Populists or revolutionaries, see E. H. Carr, *Michael Bakunin*, New York, 1937, and E. Pyziur, *The Doctrine of Anarchism of Michael Bakunin*, Milwaukee, 1955. G. P. Maximoff compiled and edited *The Political Philosophy of Bakunin: Scientific Anarchism*, Glencoe, Ill., 1953. An interesting side light on Bakunin is the story of "A Russian Anarchist Visits Boston," by O. Handlin *(New England Quarterly*, 1942). There is an excellent biography of Lavrov by way of an introduction to the translation of his famous letters in the work *Peter Lavrov: Historical Letters* by J. P.

Scanlon, Berkeley, Calif., 1967. See also the article by M. Karpovich, "P. L. Lavrov and Russian Socialism" *(California Slavic Studies,* 1963), and F. A. Walker, "The Morality of Revolution in Pyotr Lavrovich Lavrov" *(Slavonic and East European Review,* 1962). Lavrov, who was sufficiently familiar with the works of American writers to write significant comments on Whitman, Lowell, and Whittier, is the subject of an article by D. Hecht, "Lavrov and Longfellow" *(Russian Review,* 1946). The Soviet Government has published an English translation of N. G. Chernyshevsky's *Selected Philosophical Essays,* Moscow, 1953. There is a rare vignette on Chernyshevsky in R. Hare's *Pioneers of Russian Social Thought,* New York, 1964.

Terrorism and terrorists of the postreform period have attracted the attention of many writers. R. Seth's *Russian Terrorists,* London, 1967, is hardly a profound work, although the author has read the sources. *The Unmentionable Nechaev,* by M. Charol who writes under the name of Michael Prawdin, has the grossly inaccurate subtitle *A Key to Bolshevism,* New York, 1961. *The First Bolshevik, a Political Biography of Peter Tkachev* by A. L. Weeks, New York, 1968, is the most scholarly of the three. A necessary corrective to all three is D. Hardy's "Tkachev and Marxists" *(Slavic Review,* 1970). D. Footman's *Red Prelude: The Life of the Russian Terrorist, Zhelyabov,* New Haven, Conn., 1945, is really the story of the Land and Freedom and People's Will Parties.

Some of the Populists left interesting accounts of their activities. See *Underground Russia* by S. Stepniak (pseudonym for the Narodnik and later revolutionary Serge M. Kravchinsky), London, 1883, and *Memoirs of a Revolutionist* by the anarchist Prince P. A. Kropotkin, New York, 1930. Victor Serge's *Memoirs of a Revolutionary, 1901–1914,* Oxford, 1963, is the poignant and melancholy autobiography of an anarchist who fought against authoritarian regimes in France, Spain, and Russia before and after 1917.

Moderate thought, liberal and conservative, has received relatively little attention. *Geschichte des Liberalismus in Russland* by V. Leontovitsch, Frankfurt, 1957, is a work of the first importance. See also *Russian Liberalism: From Gentry to Intelligentisia* by G. Fisher, Cambridge, Mass., 1958, and "The Cadet Party," by A. Tyrkova-Williams *(Russian Review,* 1953). Another segment of the political spectrum is the subject of Hans Rogger's "Formation of the Russian Right" *(California Slavic Studies,* 1964). For one aspect of conservatism see E. C. Thaden's *Conservative Nationalism in Nineteenth Century Russia,* Seattle, 1964. On Pan-Slavism there is the scholarly study by M. B. Petrovich, *The Emergence of Russian Pan-Slavism, 1856–1870,* New York, 1956, and the learned work of H. Kohn on the broader subject, *Pan-Slavism, Its History and Ideology,* Notre Dame, Ind., 1953.

The study of foreign relations under Alexander II has produced a number of works of great stature. B. H. Sumner's *Russia and the Balkans 1870-1880,* New York, 1937, is a classic, as is W. L. Langer's *European Alliances and Alignments, 1871–1890,* New York, 1950. The Polish uprising of 1863 is the subject of R. F. Leslie's *Reform and Insurrection in Russian Poland,* New York, 1963, and of the article by K. S. Pasieka, "The British Press and the Polish Insurrection of 1863" *(Slavonic and East European Review,* 1963).

The sole biography of Alexander III, C. Lowe's *Alexander III of Russia,* London, 1895, is of little value. Nicholas II has fared slightly better, but only in the fact that there are several worthless biographies of the last tsar. The two best recent accounts of the reign of Nicholas II are to be found in *Russia in Revolution, 1890–1918* by Lionel Kochan, New York, 1966, and Sidney Harcave's *Years of the Golden Cockerel, the Last Romanov Tsars, 1814–1917,* New York, 1968, two fifths of which deals with the last tsar.

Several well-written accounts of the closing years of the monarchy are: R. Charques, *The Twilight of Imperial Russia,* New York, 1958; M. T. Florinsky, *The End of the Russian Empire,* New York, 1931; and B. Pares, *The Fall of the Russian Monarchy,* New York, 1939. There is an excellent collection of essays, edited by R. H. McNeal, entitled *Russia in Transition, 1905–1914,* New York, 1970.

There were shrewd observers of and participants in the approaching deluge who left fascinating accounts of the progress they witnessed. The Liberal leader Paul Miliukov analyzed the situation on the eve of the 1905 Revolution in a series of lectures at the University of Chicago. The lectures were published as *Russia and Its Crisis,* Chicago, 1905; reprinted London, 1969. Miliukov's *Political Memoirs, 1905–1917,* Ann Arbor, Mich., 1967, tells the story of his lifetime devotion to the principles of Western parliamentary democracy. The English historian, Russophile, and traveler Sir Bernard Pares wrote many works out of the profundity of his understanding and appreciation of Russia. The publications particularly appropriate to a study of the early twentieth century are *Russia and Reform,* London, 1907, and *My Russian Memoirs,* London, 1931. Alexander Kaun, out of his own bitter experience, roundly criticized Nicholas II and his ministers in the postscript chapters he added to the 1917 edition of his translation of A. A. Kornilov's *Modern Russian History.* Unfortunately, the 1943 reprint of Kornilov's work did not carry the additional chapters by Kaun.

The works of and about some imperial ministers under the last tsar are significant. Two foreign ministers left memoirs: A. P. Izvolsky, *The Memoirs of Alexander Izwolsky,* London, 1920, and Serge Sazonov, *Fateful Years, 1909–1916,* London, 1928. A. Yarmolinsky translated and edited *The Memoirs of Count Witte,* New York, 1921. T. H. von Laue's *Sergei Witte and the Industrialization of Russia,* New York, 1963, is a sound piece of research. There are three excellent short articles on Stolypin: A. Levin's "Peter Arkad'evich Stolypin: A Political Appraisal" *(Journal of Modern History,* 1965), "The Concept of the Stolypin Land Reform" by G. Yaney *(Slavic Review,* 1964), and L. Strakhovsky's "The Statesmanship of Peter Stolypin" *(Slavonic and East European Review,* 1959). A finance minister, V. N. Kokovtsev, wrote *Out of My Past,* Stanford, Calif., 1935. And Pobedonostsev's vitriolic fulminations appeared in English as *The Reflections of a Russian Statesman,* London, 1898.

The interest in the revolutionary movement never wanes. J. L. H. Keep's scholarly and learned *The Rise of Social Democracy in Russia,* Oxford, 1963, focuses on the Revolution of 1905, of which it is a superb account. Another excellent study of the 1905 Revolution is S. Harcave's *First Blood: The Russian Revolution of 1905,* New York, 1964. One aspect of the revolution appears in S. Schwarz's *The Russian Revolution of 1905: The Workers' Movement and the Formation of Bolshevism and Menshevism,* Chicago, 1967.

B. D. Wolfe's *Three Who Made a Revolution,* New York, 1940, is a history of Russian Marxism from its origins to 1914 as well as an excellent account of the lives of Lenin, Trotsky, and Stalin. There is no end to works on Lenin. D. W. Treadgold's *Lenin and His Rivals: The Struggle for Russia's Future,* New York, 1955, is an outstanding piece of research. Leon Trotsky's *Lenin,* New York, 1962, is an intimate and colorful treatment. Lenin's wife, a revolutionary in her own right, has left her *Memories of Lenin,* two volumes, London, 1935. The second edition of D. Shub's *Lenin,* New York, 1966, is superior to S. T. Possony's polemical *Lenin, the Compulsive Revolutionary,* Chicago, 1964, and to R. Payne's journalistic *The Life and Death of Lenin,* New York, 1964. L. Fischer's *The Life of Lenin,* New York, 1964, is reasonably sound. By far the best biography of Lenin is A. B. Ulam's *The Bolsheviks,* New York, 1965, the English version of which bore the more accurate title, *Lenin and the Bolsheviks,* London, 1965. See also the earlier study by L. Haimson, *The Russian Marxists and the Origins of Bolshevism,* Cambridge, Mass., 1955.

The best way to know Leon Trotsky, surely, is to read his *Moia Zhizn'* (My Life), two volumes, Berlin, 1930, published as a single volume in English as *My Life,* New York, 1930, and his delightfully prejudiced *History of the Russian Revolution,* three volumes, New York, 1936. The definitive biography, of which the first volume deals with his life to the death of Lenin, is I. Deutscher's *The Prophet Armed,* New York, 1954.

For recent scholarly biographies of other leaders, see S H Baron's *Plekhanov: The Father of Russian Marxism,* Stanford, Calif., 1963, and T. Riha, *A Russian European: Paul Miliukov in Russian Politics,* Notre Dame, Ind., 1969. See also A. Goldenweiser, "Paul Miliukov — Historian and Statesman" *(Russian Review,* 1957). B. M. Bekkar translated and edited Plekhanov's *History of Russian Social Thought,* New York, 1967. There is a good biography of one of Lenin's rivals in I. Getzler's *Martov: A Political Biography of a Russian Social Democrat,* New York, 1967.

The intellectuals as a force in the declining days of the monarchy are the subject of G. Fischer's essay, "The Intelligentsia and Russia," in *The Transformation of Russian Society,* Cambridge, Mass., 1960, and of an essay, "The Historical Evolution of the Russian Intelligentsia," by R. Pipes in *The Russian Intelligentsia,* New York, 1961. On constitutional developments during the reign of Nicholas II there is the definitive study by A. Levin of *The Second Duma,* New Haven, Conn., 1940, and *The Bolsheviks in the Tsarist Duma* by A. Badayev, New York, 1929. Briefer accounts of Duma activity are to be found in J. L. H. Keep's "Russian Social Democracy and the First State Duma" *(Slavonic and East European Review,* 1955); E. A. Goldenweiser's "The Russian Duma" *(Political Science Quarterly,* 1914); Bernard Pares's "The Second Duma," *(Slavonic and East European Review,* 1923); and W. B. Walsh's "Political Parties in the Russian Dumas" *(Journal of Modern History,* 1950). See also the essays in *The Transformation of Russian Society* edited by C. E. Black, Cambridge, Mass., 1960, particularly "The Patterns of Autocracy" by Z. K. Brzezinski, "The Parties and the State: The Evolution of Political Attitudes" by L. H. Haimson, and "The State and the Local Community" by A. Vucinich.

For the political police see *The Ochrana* by A. T. Vassilyev, Philadelphia, 1930, and for the dramatic career of a double agent see B. I.

Nikolaevskii's *Azeff, the Spy,* New York, 1934. W. L. Langer's *The Franco-Russian Alliance, 1890–1894,* New York, 1929, chronicles the diplomatic exchanges that committed imperial Russia to the defense of Western civilization.

The best treatments of the peasant in the early twentieth century are G. T. Robinson's *Rural Russia under the Old Regime,* New York, 1932, L. A. Owen's *The Russian Peasant Movement, 1906–1917,* London, 1937, and G. Pavlovsky, *Agricultural Russia on the Eve of the Revolution,* London, 1930. *Church and State in Russia* by J. S. Curtiss, New York, 1940, is the story of Orthodoxy under autocratic domination from 1900 to the end of the monarchy.

There were several shrewd foreign observers who studied Russia at first hand during the reigns of the last three tsars. Aside from the works of Sir Bernard Pares already mentioned, see A. Leroy-Beaulieu's *L'Empire des Tsars et les Russes,* three volumes, Paris, 1881–1889, D. M. Wallace, *Russia,* London, 1912, M. Baring, *The Russian People,* London, 1914, and S. Harper, *The Russia I Believe In,* Chicago, 1945.

Index